EARTH WISDOM

Also by Raymond Barnett:

Jade and Fire
Relax, You're Already Home
The China Ultimatum
The Return to Treasure Island
Sauntering to a New Wisdom
The Death of Mycroft
The Death of Lord Carnarvon

EARTH WISDOM

john muir, accidental taoist, charts humanity's
only future on a changing planet

Raymond Barnett

ISBN: 1532762372
ISBN 13: 9781532762376
Library of Congress Control Number: 2016917716
CreateSpace Independent Publishing Platform
North Charleston, South Carolina

For

Tam
AJ, Kyle, and Al

Boon companions on the Journey

"Wonderful how completely everything in wild nature fits into us, as if truly part and parent of us. The sun shines not on us but in us. The rivers flow not past, but through us, thrilling, tingling, vibrating every fiber and cell of the substance of our bodies, making them glide and sing. The trees wave and the flowers bloom in our bodies as well as our souls, and every bird song, wind song, and tremendous storm song of the rocks in the heart of the mountains is our song, our very own, and sings our love."
   —John Muir, *Unpublished Journals*, 1872

"The highest degree of the spiritual is to know clearly the ten thousand creatures." (*Shen ming zhi ji, Zhao zhi wan wu*)
   —Guan Zhong, 7th century BCE Taoist

"I urgently appeal, then, for a new dialogue about how we are shaping the future of the planet...Our efforts at education will be inadequate and ineffectual unless we strive to promote a new way of thinking about human beings, life, society and our relationship with nature... We do need to slow down and look at reality in a different way."
   —Pope Francis, *Laudato Si'*, 2015

"To see humanity, as four centuries of scientific investigations have enabled us to see ourselves, within the cosmic sweep of space and time is to grasp the disproportion between our needs, effects, and intentions and the movement of reality in its full majesty and complexity."
   —D.M. Yeager, *Suspended in Wonderment*, 2015

"Get thee up into the high mountains...Arise, shine, for thy light is come."
   —Isaiah, 8th century BCE Jewish prophet

Table of Contents

Introduction

As humanity faces the gravest challenge in its 200,000-year history, it is curious that the best hope of answering the threat of climate change comes from an eccentric Scotch immigrant who died a century ago. Before he died, though, John Muir left two legacies: a worldview, and a movement. With much luck, these may yet play a key role in pulling civilization back from the abyss.

Climate change's floods, famines, epidemics, and mass migrations that every credible scientific and policy institute in the world sees in humanity's near future—modern Four Horsemen of the Apocalypse—have elicited calls from Pope Francis and thoughtful analysts for a "new way of thinking," and a worldwide popular movement to persuade leaders to adopt the new approach's insights.

Muir's radical worldview, his Earth Wisdom, was forged from epic rambles in the wildest mountains and glaciers of 19th-century America. So unorthodox is it that his followers have let it remain largely hidden in his journals for a hundred years. Yet strangely enough, Muir's Earth Wisdom seems crafted to provide the new way of thinking that could inspire an effective response to the modern challenges of global climate change. And stranger still, this worldview also arose, unknown to him, two thousand years earlier half a world away, in the Taoist tradition of China. Muir was thus the first American Taoist, albeit an accidental one.

But the confluence of Muir's worldview and that of ancient China's Taoists is not really so strange. Both developed from the habit of living among the mountains and unspoiled places of the planet. Both were grounded in viewing the world through keen eyes and unbiased minds. "Open eyes, Open minds, Will travel" characterizes the approach to life of Muir in the late 19th century, and the Taoists two millennia and more before.

They saw the same thing. A world bursting with vitality and beauty, driven by the flow of grand natural processes inherent in matter itself. A world in which humans are but one component—interesting, prone to mischief, perhaps, but really nothing special in the overall scheme of things. A Gaiacentric world, rather than an anthropocentric one. And behind, under, *in* it all: the mysterious, wonderful, awesome presence of a Way, a Great Fountain, a Source of Sources, a God utterly unlike any previous conception of God in either Western or Eastern religions.

So that, oddly enough, when Pope Francis decries the modern technocratic paradigm whose "pace of consumption, waste and environmental change has so stretched the planet's capacity that our contemporary lifestyle, unsustainable as it is, can only precipitate catastrophes," he echoes Muir and Taoism. When he observes that "Our efforts...will be inadequate and ineffectual unless we strive to promote a new way of thinking about human beings, life, society and our relationship with nature," it is Muir and Taoism to which he unknowingly points.

Journalist Naomi Klein, perhaps the most thoughtful analyst of our modern dilemma, comes to the same conclusion as Pope Francis. In view of the overwhelming scientific consensus leading to the usually staid International Energy Agency's 2011 conclusion that "quite simply, climate change has become an existential crisis for the human species," Klein is persuaded that "fundamentally, the task is to articulate...an alternative worldview to rival the one at the heart of the ecological crisis."

No need to conjure this saving "alternative worldview" from raw material, though; it exists already, in cultures West and East, in two distinct versions of an earth-centered, immanent philosophy focused on the here and now of our experiences in life.

In the West, Muir's Earth Wisdom was distilled from his seven decades amongst mountains, glaciers, tycoons and presidents. His worldview is concrete and practical, resting upon what we may posit as *three pillars* that Muir saw as fundamental to the way the world works. First, the earth itself is our proper focus, and provides all we need. Second, all creatures on the planet are related in kinship, with humans but one part of the whole— a Gaiacentric stance replacing the traditional anthropocentric one. And third, females and the traits of cooperation, acceptance, and nurturing have critical roles to play in human society, a reflection of the complementary dualism intrinsic throughout the natural world.

In the East, this immanent outlook emerged two thousand years ago in the Taoist tradition. Though not hidden, as Muir's Western version, Taoism has been relegated to the margins of society, branded as superstition, and only grudgingly tolerated by the urban elite imposing their rule over the people of the culture, then as now. Even so, the various strands of the Taoist tradition have developed a rich, all-encompassing worldview over many centuries. And this Eastern version of Earth Wisdom is strikingly similar to that discovered by Muir only a century ago in the West, marked especially by its recognition of the dualism inherent in reality, the yin and the yang of the world.

Muir's second legacy is the worldwide environmental movement, of which he is the acknowledged father. The movement has grown and diversified these hundred years, and saved much of the natural world from commercial exploitation—yet its best efforts to meet the challenges of climate change have faltered. Even the December 2015 UN climate summit, widely hailed as the first of twenty-one such to achieve meaningful results, is acknowledged as failing to rescue human civilization without many more hard-fought changes.

It is now time for the hidden Muir to come fully into its own, for Earth Wisdom to partner with other immanent worldviews—China's Taoism, science's Darwinism, indigenous peoples' cosmologies, immanent strands of existing religions—to re-energize Muir's two legacies into an irresistible, worldwide mass movement transforming societies and economies, rescuing humanity from the modern Four Horsemen it has unleashed by climate change.

Join me, then, in a voyage of discovery. We shall begin with Muir, on a selection of his daunting rambles, from the post-Civil-War South, to the Sierra Nevada mountains, to Alaska's glaciers. His resulting worldview of Earth Wisdom with its three pillars will be explored. We'll delve into the Tao of Muir, the striking similarities between Muir's Earth Wisdom and the Taoism of ancient China. Then the century-long saga of Earth Wisdom's imperfect and patchy application by the environmental movement is considered. We follow its splits and rebels, its traitors and heroes, its successes and failures, from the tragic battle for the Hetch Hetchy Valley in 1913, to 2015's United Nations conference in Paris grappling with the implacable issue of climate change.

Finally, we look at what Earth Wisdom tasks us to accomplish now, and promptly, to resolve the looming threat to human civilization, including the roles to be played by city planners, economists, politicians, and environmentalists. Organized religion, surprisingly, has a part to play, if it can find theological and communal ways to incorporate Earth Wisdom's earth-centered outlook into its traditions.

Our story begins in 1867, as the young John Muir shoulders his plant press and a rucksack containing the *New Testament*, Robbie Burns' *Poetry*, and Milton's *Paradise Lost*. In long-legged strides he crosses a bridge over the Ohio River from Indiana to Kentucky, and begins a walk of a thousand miles through the war-ravaged South to the Gulf of Mexico. The walk will change Muir's life—and that of his adopted homeland, as well.

Part 1
Earth Wisdom, West: Muir's Rambles and Worldview

The Wanderer: a thousand-mile walk (1867)

"My plan was simply to push on in a general southward direction by the wildest, leafiest, and least trodden way I could find."

When in September of 1867 he scribbled "John Muir, Earth-Planet, Universe" on the opening page of his journal, Muir clearly saw his upcoming walk from Indiana to Florida's Gulf of Mexico as something special. Even so, he could not have imagined it would spark the creation of a new way of looking at the world, a stance that a century later would provide the best hope for saving human civilization from the gravest threat of its entire history on the planet.

Muir had dropped out of the University of Wisconsin after two years, fascinated with botany and geology, but restless. He had earlier spent months botanizing in Canada (prompting some in later years to accuse him of dodging the Civil War draft, a charge stoutly denied by others). To keep himself in bread during his botanical studies, he had progressed from threshing wheat by hand in the summers, at which his strength and endurance were remarkable, to working in the country's largest carriage manufacturer, in Indianapolis.

At this last enterprise his skill and sharp suggestions on efficiency had earned him rapid promotion and the offer of a partnership—until tragedy struck. While tightening a machine belt with a file, the point of the file flipped and pierced his right eye, robbing him of his sight (as well as a considerable amount of aqueous humor, which he watched puddle in his palm with his remaining eye). Muir feared he would be blind in the injured eye, and resolved during his recuperation that he would waste no more time "on the inventions of man, and devote myself to the inventions of God," by which he meant God's creation of the natural world.

To Muir's surprise and relief, most of the sight of his eye returned within several months. His resolve to devote himself wholeheartedly to exploring God's creation was unchanged, however, and he decided to introduce himself to the plants of the southern United States and then to press on to the Amazon basin. On the second day of September 1867, Muir walked across the bridge spanning the Ohio River from Jeffersonville, Indiana to Louisville, Kentucky, "joyful and free," he tells us in his journal. He traversed the city without speaking a word to anyone, and on the southern outskirts spread a map before him. "My plan was simply to push on in a general southward direction by the wildest, leafiest, and least trodden way I could find, promising the greatest extent of virgin forest … rejoicing in splendid visions of pines and palms and tropic flowers in glorious array."

Thus began a walk which would cover 1,000 miles, through Kentucky, Tennessee, North Carolina, Georgia, and Florida, ending two months later with Muir flat on his back with malaria for three further months in a sawmill outside the Gulf hamlet of Cedar Keys, Florida. Muir traveled remarkably light: his small shoulder bag contained (beside his journal) a towel, soap, comb, brush, single change of underwear, map of the South, three slim books (Burns' *Poetry*, Milton's *Paradise Lost*, the *New Testament*) and one thick one (Wood's *Botany*, for keying out plants). He also carried a plant press on his back, a light device of straps, wood slats, and rough-paper sheets with which to flatten and dry the many plants he collected, and periodically sent to his brother in Wisconsin for keeping.

Though this luggage seems singularly light to us, in fact it was more than Muir would carry on his subsequent rambles throughout the length of California's Sierra Nevada mountains, where his ever-present journal, a box of matches, and several loaves of bread typically comprised his entire load, disdaining even a blanket or overcoat.

True to his resolve to immerse himself in the forests of the South, Muir avoided towns, passing through only 22 his entire journey. He spent roughly half his nights indoors, in the attics of taverns or spare rooms of scattered farmhouses. The remainder of his nights were spent on the ground under the stars, with mosquitoes buzzing around him and beetles scurrying over his limbs. Food was many times given freely to him, usually cornbread and bacon, sometimes after suspicious questioning. But hunger was never far from Muir, and often enough desperately present. He averaged about 25 miles per day, though one day in Georgia, he writes, he "traveled to-day more than forty miles without dinner (lunch) or supper. No family would receive me, so I had to push on to Augusta."

Muir's principal object in his thousand-mile walk was encountering the forests and plants of the South. Here he was not disappointed. "Far the grandest of all Kentucky plants are her noble oaks," he proclaimed early on. "They are the master existences of her exuberant forests. Here is the Eden, the paradise of oaks."

In the Cumberland Mountains of Tennessee, Muir observes "There is nothing more eloquent in Nature than a mountain stream, and this is the first I ever saw. Its banks are luxuriantly peopled with rare and lovely flowers and overarching trees, making one of Nature's coolest and most hospitable places. Every tree, every flower, every ripple and eddy of this lovely stream seemed solemnly to feel the presence of the great Creator… Near this steam I spent some joyous time in a grand rock-dwelling full of mosses, birds, and flowers. Most heavenly place I ever entered."

It was in Florida that Muir most anticipated encountering new, exotic subtropical plants. He saw his first palmetto in a grassy opening on the edge of swampy woods. "A plain gray shaft, round as a broom-handle, and a crown of varnished channeled leaves…whether rocking and rustling in the wind or poised thoughtful and calm in the sunshine, it has a power of expression not excelled by any plant high or low that I have met in my whole walk thus far…They tell us that plants are perishable, soulless creatures, that only man is immortal, etc.; but this, I think, is something that we know very nearly nothing about. Anyhow, this palm was indescribably impressive and told me grander things than I ever got from human priest."

This first of Muir's lifetime of "saunters" was unusual in that he regularly encountered people throughout the journey. His descriptions of the people of the South, Negroes and white, are perceptive and entertaining, and give *A Thousand Mile Walk to the Gulf*, his journal entries assembled by Sierra Club friend William Frederic Bade, a different feel than Muir's other writings, as well as a valuable rendering of the South in the near aftermath of the Civil War.

Muir made this walk through the heart of the South a scant two years after the cessation of formal hostilities. The region remained racked by the war, the economy shattered, men solitary and in bands roaming the countryside murdering travelers for food and whatever money they might carry. Repeatedly Muir was warned by those he encountered, being assured that his life was in jeopardy. And repeatedly Muir ignored the good advice, and set off for yet another day through the ravaged countryside. The only danger that Muir did not face and survive was malaria, but that felled him only after he had reached the Gulf.

Early in the trip, on a level sandstone plateau amongst desolate fields in the Cumberland Mountains, Muir towards sundown came in sight of ten men watching his progress closely. "They all were mounted on rather scrawny horses, and all wore long hair hanging down on their shoulders. Evidently they belonged to the most irreclaimable of the guerrilla bands who, long accustomed to plunder, deplored the coming of peace…Without halting even for a moment, I advanced rapidly with long strides as though I intended to walk through the midst of them. When I got within a rod or so I looked up in their faces and smilingly bade them 'Howdy.' Stopping never an instant, I turned to one side and walked around them to get on the road again, and kept on without venturing to look back or betray the slightest fear of being robbed…I was not followed, however, probably because the plants projecting from my plant press made them believe that I was a poor herb doctor."

Muir's closest brush with violence came near the end of his trip, in Florida. "In a lonely, swampy place in the woods, I met a large, muscular, brawny young negro, who eyed me with glaring, wistful curiosity…He inquired where I came from, where I was going, and what brought me to such a wild country, where I was liable to be robbed, and perhaps killed. 'Oh, I am not afraid of any one robbing me,' I said, 'for I don't carry anything worth stealing.' 'Yes,' said he, 'but you can't travel without money.'

"I started to walk on, but he blocked my way. Then I noticed that he was trembling, and it flashed upon me all at once that he was thinking of knocking me down in order to rob me. After glaring at my pockets as if searching for weapons, he stammered in a quavering voice 'Do you carry shooting-irons?' His motives, which I ought to have noted sooner, now were apparent to me. Though I had no pistol, I instinctively threw my hand back to my pistol pocket and, with my eyes fixed on his, I marched up close to him and said, 'I allow people to find out if I am armed or not.' Then he quailed, stepped aside, and allowed me to pass, for fear of being shot. This was evidently a narrow escape."

Muir navigated the inherent dangers of solitary travel in the immediate postwar South through luck, bravado, and a strict prohibition of camp fires in his many nights in the open, so as not to advertise his presence to "prowling mischief makers." He was conscientious, though, to note the numerous instances of generosity and kindness to him by both whites and Negroes. On September 6, Muir "overtook an old negro driving an ox team. Rode with him a few miles and had some interesting chat concerning war, wild fruits of the woods, et cetera…I asked him if he would like a renewal of these sad war times, when his flexible face suddenly calmed, and he said with intense earnestness, 'Oh, Lo'd, want no mo wa, Lo'd no.' Many of these Kentucky negroes are shrewd and intelligent, and when warmed upon a subject that interests them, are eloquent in no mean degree."

Regarding the white folks he met, Muir praises their courtesy but does not overlook the common prejudice towards Negroes. He comments on "that open, unconstrained cordiality which is characteristic of the better class of Southern people." In Georgia, he "was received at the house of

Dr. Perkins…Heard long recitals of war happenings, discussion of the slave question, and Northern politics; a thoroughly characteristic Southern family, refined in manners and kind, but immovably prejudiced on everything connected with slavery."

Despite the bleakness of the landscape and society, Muir was ever ready to appreciate the humor in a situation. In the Cumberland Mountains, after much back-and-forth amongst "roads (which) never seem to proceed with any fixed purpose, but wander as if lost," Muir "reached the house of a negro driver, with whom I put up for the night. Received a good deal of knowledge which may be of use should I ever be a negro teamster."

And "in Murphy (North Carolina) I was hailed by the sheriff who could not determine by my colors and rigging to what country or craft I belonged. Since the war, every other stranger in these lonely parts is supposed to be a criminal, and all are objects of curiosity or apprehensive concern. After a few minutes' conversation with this chief man of Murphy I was pronounced harmless, and invited to his house, where for the first time since leaving home I found a house decked with flowers and vines, clean within and without, and stamped with the comforts of culture and refinement in all its arrangements."

Accustomed as he was to the hard-working, tidy immigrant community of his youth in Wisconsin, to which his family had emigrated from Scotland when he was twelve years old, Muir's frequent encounters with back-country living in the South, particularly in the mountains, did not impress him.

"All the machines of Kentucky and Tennessee are far behind the age," he observes. "There is scarce a trace of that restless spirit of speculation and invention so characteristic of the North. But one way of doing things obtains here, as if laws had been passed making attempts at improvement a crime…This is the most primitive country I have seen, primitive in everything. The remotest hidden parts of Wisconsin are far in advance of the mountain regions of Tennessee and North Carolina." He recounts a philosopher in the Kentucky hills mocking the uppity ways of an ambitious neighbor: "'There's a place back heah,' said my worthy entertainer, 'whar there's a mill-house, an' a store-house, an' a still-house, an' a spring-house, an' a blacksmith shop—all in the same yard! Cows too, an' heaps of big gals a-milkin' them.'" Such a thing!

Given his time amongst such places and peoples, Muir particularly relished his days among the natural beauty of trees and streams. Describing Bonaventure Graveyard outside Savannah, Muir observes that "You hear the song of birds, cross a small stream, and are with Nature in the grand old forest graveyard, so beautiful that almost any sensible person would choose to dwell here with the dead rather than with the lazy, disorderly living."

Muir's low point on his thousand-mile walk occurred in Savannah. He arrived with a dollar and a half in his pocket, and eagerly checked the post office for an expected money draft from his brother. It had not arrived. "Feel dreadfully lonesome and poor. Went to the meanest looking lodging-house that I could find, on account of its cheapness." The money package did not arrive the next day, nor the four next days. Muir could not afford even the "meanest looking" hostel again, and had noted numerous menacing bands of ex-slaves checking out travelers in the city and its environs. Where to sleep with reasonable expectation of avoiding robbery or worse? He hit upon the Bonaventure Graveyard outside of town, where "no superstitious prowling mischief maker dares venture for fear of haunting ghosts."

The graveyard was Muir's resting place for five nights, where "on rising I found that my head had been resting on a grave, and though my sleep had not been quite so sound as that of the person below, I arose refreshed, and looking about me, the morning sunbeams pouring through the oaks and gardens dripping with dew, the beauty displayed was so glorious and exhilarating that hunger and care seemed only a dream."

After several days subsisting on a few crackers in the morning and evening, though, Muir became weak and dizzy. Unable to secure employment of any sort in the town, he would trudge from graveyard to post office each morning, only to be disappointed. By the sixth morning, he was hallucinating. "I was becoming faint, and in making the journey to the town was alarmed to find myself growing staggery and giddy. The ground ahead seemed to be rising up in front of me, and the little streams in the ditches on the sides of the road seemed to be flowing up hill. Then I realized that I was becoming dangerously hungry."

Finally the funds arrived. "Gladly I pocketed my money, and had not gone along the street more than a few rods before I met a very large negro woman with a tray of gingerbread, in which I immediately invested some of my new wealth, and walked rejoicingly, munching along the street, making no attempt to conceal the pleasure I had in eating. Then, still hunting for more food, I found a sort of eating-place in a market and had a large regular meal on top of the gingerbread! Thus my 'marching through Georgia' terminated handsomely in a jubilee of bread."

Muir had originally planned to press on from the Gulf of Mexico to South America, forge Humboldt-like through the tropical forest to a tributary of the Amazon, and raft down the great river's entire length. Muir himself in later years acknowledged that the idea was foolish. Fortunately he was not able to find a ship to take him to South America, and settled instead on California, to see the Sierra Nevada's recently discovered Yosemite Valley. Muir more than reached his botanical goals on his thousand-mile walk through the South, as he encountered, keyed, pressed and collected hundreds of new plants, reveling in their splendor.

Reading Muir's journal entries during the ramble, one is struck by two things. First, of course, is how foolish Muir was to trudge solitary through the American South but two years after the devastation of the Civil War. Indeed, by his own account he was frequently in real danger of his life. Only luck and his steely courage in tight situations brought him through.

Second, one is struck by how winning Muir's ways were with the vast majority of the people he met, white and Negro. With the Negroes, he is usually freely given food and lodging and enjoys the company. With the whites, sometimes the same is the case, though often there is initial refusal and considerable questioning before his acceptance. This ability of Muir to attract and win over his fellows was a constant throughout his life, from postbellum South to, later, the elegant salons of San Francisco, New York, and London.

That there were limits to Muir's likability and luck is clear, though. The marauding bands of whites and Negroes, thick in all the lands he traversed, were immune to Muir's charm. He recognized this and avoided the dangers, for the most part, by eschewing camp fires, sleeping in a graveyard, and brazenly bluffing his way through the threat if all else failed.

His journal entries reveal that the experience of wandering freely through new lands and societies, often braving danger, hunger, and loneliness, opened Muir to perspectives and possibilities not previously considered in his 29 years of life. To a worldview, indeed, not previously well explored anywhere in the West.

In Muir's journal of this thousand-mile walk we find startling observations and thoughts regarding death, the nature of creation, the rights and roles of alligators, the place of humans in the world, and man's curious concept of God as "a civilized, law-abiding gentleman in favor either of a republican form of government or a limited monarchy."

We will consider these radical, new views in later chapters. Suffice it for now to note that his long ramble to the Gulf opened Muir's eyes and his mind, and took him a giant first step toward a way of viewing the world unknown in the Western tradition beyond hints and anomalies. A way of viewing the world that would, over a century later, provide a ray of hope to rescue the human enterprise from an existential danger it was signally failing to resolve.

Sierra Nevada Geologist, Botanist (1869)

*"His open blue eyes of honest questioning, and glorious auburn
hair might have stood as a portrait of the angel Raphael."*

—THERESE YELVERTON, VISCOUNTESS AVONMORE

Muir arrived in San Francisco harbor in spring of 1868. Much as he did to begin his thousand-mile walk, he promptly traversed the city, took the ferry to Oakland, walked south to Pacheco Pass, and then down into the San Joaquin portion of California's great Central Valley, "the floweriest piece of world I ever walked." Trampling upon scores of golden flowers with each step, he followed the Merced River across the valley, up into the foothills, and through the lower montane forest to Yosemite Valley (a mere two-hundred-mile walk).

To provide his daily bread he soon secured employment as a shepherd back at the edge of the foothills, overseeing a flock of sheep through the fall and winter. The next spring he helped drive the flock to its winter pasturage in Tuolumne Meadows and back (recounted in *My First Summer in the Sierras*), and formed the resolve to spend time in the great Yosemite Valley he had gazed upon wistfully from its north rim.

From the summer of 1869 to the summer of 1871 Muir was a sawyer and handyman in Yosemite Valley for James Hutchings, an early promoter of the valley and owner of a lodge for visitors there. Muir had early noted evidence of glaciation in the valley and surrounding high country, and soon was entertaining visitors with his claim that glaciers had shaped the stunning landscape, a view starkly at variance with the official dictum in guidebooks. Muir's brilliance and winning ways soon established him as the authoritative guide to the valley, much to the annoyance of Hutchings. Many visitors arrived in the valley from San Francisco and Oakland with specific instructions to see Muir, given them by Jeanne Carr, a prominent Bay Area civic leader.

Mrs. Carr, also newly a Californian, was a Muir admirer from his Madison days, being captivated by him from the moment she judged his mechanical inventions in the 1860 Wisconsin State Fair (which garnered ribbons and widespread acclaim). Muir took geology and chemistry courses from her husband at the University of Wisconsin, and soon was sharing meals with the Carrs and entertaining their children with his stories and impersonations. Muir and Mrs. Carr already corresponded frequently when Professor Ezra Carr moved to the new University of California. Everyone, or at least everyone important, was known by Mrs. Carr.

When the old and much-lionized Ralph Waldo Emerson visited California in 1870, Mrs. Carr insisted that he see Muir in his visit to Yosemite Valley. The old man did, and was as taken with Muir as plantation masters and Negro teamsters had been earlier. Emerson tried to convince Muir to move to Boston and become the editor of Henry David Thoreau's papers, but Muir declined. Arriving back in Boston, Emerson made one last addition before his death to a short list of "My Men" whom he greatly admired: John Muir.

Others won over by Muir in these two years included Joseph Le Conte, geology professor at the University of California. On a field trip with students, Le Conte invited Muir to join them on a trek to the Sierra high country above Yosemite Valley. By the time they had reached Tuolumne Meadows, Le Conte was convinced by Muir's ideas of glacial sculpturing of the terrain (though he disagreed with Muir on the exclusive importance of the role of glaciers).

Another Yosemite visitor was Therese Yelverton, Viscountess Avonmore, a glamorous adventuress who had won fame (of sorts) in England and was on a world tour. The countess too fell under Muir's spell, though perhaps in a different manner than Emerson and Le Conte, and promptly wrote a novel depicting a charismatic protagonist named Kenmuir: "His open blue eyes of honest questioning, and glorious auburn hair might have stood as a portrait of the angel Raphael." She solicited Muir to join her on her globe-circling trip's next leg, to China, as her "secretary." Muir promptly fled the valley, and stayed away until the disappointed countess' ship was several days at sea.

His two years at the University of Wisconsin had conspired with his own inclinations to render Muir a nascent scientist. He was already a competent botanist when he arrived in California, and the glacial clues in Yosemite permitted him the application of his geological studies and their furtherance through extensive readings. In July of 1871 the frugally living Muir had saved enough money (even regularly sending portions to his family in Wisconsin) to quit his job as sawyer, and devote himself full-time to exploring Yosemite and its high country over the next three years, with the aim of gathering conclusive evidence of glaciation and presenting it in a scientific paper.

One suspects several, equally important motivations. Muir's journals reveal an intense, ecstatic joy in his mountain rambles. His sawyer employment restricted these rambles to Sundays and the occasional guiding of visitors; Muir wanted more. In addition, as his glacial ideas became widely known and commented upon, he had drawn the icy disapproval of California's state geologist, the eminent Harvard professor Josiah Whitney, who rejected Muir's claim in withering tones. Whitney moreover dismissed Muir himself as an "ignorant shepherd." Muir doubtless felt impelled to defend his views, and himself, with a meticulously researched scientific presentation.

We will trace two of Muir's rambles in this period of his life, from July 1871 to the fall of 1874. First, his October 1871 penetration of one of the most inaccessible of the high country's mountain redoubts, where he discovered the first living glacier in the Sierra Nevada. And second, his September 1873 traverse of the entire Sierra Nevada range (much of this along what would become The John Muir Trail) from Yosemite Valley to Mr. Whitney (yes, the same geologist Whitney), where he survived perhaps the most harrowing night of his life atop an icy promontory now called Mt. Muir.

Muir's extended trips into the high country soon took on a pattern. He traveled light, lighter even than on his thousand-mile walk. Typically he would clamber Indian Canyon's steep three-thousand-foot ascent out of Yosemite Valley (just east of Yosemite Falls) with neither overcoat nor blanket, taking with him only matches, tea bags, his journal tied to his belt, and as many loaves of bread as he could carry. Once in the high country, he ranged far and wide in a swift, mile-eating gait. Wherever he was when darkness fell, that was his camp. He would gather some leafy (or needly) boughs between him and the bare earth (incense cedar was his favorite, though he made do with any conifer), scavenge downed branches with which to start a fire (often in the protection of a rock or toppled tree), and munch some bread with his tea.

He would spend much of the night admiring the stars and the firelight's reflection off nearby trees, then build up the fire and sleep until his side away from the fire was cold enough to wake him. Awake, he built up the fire again, and lay down with his formerly cold side now facing the fire. He repeated this procedure through the night. When morning came he'd brew tea, allow himself a bit of bread as he admired the gathering beams of the sun spreading over the landscape, then douse the fire and set off again in his long, springy strides.

Muir would remain in the high country until his bread ran out, typically stay another day, then reluctantly head back to Yosemite Valley. There he'd rest a day or two, catch up on correspondence from Mrs. Carr, perhaps greet yet another visitor wishing to see him, then impatiently set off for the high country again.

3

Discovery of a Living Glacier (1871)

"Ice creations of this kind are perfectly enchanting, notwithstanding one feels so entirely out of place in their pure fountain beauty."

As he relentlessly explored the mountains and canyons in all directions from Yosemite Valley, noting scores of locations where the signs of glacial activity could be plainly seen—striations, polished surfaces, moraines, erratics left as the glaciers shrank—one wish came to dominate his mind, a dark desire as close to lust as Muir would apparently ever get. Every fiber of Muir's lean body ached to find the single phenomenon that would irrefutably prove his thesis.

Muir wanted badly to find a *living glacier*. Not a huge, hulking glacier filling an entire valley—the day was long since past for that—but the diminished remnant of one of those former glaciers, hidden away in some remote, cold mountain refuge, so rugged and high that no one had ever fought their way to see it. Muir felt in his bones that if a living glacier existed in the Sierra, he was the man to penetrate to its lair and introduce himself.

So he forged on, day after day through the summer months of 1871 and into the fall, pushing himself into the high canyons and up tributaries of the Merced, the Tuolumne, the Tenaya, the Illilouette, the Yosemite Rivers, climbing higher and higher into the great mountain ranges. He drove himself mercilessly, begrudging every return to the valley for bread, lamenting his weakness to need food to carry on. In early October he climbed east up the Merced River past Vernal Fall and Nevada Falls into Little Yosemite Valley, pressing eastward along the river past Clouds Rest to the north, past Echo Creek coming down from Cathedral Peak, past Merced Lake, continuing to follow the Merced as it turned southeast where Lewis Creek flows into it from Vogelsang Peak.

Still Muir pushed on; the morning of October 6 he came into sight of the great amphitheater of peaks where a dozen falling creeks and forks of the Merced came together to form the river. The river canyon deepens here, with the peaks of the Cathedral Range looming to the northeast (Simmons, Lyell, Florence, Forester) and those of the Clark Range to the southwest (Clark, Gray, Red, Black (now Merced) and Triple Divide). Muir drove himself on, past an enchanting little lake that he would come back to and call Shadow, or Nevada, and we now call Washburn.

He plunged up the side canyons on the north side of the Clark Range, canyon by canyon. In the canyon between Red Mountain and Black Mountain he followed a stream up and up, and on a whim struck off along a small tributary. On a stretch of the creek where the water slowed as it emerged from a line of rocks, Muir caught a glimpse of silt on the bottom. Splashing into the creek, he knelt and scooped some of the silt into his palm, a silvery silt fine as flour. Muir flushed. "Glacial mud!" he breathed, his voice breaking. "Mountain meal!"—the characteristic product of glacial ice grinding over rock.

Muir jerked upright, glanced about wildly, and crashed through underbrush to mount what he now knew was the moraine of a glacier. Cresting the line of rocks, he caught his breath—before him stretched a small glacier, butting up against the ramparts of Black Mountain. "A living glacier!" he shouted to the mountains. Feverishly he launched himself onto the glacier as his cry echoed, running until he came to a crevasse. Looking in, he could see the blue-green gleam of ice. Muir plunged up the snow atop the glacier to the Black Mountain cliff face, and saw the *bergshrund*, the space where the moving glacier pulled itself away from the cliff, creating the opening into which fresh snow would pile every winter and be compressed into new ice.

Looking into the icy depths, he was aware of his heart's wild pounding. Muir breathed hard, and without thinking began the dangerous navigation down the ice wall into the very womb of the glacier. "A series of rugged zig-zags enabled me to make my way down into the weird ice world of the *Shrund*. Its chambered hollows were hung with a multitude of clustered icicles, amidst which thin subdued light pulsed and shimmered with indescribable loveliness. Water dripped and tinkled overhead, and from far below there came strange solemn murmurs from currents that were feeling their way among veins and fissures on the bottom.

"Ice creations of this kind are perfectly enchanting, notwithstanding one feels so entirely out of place in their pure fountain beauty. I was soon uncomfortably cold in my shirt sleeves, and the leaning wall of the *Shrund* seemed really to ingulph me. Yet it was hard to leave the delicious music of the water, and still more intense loveliness of the light."

Muir would in following months discover two more glaciers, abutting the Cathedral Range's Mt. Lyell and Mt. Maclure. And in the next two years he would record a total of 65 residual glaciers in the northern Sierra Nevada. All were exciting, but none so magical as this first one deep in the amphitheater of peaks giving birth to the Merced River.

4

Tracing the Sierras to Mt. Whitney (1873)

"I had to dance all night to keep from freezing, and was feeble and starving next morning."

By the fall of 1873, Muir's geological studies around Yosemite were substantially complete. He had traversed more of the Merced and Tuolumne River basins than any man alive, and no one knew more of this area's geology and botany. But the great basins of the San Joaquin, Kings, Kaweah, and Kern Rivers to the south were a tantalizing blank to Muir. Add in that the southern Sierras had the highest mountains of the range, including all the towering 14,000 foot peaks culminating in Mt. Whitney, the highest point in the contiguous 48 states—being ignorant of all this was intolerable to Yosemite's most famous mountaineer. When the California Academy of Sciences botanist Albert Kellog asked Muir to join him on a survey of the southern Sierras, Muir gladly agreed, and enlisted Galen Clark to come along.

Clark, whom Muir claimed was the best mountaineer he had ever met, had grown up sickly back East and failed at any number of attempts to earn a living. After coughing up copious amounts of blood at age 42, and being told by physicians that he had less than a year of life remaining, Clark decided to live out the brief time left to him in a beautiful place. He set up camp in a sunny meadow some 35 miles south of Yosemite Valley, surrounded by soaring pines and cedars in the pure mountain air. The place must have agreed with him, for instead of dying within the year, he lived there for another 54 years, nearly reaching his 96th birthday.

Clark's stewardship of Yosemite Valley and his discovery of the Mariposa Grove of Giant Sequoias near his meadow (which he named Wawona, after the Miwok name for "big trees") led to his being appointed the official "Guardian" of what was then the California state reserve of Yosemite Valley and Mariposa Grove.

Muir had taken many jaunts into the high country with Clark, who had gained both health and strength in the mountains. While he could outstrip Clark "up talus slopes and across slippery cobbles," Muir admitted that the now-burly Clark could outpace him in bulling his way through thick streamside underbrush. Like Muir, Clark was indefatigable in the high country, and even less concerned with comfort, having developed the habit of just lying on the bare ground to sleep at night, disdaining Muir's gathering of conifer boughs for a "bed." The perfect companion for a long trek the length of the Sierra Nevada, in other words.

The company was completed by Billy Sims, a young artist eager to see the mountains, particularly in the company of the increasingly famous John Muir. In retrospect, such a diverse group guaranteed tension, at least, discord possibly, though Muir's harrowing brush with disaster at 14,000 feet at the very end was unforeseen. They would not be traveling as Muir did when alone. Several mules and horses carried their food, gear, and Kellogg's plant presses. The disparate group and its caravan of support beasts set out from Wawona, in what is now the southern portion of Yosemite National Park, on September 19 of 1873.

Muir journaled their trip in laconic entries, indicating their route by the waterways they followed and the divides between basins they traversed. Muir perceived landscape in terms of rivers and mountains; he would gaze upon a scene and see great basins (watersheds, in today's terms) demarcated by divides between ranges of peaks. This organic sense of how the land arranged itself did not preclude appreciation of the sheer beauty of the scene, but it revealed Muir's deep, instinctive ability to "read" the land more accurately and thoroughly than any of his contemporaries.

So the grand journey revealed itself to Muir as a southerly sequence of river basins to cross: the Merced, then the San Joaquin, then the Kings, with a view of the Kaweah before the final push to the Kern River canyon and the great mountain due east of it. The general procedure would be to follow a river fork upstream, cross a high dividing range into the next river basin to the south, follow the southernmost fork to the next basin, and repeat until they arrived at Mt. Whitney, the top of the (American) world.

"On divide between Chiquito Creek and South Fork Merced" reads his September 19 entry, indicating that he has led the company from "Camp Clark" at Wawona, up the South Fork of the Merced River early in the day, then ascended the ridge which divides the Merced drainage from that of the San Joaquin River to the south, at the point that Chiquito Creek runs down the south side of the divide toward the San Joaquin. "From the divide we obtained a glorious view of all the heads of the San Joaquin River excepting the north forks," Muir notes in his journal.

The San Joaquin drains a large expanse of the north-central Sierra, its north and middle forks originating on Mt. Ritter's flanks, and its south fork flowing from Mt. Darwin's slopes in the upper reaches of today's Kings Canyon National Park—a spread of some 50 miles north to south. Once they had left the Merced basin and entered into that of the San Joaquin at Chiquito Creek, Muir's band followed what he termed the San Joaquin Middle Fork upstream (east) for several days. We assume that where trails existed alongside the river, those were taken; but Muir and Clark would probably strike out cross-country more often than Kellogg and the artist Sims would have preferred.

They found the canyons alongside the San Joaquin steep and difficult to traverse; "Made tedious progress, horses and mules tending constantly to roll down canyon...The average slope of San Joaquin Canyon, Middle Fork, is twenty-three degrees for a height of seventy-five hundred feet," Muir recorded on September 22. Hot and doubtless annoyed at the steep going, they turned south onto the South Fork, passing on September 23 the point where Mono Creek enters that fork. "We pass a lake lovely with ducks and rippling glassy dark mountains nobly sculptured, sheer to the water. Pines and junipers stand picturesquely on the rock headlands… Hum of bees, and dragonflies…Altitude seventy-one hundred feet."

Now they pushed on south alongside the San Joaquin's south fork, with Muir characteristically appreciating that "In this poor rocky wilderness…View very grand and universal. Ritter (some 25 miles to the northeast) the noblest and most ornate of all…Snowy peaks loom yet beyond at the head of Kings River forest (some 20 miles to the south)." What Kellog and Sims, or Clark for that matter, thought of the grinding journey is lost to us, though strong hints will soon emerge.

On September 26, the eighth day, Muir tires of their slow, beast-dictated pace, and leaves the others near Florence Lake to explore "the icy summits" ahead, taking a week's worth of provisions. Presumably Kellog will spend the time collecting plants, Sims sketching scenery. Clark's choice not to accompany Muir is puzzling. We know that Clark took his guardianship seriously; possibly he was chafing to return to his duties in Yosemite. We also know that Clark was at this time depressed at growing debt from his inn at Wawona catering to travelers to the valley. Though he had become a superb mountaineer, Clark was still as poor at business matters as ever.

On his own now, Muir a day later encountered a band of mountain sheep: "They crossed the river between the steps of the cascade where the channel was blocked and bridged with big boulders…making leaps on glacial bosses that made me hold my breath…they leaped up the face of the mountain just where I thought they wouldn't, and perhaps couldn't, go. I could have scaled the same precipice, but not where they did…Like the true mountaineers they are, they never seemed to hurry…Looking at them I often cried out, 'That was good!'…I exulted in the power and sufficiency of Nature, and felt like saying aloud to God as to a man, 'Well done!'… These noble fellows—I would like their company!"

After several more days scaling today's Mount Darwin and Mount Goethe, Muir rejoined the party back on the south fork of the San Joaquin upstream from Florence Lake, and with Clark climbed to the divide between the San Joaquin and the Kings basins "to view the landscape and plan the route. The view is awful—a vast wilderness of rocks and canyons. Clark groaned and went home," his old adventuring days crushed by cares.

Without Clark, then, Muir leads the group southeast over the divide into the Kings River basin on October 1, probably over the 11,296-foot Hell for Sure Pass (named by someone who clearly had not climbed the much tougher Forester Pass further south, at 13,160 feet). They then followed the King's north fork down into the oaks of the foothills to the west, arriving at Thomas Mills five days later, doubtless to replenish their provisions and allow Kellogg to ship bales of plant specimens back to civilization.

Following "Mill Creek" upstream to the east (probably today's Mill Flat Creek), Muir and the others visited the already-famous General Grant tree several days later, judged today to be the second largest Giant Sequoia, and thus the second largest creature on the planet (by weight). They camped that night on the divide between the Kings River basin and that of the Kaweah to the south.

With doubtless a wistful look at the Kaweah basin (he would return and explore it fully in 1875 on his survey of Giant Sequoia groves), Muir led the group north for a day and a half to the South Fork of the Kings River, camping in the Grand Canyon of the Kings, which reminded Muir much of Yosemite Valley in many details. They journeyed east up the South Fork, doubtless on the rim of the deep, rugged canyon rather than actually alongside the river, and camped that night "At mouth of first tributary of South Fork Kings River," which would be Bubbs Creek flowing west from Vidette Meadow below Kearsarge Pass, on the other side of the range.

Here Muir again feels the call of the surrounding icy summits, and leaves the likely disgruntled Kellogg and Sims "at camp with the animals" while he makes a dash for "Mt. Tyndall". En route he spends a moonlit night high amongst the peaks: "A grand mountain towers above my camp. A rushing stream brawls past its base. Willows are on one side, dwarf *flexilis* on the other. The moon is doing marvels in whitening the peaks with a pearly luster, as if each mountain contained a moon. I have leveled a little spot on the mountain-side where I may nap by my fireside. The altitude of my camp is eleven thousand five hundred feet and I am blanketless."

Muir rises early the next day and reaches the peak of "Mt. Tyndall" by nine. Early Muir biographer Linnie Marsh Wolfe in a footnote says "Not the present Mount Tyndall. Perhaps it was a peak on the Kings-Kern divide, or perhaps Mount Brewer." Since Muir on the peak writes "Had grand views of the valley of the Kern…and north and south along the axis of the range, and out over the Inyo Range and the Great Basin," it was more likely today's Mount Geneva he climbed, on the Kings-Kern divide, from whence the described views may be had.

Perhaps realizing that he is straining the patience of his colleagues, Muir "descended and pushed back to the main camp. Arrived about noon to find Billy and Dr. Kellogg gone, though they promised to wait three days for me. They left me neither horse nor provisions." Whatever pent-up frustration prompted this extraordinary abandonment of Muir by the others, it must have been of considerable magnitude. Leaving anyone without food in the middle of the wildest part of the Sierra Nevada, particularly late in the season, was a grievous insult, potentially a lethal one—at least for anyone other than Muir (or Galen Clark, perhaps). As it was, Muir promptly struck off on the trail of his colleagues in his long strides, crossed the central Sierra Nevada in a day, climbed the formidable 11,823-foot Kearsarge Pass, and finally caught up with his erstwhile colleagues (and food!) a mile on the far side of the pass as dusk fell.

"When asked why they had left me," Muir records, "they said they feared I would not return. Strange that in the mountains people from cities should so surely lose their heads." We can well imagine the scene may have been more dramatic than Muir's record of it. Muir seems not to have any idea that his frequent abandoning of his colleagues to climb nearby peaks might have contributed to their extraordinary behavior toward him.

On October 13 "We descended the long pass, which is one steep declivity scarce broken from top to bottom" (to which I can only say "Amen!", having struggled up Kearsarge Pass the opposite direction several times). "In a few hours we passed from ice and snow to the torrid plain. I took some provisions and my horse and left the party at the foot of the pass to make an excursion to Mount Whitney, while the rest of the party went to Independence."

The formal journey was done; Kellogg had his plants from the southern Sierra Nevada, Billy Sims his sketches (including a fine study of Muir), and all parties were doubtless relieved. Once again Muir took off alone to climb the peaks, but this time his goal was Mt. Whitney, the highest point in the Sierras (and North America, south of Alaska).

Unknown to Muir at the time, what Clarence King had described as Mt. Whitney when he became the first man to climb it two years earlier was not the range's highest peak, but rather what today we call Mt. Langley, at a mere (!) 14,042 feet some 5 miles south of today's Whitney. It was following King's published directions that Muir directed his path south along the east base of the range, then "over into the valley of the Kern by the Hockett Trail." That is, in a mere two days Muir descended from Kearsarge Pass on the spine of the Sierra Nevada, pushed south past the roads to the hamlets of Independence and Lone Pine to a point south of the purported Mt. Whitney, then climbed back up to the divide again, probably near Army Pass at 11,475 feet, and into the Kern basin west of the spine, where he camped the night of October 14. Such a trek would exhaust even Muir, and probably contributed to the near-disaster that was about to unfold.

His journal tells us that Muir rose October 15, left the horse and provisions in his camp, and climbed to the summit that had mistakenly been proclaimed Mt. Whitney. Arriving on that summit after a challenging climb in rough terrain, the sharp-eyed Muir observed another peak about five miles to the north that, strangely, seemed higher. His hand-held spirit-level indicated that northern peak (today's Whitney) was indeed five hundred feet higher—an astonishingly accurate estimate, considering the relatively crude instrument he was using; today's GPS satellite reckoning puts the actual number at 468 feet higher.

Predictably, Muir immediately set out to reach the higher peak. "The way was very rough, up and down canyons," he writes in his journal with typical vast understatement. I can attest that making your way along the spine of the Sierra Nevada in the vicinity of Mt. Whitney is a grueling challenge. Even today, the trail along the spine to Whitney from Trail Crest junction hardly warrants the term, so rough is the terrain, so strewn with jagged giant boulders. And of course you are climbing at 14,000 feet—another world altogether, thousands of feet above tree line or water, where temperatures quickly plunge below freezing as daylight wanes through most of the year, certainly in mid-October. Beyond all this, the thin atmosphere clouds the mental process, even for a hiker fresh and rested.

On Muir climbed over the brutal landscape at the top of the world, as the temperature plunged and gale winds buffeted him. Darkness fell, and he foolishly persisted. "Though tired, I made up my mind to spend the night climbing, as I could not sleep. I took bearings by the stars." Around midnight he found himself on a peak still south of the true Mt. Whitney by 2.5 miles or so.

Even Muir was by now too exhausted to go further. He sank down upon the peak—which today we call Mount Muir, at 14,015 feet—to his knees, then his side. His head swam, and he began to slip into the blessed darkness of sleep. The temperature was far below freezing, 22 degrees below zero, biographer Wolfe claims. Abruptly Muir jerked awake. Sleep meant death, he realized with a gasp. He staggered to his feet. His jaw was aching, the last several day's exertions having brought on an ulcerated tooth. His life depended on his staying awake. His legs began jerking into old Scottish patterns. He flung his arms up and danced a Highland fling, dancing until he fell exhausted. He lay panting on the rocky summit of Mt. Muir, then as sleep beckoned he forced himself up and danced some more. Through the long, frigid night he kept himself alive by dancing and waving his arms and bellowing old Scottish ballads.

Daybreak came to the jagged peaks, mercifully bringing to a close perhaps the most harrowing night of his life. "In the cold dawn," Wolfe tells us, drawing on Muir's later journals, "he set out again for the summit. Half out of his mind with cold, hunger, and the blazing pain in his jaw, he struggled on. Suddenly he stopped and clung to the rocks, with everything swimming about him. Then, as in previous emergencies, the other self took control. 'I felt,' he related, 'as if Someone caught me by the shoulders and turned me around forcibly, saying "Go back" in an audible voice.' So he went resignedly down the mountainside."

In his journal, Muir simply noted for October 15 that "I had to dance all night to keep from freezing, and was feeble and starving next morning." And only two sentences for October 16: "I had to turn back without gaining the top. Was exhausted ere I reached horse and camp and food." Muir rode and walked down the mountain to the little town of Independence, where he slept and ate for two solid days.

Then, of course, he returned to Mt. Whitney. Even though the California Geological Survey flatly stated that the 14,000-foot peaks here could not be reached from the east side, and never had been, Muir approached what he now knew was the true Mt. Whitney from the east and a bit north of the peak, surveying the landscape. He took his time.

"October 19. Set out afoot for the summit by direct course up the east side. Camped in the sage at a small spring the first night.

"October 20. I pushed up the canyon which leads past the north shoulder of the mountain. Camped at the timber line."

Muir was avoiding the treacherous southern approach which had nearly cost him his life days before. His probable route was up the North Fork of Lone Pine Creek, camping perhaps at today's Upper Boy Scout Lake on the 19th, then up through Iceberg Lake Canyon and reaching the spine of the range north of Whitney, between Whitney and Mount Russell (itself at 14,086 feet).

"October 21. I climb to the summit by 8 a.m., sketch and gain glorious views, and descend to the foot of the range."

Unmentioned in his journal, but described in later writings, at the peak of the true Mt. Whitney Muir noticed a yeast-powder can containing two notes. One was from a fisherman who had reached the peak a month and a half before Muir. The second note was from Clarence King himself, who had realized his mistake of two years ago, and returned to rectify the situation but a month and two days before Muir.

As he gazed at the "glorious views" from atop Whitney—the Great Basin shimmering hot and purple-tinged to the east, the procession of magnificent, snowy 14,000-foot summits to the south and north—Muir had to be overwhelmed by a quiet exultation in the midst of his exhaustion. He had added the great basins and peaks of the San Joaquin, the Kings, and the Kern rivers to his experiences. He had gazed into the Kaweah basin (and would return to it two years later). He had summited many of the icy peaks surrounding him, and survived a terrible night atop one directly south of where he stood, that one day would bear his own name. And he stood on the highest peak in the lower 48 United States, where but a handful of men had preceded him.

Even Muir had to realize that he had not made fast friends of Albert Kellogg or Billy Simms. But the journey was not for forming friendships. The journey was for introducing himself to the peaks and basins of the Sierra Nevada, the entire Sierra Nevada. For probing deep into the heart of mountains and rivers, ice, stone, and water. And that he had done in fine style. He glanced at the peak to the south on which he'd spent that long night. Muir shook his head, and uttered a soft laugh. He stiffly tried a step of Highland fling, failed, and with a wry smile turned to begin his descent.

A Jubilee of Mountains and Rivers (1877)

"They made me eat and sleep, stuffing me with turkey, chicken,
beef, fruits and jellies in the most extravagant manner."

Even by Muir standards, the fall of 1877 was full of outdoor adventures, much of it beyond the Sierra Nevada. Ever since giving *The Overland Monthly* the seven-part article setting forth his Yosemite glacial studies in September of 1874, Muir felt his time of intense immersion in Yosemite Valley and its environs was at an end. "No one of the rocks seems to call me now, nor any of the distant mountains. Surely this Merced and Tuolumne chapter of my life is done," he wrote to Jeanne Carr.

By November of 1874 Muir had ventured beyond the Sierra Nevada on a trip to 14,142-foot Mount Shasta in northern California, a southern peak of the Cascade Range. He returned to Shasta in April of 1875, where he was caught atop the peak in a storm and spent the night lying half-in boiling hot springs as snow pelted the other side of his body—freezing above, scalding below, a long, trying night approaching the earlier one atop Mt. Muir in discomfort and danger. So he knew Mt. Shasta reasonably well. Returning from trips to Nevada's Wasatch Mountain and southern California's San Gabriel Mountains in the fall of 1877, he found the Harvard botanist Asa Gray in San Francisco with a plea to lead him, Mrs. Gray, and the Englishman Sir Joseph Hooker on a botanizing expedition to Mt. Shasta. Muir eagerly accepted.

Muir's company on this trip reflected his rise on the national stage. Gray was America's leading botanist, a friend and correspondent of Charles Darwin, and the acknowledged American champion of Darwin's new theory of evolution by natural selection. Muir had spent a week collecting plants in Yosemite with Gray in the summer of 1872, and both men were impressed with the other. Gray lauded Muir as among the best "plant finders" he knew, and Muir allowed that Gray had the best "travelling legs" in the field of anyone beside himself and Galen Clark, which was saying a lot. Gray would later name two new-found plants after Muir, a signal honor.

Gray's companion Hooker was Darwin's closest friend in England, and as director of the prestigious Kew Gardens, England's most prominent botanist. Heady company, indeed, but by this fall of 1877 Muir's steady stream of articles in the *New York Tribune*, and national magazines such as *Scribners, Harpers, The Century*, and *Atlantic Monthly* had garnered him a devoted following from California to New York among scientists, naturalists, educators, and politicians alike.

On their way north to Shasta, the company stopped in the small town of Chico to pick up John and Annie Bidwell, and Annie's sister from Washington, D.C. Bidwell had wooed and won Annie while in Washington D.C. serving in the House of Representatives; wedding guests included President Andrew Johnson and future president Ulysses S. Grant. Bidwell himself would run for president as the Prohibition Party candidate in 1892. The Bidwell ranch in Chico, a huge tract of land formerly a Mexican land grant, was a leading innovator in agricultural techniques and plant introductions. Annie, particularly, was an admirer of Muir's writings, and they had long importuned him to visit them.

It was quite a grand party, then, that set out from Bidwell's "Rancho Chico" for Mount Shasta. Muir, Gray, and Hooker did most of the serious botanizing, and the cosmopolitan group thoroughly enjoyed themselves back at the camp, which was considerably more comfortable than the three botanists were accustomed to. In both his previous trips to Shasta, Muir had been caught on the mountain by snowstorms, and a consequent frostbite of his right leg would have slowed down any man other than Muir.

This trip, however, the weather held, and the only adventures were in the social realm, where Muir's lively stories and warm, bantering style with both ladies and men were thoroughly congenial.

One night around the campfire, Muir had stoked the flames prodigiously and waxed dramatic on the beauty of the firelight reflected in the foliage of the surrounding silver firs. "Look at the glory! Look at the glory!" he exclaimed as he waved his arms. Gray and Hooker sat calm and silent, prompting Annie Bidwell to demand whether they thought the scene beautiful. "Of course it is," the men responded with twinkling eyes. "But Muir is so eternally enthusiastic, we like to tease him."

Afterwards, when the Grays and Hooker departed, the Bidwells persuaded Muir to stay at their elegant 26-room Italianate mansion in Chico. Doubtless Muir eagerly soaked up Bidwell's agricultural expertise; half a decade later Muir found himself in charge of a large orchard operation through marriage, and made a fortune from his deft management. But clearly it was Annie Bidwell that was most keen on Muir, and one wonders if she were not wondering about a match between the charismatic naturalist and her sister.

After a week with the Bidwells, though, Muir heard adventure calling. When he expressed a wish to float down the nearby Sacramento River to the Delta region, Bidwell promptly had his carpenter throw together a crude boat. (I can imagine Bidwell was tiring of his wife's gushing admiration of Muir, and was not unhappy to facilitate his guest's departure.) With blankets and prodigious amounts of food, Muir set off from Bidwell's river landing on October 2, little flags fluttering fore and aft.

The 195 river miles to Sacramento were idyllic, a good approximation of Mark Twain's descriptions of Huck and Jim's days and nights on the Missisippi a decade later. I can attest to the languid joys of this aquatic journey from Chico, with its bucolic scenery and abundance of great blue herons, osprey, egrets, brown pelicans, red-shouldered hawks, beavers, otters, muskrats, and various ducks on the great, rolling river—all of whose numbers would have been much greater for Muir than for me and my comrades a century later.

This voyage is never dull, due to the abundant downed trees in the river, then as now. I have had many anxious moments on the Sacramento avoiding (barely) the pull of whirling water around great snags. Muir navigated them all, and christened his boat *Snagjumper*. When his little craft began to take on water due to a swollen board, Muir rowed to shore, removed the too-wide plank, whittled it down with his knife, then banged it back into place with a rock and was off again.

Arriving in Sacramento a week later, his appetite whetted for more watery adventure, Muir took a stage south to Visalia, in the Sierra foothills near where the mighty Kings River emerges from the mountains. Clarence King had declared the great canyon of the Middle Kings River "inaccessible"—that is, too rugged to be traversed along its length by humans. Muir, who had viewed the canyon in 1873 on his way to Mt. Whitney, reckoned otherwise.

With a young man who had heard of Muir's intentions and begged to be included, Muir traveled into the southern Sierras to the head of the great canyon, climbed down the steep gorge to the river, and headed downstream. Down the canyon he and the young man walked, crawled, jumped, dropped, slid, and often swam. They emerged at the foot of the gorge some twelve days later, having gone the last several days with no food. Muir had to half-carry his young companion the last couple of days, who was not as accustomed as Muir to rough travel on an empty stomach. But Muir had proved that the Kings River canyon was, indeed, accessible—to John Muir, at least.

But Muir wasn't through. After gorging himself with food and leaving his exhausted companion, Muir took train and stage north to Hopeton, where the Merced River emerges from the mountains (and where Muir had looked after sheep his very first months in California, nearly a decade earlier). After a reunion with friends from those early days, Muir constructed himself the *Snagjumper II* from weathered fence boards he found, assisted by a bag of nails and a rock. Promptly he launched himself onto the Merced for another float trip.

Down the Merced he went, to its confluence with the (then) great San Joaquin River, which flows north up the southern portion of California's Central Valley, the southern analog to the Sacramento River in the north. Muir floated and rowed down the San Joaquin north to Stockton, then through the Delta formed by the confluence of the San Joaquin and the Sacramento Rivers. After two weeks and 250 river miles from Hopeton, he reached the junction of Suisin Bay and San Francisico Bay, where he finally docked his boat at Martinez, and walked the two miles to the Alhambra Valley and the orchards of Dr. John Strentzel.

The Strentzels, like the Bidwells, had for years issued a standing invitation to Muir to visit their ranch and orchards. The physician Strentzel was an immigrant from Hungary, who had knocked around Texas before arriving in California and securing 2,600 acres north of San Francisco, where he experimented with various fruit trees. Strentzel and his wife had a very eligible daughter, Louie, who had resolutely refused numerous offers of marriage, waiting for the right man. Muir arrived out of the blue just before Thanksgiving, looking more like a scarecrow than a suitor, his clothes nearly to rags, his beard and hair long and wild. The Strentzels happily took him in.

"They made me eat and sleep," Muir wrote, "stuffing me with turkey, chicken, beef, fruits and jellies in the most extravagant manner." He toured the orchards with Dr. Strentzel and talked science and agriculture with him into the night. Muir must have also paid some attention to the daughter Louie, for he would marry her three years later, and be blessed with two daughters by her. After two days, though, Muir thanked his hosts, nonchalantly walked the twenty miles to Oakland, caught the ferry, and settled in San Francisco to resume his writing.

Some fall!

6

Alaska, Land of Glaciers (1879-1890)

"My bed was two boulders, and as I lay wedged and bent on their up-bulging sides, beguiling the hard, cold time in gazing into the starry sky and across the sparkling bay, magnificent upright bars of light in bright prismatic colors suddenly appeared (in the sky)…and the blessed night circled away in measureless rejoicing enthusiasm."

By 1879, Muir was eager to expand his horizons beyond the American West, where the mark of the expanding nation was everywhere. Grazing herds of sheep and logging operations were common through the length of the Sierra Nevada and elsewhere. It would be a decade before Muir would pitch himself wholeheartedly into the protection of what remained of the American wilderness. But for now, Muir hungered for a wilder slice of the natural world, and a pristine wilderness beckoned not far to the north of California.

The United States had purchased Alaska from Russia in 1867, as Muir was on his thousand-mile walk. Twelve years later, not much had changed in the far north. Alaska was particularly alluring to Muir because it contained a glorious array of full-bodied glaciers. Though he always insisted, rightly, that the glaciers he had discovered in the Sierra Nevada were true glaciers, Muir was fully aware that these were residual glaciers, much-diminished remnants. In Alaska, glaciers in all their youthful glory awaited him, glaciers still actively involved in their awesome sculpting of valleys, creating soil for forests and basins for lakes centuries in the future. He must see them and study them.

So it was that when Muir formally asked Louie Strentzel for her hand in marriage in the spring of 1879, he had a curious stipulation. *I love and admire you ardently, Miss Strentzel, but may we postpone the wedding until after I explore Alaska this summer and fall?* Louie knew well the man she had agreed to marry. She loved Muir as he was, the wild Muir, the sojourner in wild places. *Of course, my love. How shall we explain it to my parents?*

Although Dr. and Mrs. Strentzel never fully approved of Muir's frequent adventures in far-away places during his marriage to their daughter, they learned to accept it. Muir's first trip to Alaska that summer was indeed an epic exploration. He traveled as far up the Alaska coast as commercial boats would take him, had a host of adventures on mountains and glaciers, then hired a crew of Tlingit Indians and their huge canoe to venture another 400 miles up the uncharted Alaska coast—not returning until late November!

On this daring trip Muir discovered and named Glacier Bay, described the largest glacier facing it (which would later be named Muir Glacier), discovered and studied hundreds of other mature glaciers debouching into the ocean, and came to admire and enjoy the company of the Stickeen, Taku, Chilcats, Hoona, Chinook, and Tlingit Indian tribes along the way—though he also observed first-hand the devastating effects of the introduced whiskey on some of these tribes.

After this first trip, Muir was hooked on Alaska, its snowy mountains, its pristine steep-walled fiords, the glaciers calving huge icebergs into the ocean with stupendous roars and waves. He returned to Alaska the following summer of 1880, just months after his and Louie's spring wedding (not realizing that Louie was newly pregnant with their first child). Again he hired an Indian crew and pushed north in a canoe with a newly-made missionary friend, S. Hall Young. He re-charted Glacier Bay, and pushed on to Taylor Bay. He wanted to measure the extent of the Brady Glacier there, which meant traversing the width and breadth of it.

Awakening one morning in his camp beside the glacier, as a driving rainstorm howled around him, Muir put aside his overcoat on a rock, "knowing I would be drenched anyhow, and firmly tied my mountain shoes, tightened my belt, shouldered my ice-axe, and thus free and ready for rough work, pushed on, regardless as possible of mere rain." He was accompanied by Stickeen, Young's camp dog he could not shoo away. Muir and Stickeen followed the wracked forest at the edge of the glacier for four miles, then using his ice-axe Muir hacked footholds into the ice and mounted onto the glacier itself. Finding relatively few and narrow crevasses in this portion, Muir set off in the continuing storm toward the glacier's far side some seven miles away. Carefully he took frequent compass readings to facilitate his return. In the late afternoon, with the glacier's opposite side charted, Muir and the dog began their return.

"After two hours of hard work I came to a maze of crevasses of appalling depth and width which could not be passed apparently either up or down. I traced them with firm nerve developed by the danger, making wide jumps, poising cautiously on dizzy edges after cutting footholds, taking wide crevasses at a grand leap at once frightful and inspiring."

The failing light of dusk found Muir running between crevasses to make better time, snow now beginning to fall in the plunging temperature. He made the mistake of jumping one wide crevasse to a lower level on the far side, thus cutting off the possibility of retracing his steps. He pushed on, to discover to his dismay "the very widest of all the longitudinal crevasses we had yet encountered. It was about forty feet wide." Reconnoitering up and down the crevasse, he spotted a feature that presented his only hope of survival: a sliver-thin bridge of ice that spanned the crevasse at a point where it was now seventy five feet wide, seemingly bottomless depths yawning blue-black to either side of the narrow bridge. The prospect daunted even Muir; it seemed impossible to contemplate.

Yet spending the night on the glacier in the storm seemed even more dangerous, probably deadly.

With a shiver, Muir decided on "venturing ahead across the giant crevasse by the very worst of the sliver (ice) bridges I had ever seen. It was so badly weathered and melted down that it formed a knife-edge, and extended across from side to side in a low, drooping curve like that made by a loose rope attached at each end at the same height. But the worst difficulty was that the ends of the down-curving sliver were attached to the sides at a depth of about eight or ten feet below the surface of the glacier. Getting down to the edge of the bridge, and then after crossing it getting up the other side, seemed hardly possible. However, I decided to dare the dangers of the fearful sliver rather than to attempt to retrace my steps.

"Accordingly I dug a low groove in the rounded edge for my knees to rest in and, leaning over, began to cut a narrow foothold on the steep, smooth side (with my ice-axe)…After getting down one step I cautiously stooped and cut another and another in succession until I reached the point where the sliver was attached to the wall. There, cautiously balancing, I chipped down the upcurved end of the bridge until I had formed a small level platform about a foot wide, then, bending forward, got astride of the end of the sliver, steadied myself with my knees, then cut off (i.e. shaved down) the top of the sliver, hitching myself forward an inch or two at a time, leaving it about four inches wide for Stickeen. Arrived at the farther end of the sliver, which was about seventy-five feet long, I chipped another little platform on its upcurved end, cautiously rose to my feet, and with infinite pains cut narrow notch steps and finger-holds in the wall and finally got safely (up the ten-foot wall and) across."

And the dog Stickeen? Muir exhorted him to follow. After howling and whining anxiously on the far side for some minutes, the dog "hushed his cries, slid his little feet slowly down into my footsteps (and) out on the big sliver, walked slowly and cautiously along the sliver as if holding his breath, while the snow was falling and the wind was moaning and threatening to blow him off. When he arrived at the foot of the slope below me, I was kneeling on the brink ready to assist him in case he should be unable to reach the top. He looked up along the row of notched steps I had made, as if fixing them in his mind, then with a nervous spring he whizzed up and passed me out on to the level ice, and ran and cried and barked and rolled about fairly hysterical in the sudden revulsion from the depth of despair to triumphant joy."

Muir had survived yet another of his narrow escapes from death.

After accompanying the U.S. Corwin to Alaska searching for a lost ship in 1881, Muir spent the rest of the 1880s running the Strentzel family ranch and orchard in Martinez. Though he was fabulously successful at the enterprise, setting aside enough funds in various banks to assure Louie and their two daughters financial independence for the rest of their lives, his health was wretched throughout the lowland-dwelling decade. In addition, his slavish attention to commerce made him depressed.

Louie finally prevailed upon Muir to hand the management of the ranch over to other hands. "A ranch that needs and takes the sacrifice of a noble life, or work, ought to be flung away beyond all reach and power for harm" she wrote to him in 1888, while he was traveling to Mt. Rainier in Washington State. "The Alaska book and the Yosemite book, dear John, must be written, and you need to be your own self, well and strong, to make them worthy of you. There is nothing that has a right to be considered beside this except the welfare of our children."

With portions of the ranch sold or leased and the rest managed by another, Muir eagerly returned to Alaska in 1890. He traveled up to Glacier Bay and the newly-named Muir Glacier. On July 11 he set off on the mammoth glacier on a solitary trip, pushing a small sled containing his compass, journal, bread, tea bags, and a bear skin that served as sleeping bag. His joy at the scenery and adventure is recorded in often-ecstatic journal entries over his eleven days atop the glacier:

"The clearest way into the Universe is through a forest wilderness… A dewdrop in every Cassiope (heather) cup and on the end of every bent grass glade, birds feeding their young, singing with full heart in the sweetness and majesty of Nature's love…In such mornings it is easy to see that the world is a-making. In this celestial day heaven and earth, radiating beauty each to each, beautify each other.

"This is one of the still, hushed, ripe days when we fancy we might hear the beating of Nature's heart…There is love of wild Nature in everybody, an ancient mother-love ever showing itself whether recognized or no, and however covered by cares and duties…To dine with a glacier on a sunny day is a glorious thing and makes common feasts of meat and wine ridiculous. The glacier eats hills and drinks sunbeams…In God's wildness lies the hope of the world—the great fresh unblighted, unredeemed wilderness. The galling harness of civilization drops off, and the wounds heal ere we are aware.

"*Camping on top of quarry Mountain, seven or eight miles from the front of Muir Glacier. July 18.* How hard to realize that every camp of men or beast has this glorious starry firmament for a roof! In such places standing alone on the mountain-top it is easy to realize that whatever special nests we make—leaves and moss like the marmots and birds, or tents, or piled stone—we all dwell in a house of one room—the world with the firmament for its roof—and are sailing the celestial spaces without leaving any track."

But then his journal entry of July 19: "Nearly blind. The light is intolerable and I fear I may be long unfitted for work. I have been lying on my back all day with a snow poultice bound over my eyes. Every object I try to look at seems double…This is the first time in Alaska that I have had too much sunshine." After several days, he regained his vision, though it was weak.

Muir was close to the end of his stumbling return when he stepped into a crevasse hidden by a thin crust of blown snow. He pitched head-first into an icy pool of frigid water in the crevasse. "Down I plunged over head and ears, but of course bobbed up again, and after a hard struggle succeeded in dragging myself out over the farther side. Then I dragged my sled over… made haste to strip off my clothing, threw it in a sloppy heap and crept into my (bearskin) sleeping bag to shiver away the night as best I could."

Several days later, the indefatigable Muir was exploring a side fiord off Glacier Bay by canoe, again with no companions: "After a hard, anxious struggle, I reached the mouth of the Hugh Miller fiord about sundown, and tried to find a camp-spot on its steep, boulder-bound shore. But no landing-place where it seemed possible to drag the canoe above high-tide mark was discovered after examining a mile or more of this dreary, forbidding barrier, and as night was closing down, I decided to try to grope my way (in the canoe) across the mouth of the fiord in the starlight to an open sandy spot on which I had camped in October, 1879, a distance of about three or four miles.

"With the utmost caution I picked my way through the sparkling (ice) bergs, and after an hour or two of this nerve-trying work, when I was perhaps less than half-way across (the fjord) and dreading the loss of the frail canoe which would include the loss of myself, I came to a pack of very large bergs which loomed threateningly, offering no visible thoroughfare. Paddling and pushing to right and left, I at last discovered a sheer-walled opening about four feet wide and perhaps two hundred feet long, formed apparently by the splitting of a huge iceberg. I hesitated to enter this passage, fearing that the slightest change in the tide-current might close it, but ventured nevertheless, judging that the dangers ahead might not be greater than those I had already passed. When I had got about a third of the way in, I suddenly discovered that the smooth-walled ice-lane was growing narrower, and with desperate haste backed out. Just as the bow of the canoe cleared the sheer walls they came together with a growling crunch.

"Terror-stricken, I turned back, and in an anxious hour or two gladly reached the rock-bound shore that had at first repelled me, determined to stay on guard all night in the canoe or find someplace where with the strength that comes in a fight for life I could drag it up the boulder wall beyond ice danger. This last was happily done about midnight, and with no thought of sleep I went to bed rejoicing.

"My bed was two boulders, and as I lay wedged and bent on their up-bulging sides, beguiling the hard, cold time in gazing into the starry sky and across the sparkling bay, magnificent upright bars of light in bright prismatic colors suddenly appeared (in the sky), marching swiftly in close succession along the northern horizon…How long these glad, eager soldiers of light held on their way I cannot tell; for sense of time was charmed out of mind and the blessed night circled away in measureless rejoicing enthusiasm."

The wilderness adventures recounted above do not by any means exhaust (or even dent!) the store of those that could be related for Muir, but they hopefully illustrate his astonishing vitality, toughness, strength, and complete immersion in the natural world. Many writers of the late nineteenth century wrote powerfully of nature and wildness—Thoreau, Emerson, Burroughs chief amongst them—but none remotely approach Muir in actual experience in the wildest regions of the natural world, often solitary. None routinely kissed the cheek of death in their wilderness experiences as did Muir. Let us now turn to what this intrepid survivor of wilderness rambles saw in the natural world.

In tracing the worldview which arose from Muir's explorations, we will rely primarily on the journal entries he made on every trip, from his 1867 thousand-mile walk to the Gulf to his 1911 journey to South America and Africa, supplemented by letters to friends. In this material we have the inner Muir revealed in spontaneous, rich observations on a wide range of phenomena. What emerges is a largely unknown Muir, one emphasized neither in the edited articles and books by which he first became known, nor in the public *persona* which has been shepherded by environmental organizations in the century since his death. This hidden Muir of his journals, for the most part published only posthumously, is a far more challenging figure, and his worldview is particularly relevant to the crisis facing early 21st-century humanity, as we shall see.

7

Singing the World's Heart

"I'll acquaint myself with the glaciers and wild gardens and get as near the heart of the world as I can."

John Muir was recognized and feted in the world of humans beginning the day of his emergence from the Wisconsin farm of his boyhood. His ingenious inventions exhibited at the 1860 Wisconsin State Fair in Madison were described on the front page of the local newspaper as "surprising, and could only have been executed by genuine genius." More practically, they earned him the prodigious prize of $15 and the instant, fervent admiration of crowds and one of the judges: Jeanne Carr, wife of a University of Wisconsin professor, who corresponded with Muir frequently for decades thereafter.

Those whom Muir met in his post-university time in Canada and Indiana were thoroughly charmed by him and became life-long friends and visitors, even to California decades later. The owners of the Indianapolis carriage factory—the nation's largest—at which he worked soon offered him a partnership in the business. A few years later, the eminent Ralph Waldo Emerson met the young Muir in Yosemite Valley, and urged him to come to Boston and edit Thoreau's writings. Upon

42

Emerson's return to Boston, he made one last entry in a short list of "My Men:" John Muir.

"I could have been a millionaire," Muir admitted as he looked back at his early experiences in the world of humans, "but chose instead to be a tramp."

Muir decisively turned away from the human world and its glittering promise and advantages. He was for "the heart of the world," and he had no doubt where that lay. Not in cities, not amongst humans, regardless of how convivial their company was to him. From the moment he was on his own, Muir was utterly convinced that the heart of the world, rather, lay in the trees, animals, rivers, mountains, and stars of the natural world.

He summarized his view in a letter to Emerson, gently declining the offer to join him in Boston: "As long as I live, I'll hear waterfalls and birds and winds wing. I'll interpret the rocks, learn the language of flood, storm, and avalanche. I'll acquaint myself with the glaciers and wild gardens and get as near the heart of the world as I can." This conviction had not swayed two decades later, on his eleven glorious days sledding alone on what was already known as Muir Glacier in Alaska. "The clearest way into the Universe is through a forest wilderness," we have seen him writing in his journal on that trip.

Muir eloquently espouses a thoroughly *immanent*, this-worldly view of life, emphasizing the physically-manifest here and now. The heart of existence resides on the earth, in experiencing the elements making up the earth, and the great cycles and transformations linking them all. The earth is sufficient, is our foundation, our life-giving and nourishing mother.

"There is love of wild Nature in everybody, an ancient mother-love ever showing itself whether recognized or no, and however covered by cares and duties," he writes while on Muir Glacier in 1890. The same insight was voiced two decades earlier, after an 1871 snowstorm buffeted Yosemite Valley: "Nature, while urging to utmost efforts…presenting cause beyond cause in endless chains, lost in infinite distances, yet cheers us like a mother with tender prattle words of love, ministering to all our friendlessness and weariness."

Muir requires no recourse to a *transcendent*, other-worldly viewpoint to arrive at the bedrock of existence. His journals are packed with minute, glowing descriptions of the natural world and its wonders, from incense cedars to storms to montane peaks. In his *Mountains of California* he spends whole chapters describing the lives of the Douglas Squirrel and the Water Ouzel bird in loving and admiring detail. This focus of concern and value on the natural world, and the insight that humans thrive only in contact with its elements, is remembered and reflected in the Sierra Club that Muir founded and the myriad other environmental groups around the world today.

What is not so well remembered these days, though, is Muir's keen spiritual root that somehow accompanied this immanent view. We today, conditioned by millennia of a transcendent worldview in which the spiritual is held to be opposed (and superior) to the physical, find it difficult to entertain the notion that an immanent, this-worldly viewpoint might include spiritual elements, but in Muir it certainly did.

Muir accomplished this juxtaposition by wrenching the spiritual from its transcendent "location" down to the earth. He claimed over and over that matter had a spiritual dimension as one of its several aspects. Spirituality was a *natural* feature of matter—trees, plants, animals, rocks, water—if we but had the keen eyes to perceive it. Muir had those eyes.

This view of matter having an inherent spiritual dimension is at variance with the Christian religion of Muir's family, and Western culture in general, of course. Muir arrived at the conviction as a result of his experiences in the natural world, the same route that the Taoist religion in China took two thousand years earlier, and that California's native-Americans took even earlier. All were convinced, with Muir, that the everyday, immanent world included the spiritual. Let us trace how Muir expresses it.

Not surprisingly, Muir uses the approach and terminology of his father's Calvinist religion in which he was raised. There exists a "God" who created the universe, and thus can also be termed the "Creator." Muir never doubts this. But he adopts this terminology in ways that are utterly unorthodox, revealing a conception of "God" and "Creator" at variance with that of his father's Christian tradition.

Muir ringingly declares that nature is God's beauty and love made manifest. "These blessed mountains are so compactly filled with God's beauty, no petty personal hope or experience has room to be," he writes in 1869. In his first spring in Yosemite Valley in 1870, Muir exclaims that "God's glory is over all His works, written upon every field and sky, but here it is in larger letters—magnificent capitals."

Two decades later, in Alaska, his terminology has not changed: "Every excursion that I have made in all my rambling life has been fruitful and delightful, from the smallest indefinite saunter an hour or two in length to the noblest summer's flight…All the wild world is beautiful, and it matters but little where we go…everywhere and always we are in God's eternal beauty and love."

Even places seemingly barren reveal themselves witness to the Creator when examined more closely. Describing the top of Mt. Hoffman northwest of Yosemite's Tenaya Lake during his first summer in the High Sierra, Muir observes that "the surface of the ground so dull and forbidding at first sight, besides being rich in plants, shines and sparkles with crystals: mica, hornblende, feldspar, quartz, tourmaline. The radiance in some places is so great as to be fairly dazzling, keen lance rays of every color flashing, sparkling in glorious abundance, joining the plants in their fine, brave beauty-work—every crystal, every flower a window opening into heaven, a mirror reflecting the Creator."

Muir is sometimes moved to ecstatic outbursts in his wanderings. He describes the solemn energy of a storm at Lake Washburn in 1871, in the upper reaches of the Merced River above Yosemite Valley:

"Nearby a clump of tall pines at bend of lake shuts off all the distant mountain, leaving nothing but the clear, present, living, soul-awakening purity of heaven…It is as if the lake, mountain, trees had souls, formed one soul, which had died and gone before the throne of God, the great First Soul, and by direct creative act of God had all earthly purity deepened, refined, brightness brightened, spirituality spiritualized, countenance, gesture made wholly Godful!…I spring to my feet crying 'Heaven and earth! Rock is not light, not heavy, not transparent, not opaque, but every pore gushes, glows like a thought with immortal life!'"

Lakes, mountains, trees, even rocks are here seen as saturated with spirituality, conferred upon them at the very throne of God. The natural world is alive, glowing with spirituality as well as beauty—and it's all immanent, an inherent property of things.

Verses from the Bible are sprinkled throughout Muir's writings, especially his journals. Muir was raised in a home drenched with Scotch Calvinism. His religiously-zealous father required Muir to memorize large chunks of the Bible, whipping him throughout his teens and early twenties if he made mistakes—or if his work on the farm seemed to lack enthusiasm. As a result, by his teens Muir could quote "by heart and by sore flesh" two-thirds of the Old Testament and all the New.

Quotations from the Old Testament definitely predominate, with references to Mt. Sinai, Jacob on the dry plains of Padanaram, the trials of Job, and Sampson's riddle, for example. Though not as frequent, allusions to the New Testament are also present, with Revelation's "a new heaven and a new earth" mentioned several times. Muir at one point compares his unruly flock of sheep in the winter of 1868 to Gadarene swine, and there is a lone early reference to Jesus' observation that lilies toil not, and a brief allusion to Jesus discussing winds with Nicodemus. But other than these, mentions of Jesus are conspicuously rare from his California days on.

A recurring note is the insight that creation is not just something that happened long ago, but is rather a phenomenon that recurs every season, indeed every day in the present. "The last days of this glacial winter are not yet past; we live in 'creation's dawn.' The morning stars still sing together, and the world, though made, is still being made and becoming more beautiful every day."

The ever-present creation in wilderness inspires Muir to this paean bringing together Revelation and Job, New Testament and Old: "(Wanting to linger in the Sierras) what glorious cloud-lands I should see, storms and calms,—a new heaven and a new earth every day...One would be at an endless Godful play, and what speeches and music and acting and scenery and lights!—sun, moon, stars, auroras. Creation just beginning, the morning stars 'still singing together and all the songs of God shouting for joy.'"

While all the natural world is touched by the beauty of creation's dawn, certain spots seem more obviously marked. In his first summer in the Sierra, Muir encounters a large flood-transported cubical boulder (reminding us of Islam's Kaaba) sitting at the foot of a waterfall in a tributary of the North Fork of the Merced River:

"One of these ancient flood boulders stands firm in the middle of the stream channel, just below the lower edge of the pool dam at the foot of the fall nearest our camp. It is a nearly cubical mass of granite about eight feet high, plushed with mosses over the top and down the sides…like an altar… The place seemed holy, where one might hope to see God. After dark, when the camp was at rest, I groped my way back to the altar boulder and passed the night on it,—above the water, beneath the leaves and stars,—everything still more impressive than by day, the fall seen dimly white, singing Nature's old love song with solemn enthusiasm, while the stars peering through the leaf-roof seemed to join the white water's song. Precious night, precious day to abide in me forever. Thanks be to God for this immortal gift."

Caught in one of the Yosemite high country's typical afternoon summer storms, Muir traces in his imagination the journey of a drop of rain: "How interesting to trace the history of a single raindrop!…every drop in all the blessed throng a silvery newborn star with lake and river, garden and grove, valley and mountain, all that the landscape holds reflected in its crystal depths, God's messenger, angel of love sent on its way with majesty and pomp and display of power…Now the storm is over…in winged vapor rising some (drops) are already hastening back to the sky, some have gone into the plants…some have gone journeying on in the rivers to join the larger raindrop of the ocean. From form to form, beauty to beauty, ever changing, never resting, all are speeding on with love's enthusiasm, singing with the stars the eternal song of creation."

The passages quoted above make explicit Muir's conviction that the natural world was a glorious manifestation of God's beauty and love, showing us windows, mirrors, and sparks of the Creator. It is important to note that in all this, Muir's emphasis is not on God *per se*, but rather the specific expression of God's beauty in the natural world, whether drops of water, mountains, ouzels, or flowers. *This* world, in all its inherent beauty, is Muir's focus. He does not refer to the natural world as a means of dwelling on God; he revels in the natural world for its *own* sake, for its own God-given beauty and vitality. He has transferred these God-given attributes from the transcendent, "spiritual" realm down to earth and made them an intrinsic, in-dwelling aspect of the immanent world.

We have here been highlighting Muir's use of his father's terminology in many quotations linking the beauty of the natural world to God and the creation. But much more often, indeed typically, Muir sings the beauty and glory of the natural world without reference to God or the Creator. Always, though, the primary focus is on the immanent phenomena *themselves*—this world. And as we have noted, when Muir does use his father's theological terms from his youthful upbringing, they are set in the utterly unorthodox position of being merely descriptive of the beauty of immanence, never a Deity dominating the phenomenon itself.

Muir's attention and devotion directed to the actual, physical plants, animals, rocks, waters, clouds, and sky themselves contrasts with the transcendent view of classic Christianity. In the poetry of Muir's contemporary Gerard Manley Hopkins, for example, the emphasis is typically on the God behind (or above) His creation, rather than the created work itself. For the priest Hopkins the world is glorious *because* it illustrates the glory of the Creator, rather than in its own right, as Muir proclaims.

Using Hopkins as our example, consider his poem *Pied Beauty*. He begins the poem by making sure that everyone knows and recognizes the sole source of earth's beauty: "Glory be to God for dappled things—". With this firmly established, he commences with his sharp-eyed tribute to the beauty in brilliant lines:

For skies of couple-colour as a brinded cow;
For rose-moles all in stipple upon trout that swim;
Fresh-firecoal chestnut-falls; finches' wings;
Landscape plotted and pieced—fold, fallow, and plough;
And all trades, their gear and tackle and trim.
All things counter, original, spare, strange;
Whatever is fickle, freckled (who knows how?)
With swift, slow; sweet, sour; adazzle, dim;

Hopkins concludes the poem with another reminder that places all these earthly beauties in firm perspective, that of the transcendent God whose beauty does not change or fade:

> *He fathers-forth whose beauty is past change:*
> *Praise him.*

Without diminishing our respect and enjoyment of Hopkins as poet, the contrast with Muir's approach to the beauties of the earth is plain. For Hopkins and the orthodox Christian, the created world fades upon comparison to its Creator, or shines primarily by virtue of its being a manifestation of the Creator. Muir's approach is quite different: the created world shines brilliantly in its *own* right. He typically does not qualify the beauty and grandeur of the natural world with reference to God or Creator; and in those instances in which he does, the immanent flower, creek, or birdsong remains paramount, not as an illustration of the greater glory of a transcendent God.

Muir was not, of course, the first person raised in the Christian tradition to elevate the immanent world as the focus of God's love and beauty. One thinks of St. Francis of Assisi and Albert Schweitzer as doing much the same. In earlier Western tradition, there were Heraclitus and other pre-Socratics, who focused on the immanent world rather than transcendent archetypes. All these left their mark, of course, but only Muir founded a movement which spread worldwide and became a public force to be reckoned with in today's world.

But we are getting ahead of ourselves. Suffice it to observe that Muir's travels and observations engendered an immanent, this-worldly view, which finds ultimate meaning and glory in the natural world itself, in its physical array of creatures, elements, and processes—which included spirituality, beauty, and love. To get to what mid-twentieth-century theologian Paul Tillich calls "the ground of being," his equivalent to "the heart of the world," Muir does not close his eyes and meditate, or enter a chapel, much less open a book. No, Muir gets "as near the heart of the world as I can" by taking a saunter into a forest or along a creek or glacier, eyes wide open.

8

Nature as Healer of Broken Humans

"…a kind of terrestrial immortality."

His experiences convinced Muir that the central task of human life is to engage the natural world, and thus discover our true home. Experiences in the natural world make us whole, and "we feel how true it is that going to the mountains is going home." And not just "home" in a metaphorical sense: "home" in a very concrete, physical sense. "Wonderful how completely everything in wild nature fits into us, as if truly part and parent of us," he observes in his journal.

"The sun shines not on us but in us. The rivers flow not past, but through us, thrilling, tingling, vibrating every fiber and cell of the substances of our bodies, making them glide and sing. The trees wave and the flowers bloom in our bodies as well as our souls, and every bird song, wind song, and tremendous storm song of the rocks in the heart of the mountains is our song, our very own, and sings our love."

Muir had a very low opinion of 19th-century cities and their "civilization." In his experience, city-bound humans were "asleep," crushed by care and anxiety, overwhelmed by schedules and stifling duties, ineluctably cut off from the zest of life basic to authentic human existence. The solution: go to a forest or a creek, where the beauty of the world is brimming and inescapable, transformative, health-giving.

After some months in the company of new friends in the education and artistic elite in Oakland and San Francisco while he wrote up his articles on glaciation, Muir eagerly returned to the mountains in the fall of 1874, confiding this in his journal:

"Tell me what you will of the benefactions of city civilization, of the sweet security of streets—all as part of the natural upgrowth of man towards the high destiny we hear so much of. I know that our bodies were made to thrive only in pure air, and the scenes in which pure air is found. If the death exhalations that brood the broad towns in which we so fondly compact ourselves were made visible, we should flee as from a plague. All are more or less sick; there is not a perfectly sane man in San Francisco."

As early as 1871, just two years after arriving in California, Muir observes that "toiling in the treadmills of life we hide from the lessons of Nature. We gaze morbidly through civilized fog upon our beautiful world clad with seamless beauty...Civilized man chokes his soul as the heathen Chinese their feet."

In his visit to the Sierras in the summer of 1869, Muir the reluctant shepherd is sketching Yosemite Valley from its rim, when suddenly he is struck by the conviction that a favorite professor of his from the University of Wisconsin three years previous was in the valley below him. (Muir already knew only that the professor planned to travel to California sometime that summer.) He makes his way into the valley the next morning, incredibly finding the professor visiting there with a distinguished general. (This is one of three instances of Muir receiving seemingly telepathic insights.)

After his visit with the astonished professor and the general, Muir climbs back to the high country through a canyon, and notes that night in his journal: "I scrambled home through the Indian Canyon gate, rejoicing, pitying the poor Professor and General, bound by clocks, almanacs, orders, duties, etc., and compelled to dwell with lowland care and dust and din, where Nature is covered and her voice smothered,—while the poor, insignificant wanderer (Muir) enjoys the freedom and glory of God's wilderness."

Muir is particularly galled by those who bring the cares and "civilized fog" of the cities with them into the mountains and wander blinded to the glories about them. In the following passage, written after his visit with the professor and the general, we are treated to a taste of Muir's frequently employed dry Scotch wit:

"It seems strange that visitors to Yosemite should be so little influenced by its novel grandeur, as if their eyes were bandaged and their ears stopped. Most of those I saw yesterday were looking down as if wholly unconscious of anything going on about them, while the sublime rocks were trembling with the tones of the mighty chanting congregation of waters gathered from all the mountains round about, making music that might draw angels out of heaven. Yet respectable-looking, even wise-looking people were fixing bits of worm on bent pieces of wire to catch trout. Sport they called it. Should church-goers try to pass the time fishing in baptismal fonts while dull sermons were being preached, the so-called sport might not be so bad; but to play in the Yosemite temple, seeking pleasure in the pain of fishes struggling for their lives, while God himself is preaching his sublimest water and stone sermons!"

A decade later, on his first trip to Alaska in 1879, Muir makes the same lament: "So truly blind is lord man; so pathetically employed in his little jobs of town-building, church-building, bread-getting, the study of the spirits and heaven, etc., that he can see nothing of the heaven he is in. Place (these blind) people who sing heaven and explore it so zealously here (in the mountains), and they would still be seeking it without guessing for a moment their present whereabouts."

But to those who will open themselves to the beauty of the natural world, Muir assures us that the dull sleep of the valley cities will be banished:

"Californians have only to go east a few miles (to the Sierra Nevada) to be happy. Toilers on the heat plains, toilers in the cities by the sea, whose lives are well-nigh choked by the weeds of care that have grown up and run to seed about them—leave all and go east and you cannot escape a cure for all care. Earth hath no sorrows that earth cannot heal, or heaven cannot heal, for the earth as seen in the clean wilds of the mountains is about as divine as anything the heart of man can conceive!"

What is the mechanism by which the natural world, and particularly mountains, heal humans broken and lulled to sleep by city life and its cares? Muir expresses it in varying metaphors, shown in the following three quotations, spanning two decades from 1872 to 1895:

"Snatch a pan of bread and run to the Tuolumne (Canyon, *i.e.* Hetch Hetchy). In whatever mood the lover of wilderness enters the Canyon, he speedily yields to the spell of the falling, singing river, and listens and looks with ever-growing enthusiasm until all the world besides is forgotten... Nature's best gardens are here in deepest repose, fountains of wild ever-playing water falling in every form—the endless song of Creation shaking the devout listener into newness of life. He who enters will hear a music which will never cease to vibrate in his life throughout all its blurring moil and toil."

"The storms of winter which so exalt and glorify mountains strike terror into the souls of those who are unacquainted with them, or who have only seen the lights of cities, but to anyone who is in actual contact with the wilderness, these storms are only emphatic words of Nature's love. Every purely natural object is a conductor of divinity, and we have but to expose ourselves in a clean condition to any of these conductors, to be fed and nourished by them. Only in this way can we procure our daily spirit bread."

"Yosemite Park is a place of rest, a refuge from the roar and dust and weary, nervous, wasting work of the lowlands...It is good for everybody, no matter how benumbed with care, encrusted with a mail of business habits like a tree with bark. None can escape its charms. Its natural beauty cleanses and warms like fire...The park is the poor man's refuge. Few are altogether blind and deaf to the sweet looks and voices of nature. Everybody at heart loves God's beauty because God made everybody."

Because mountains are so often untrammeled and not disfigured by human activity, they retain this ability to heal the broken lives of humans. One of Muir's most famous quotes occurs at the end of the journal entry of July 30, 1895, as he is climbing through the foothills: "At Grub Gulch a knoll is crowned with a group of noble oaks—a good cause for a town. From here we soon begin to rise, and the grand mountain-ridges with the spires of yellow pine thronging the long slopes come to view, and one's heart burns, and we feel how true it is that going to the mountains is going home."

Later in his life, Muir admits that while the mountains most vividly embody the healing environment of nature, to the open eye every place free of the scars and burdens of unbridled human activity can heal. He confides to his journal while on the Muir Glacier in Alaska in 1890: "All the wild world is beautiful, and it matters but little where we go...everywhere and always we are in God's eternal beauty and love."

In a journal entry from 1895, the married Muir writes from the Strentzel family orchard in Martinez: "Fine balmy day. Mount Diablo one mass of purple in the morning. Nature is always lovely, invincible, glad, whatever is done and suffered by her creatures. All scars she heals, whether in rocks or water or sky or hearts."

In another oft-quoted journal entry, in 1890 Muir generalizes the healing power of the natural world, and calls it the great hope of the (human) world: "In God's wildness lies the hope of the world—the great fresh un-blighted, unredeemed wilderness. The galling harness of civilization drops off, and the wounds heal ere we are aware."

To Muir's mind, the mechanism of healing is not just, or even mainly, a spiritual transformation, but rather an intriguingly *physical* effect of the natural world upon the body of the pilgrim. His outlook on healing, in other words, is thoroughly this-worldly and immanent, not the least tran-scendent. A previously-quoted passage is worth repeating here, from his 1872 journal:

"The Sierra. Mountains holy as Sinai...Wonderful how completely ev-erything in wild nature fits into us, as if truly part and parent of us. The sun shines not on us but in us. The rivers flow not past, but through us, thrill-ing, tingling, vibrating every fiber and cell of the substance of our bodies, making them glide and sing. The trees wave and the flowers bloom in our bodies as well as our souls, and every bird song, wind song, and tremendous storm song of the rocks in the heart of the mountains is our song, our very own, and sings our love. The Song of God, sounding on forever."

Many similar passages recur in his journal entries, the following selections culled from the late 1860s, his first years in the Sierra Nevada:

"Plain, sky, and mountains ray beauty which you feel. You bathe in these spirit-beams, turning round and round, as if warming at a campfire. Presently you lose consciousness of your own separate existence: you blend with the landscape, and become part and parcel of nature."

"We are now in the mountains, and they are in us, kindling enthusiasm, making every nerve quiver, filling every pore and cell of us. Our flesh-and-bone tabernacle seems transparent as glass to the beauty about us, as if truly an inseparable part of it, thrilling with the air and trees, streams and rocks, in the waves of the sun,—a part of all nature, neither old nor young, sick nor well, but immortal."

"Sketching on the North Dome. It commands views of nearly all the (Yosemite) valley besides a few of the high mountains...These blessed mountains are so compactly filled with God's beauty, no petty personal hope or experience has room to be. Drinking this champagne water is pure pleasure, so is breathing the living air, and every movement of limbs is pleasure, while the whole body seems to feel beauty when exposed to it, as it feels the camp-fire or sunshine, entering not by the eyes alone, but equally through all one's flesh like radiant heat, making a passionate ecstatic pleasure-glow not explainable. One's body then seems homogeneous throughout, sound as a crystal."

Moreover, this physical transformation, this physical incorporation of God's beauty and love consequent to immanent exposure to the natural world, this healing of the care and distractions and dullness of lowland city life, stays with the pilgrim as an immortal gift, claims Muir, and is not lost when one leaves the mountain. Consider these journal entries, ranging from the late 1860s in the Sierra Nevada to 1890 in Alaska:

"Another of those charming exhilarating days that makes the blood dance and excites nerve currents that render one unweariable and well-nigh immortal."

"These beautiful days must enrich all my life. They do not exist as mere pictures—maps hung upon the walls of memory to brighten at times when touched by association or will, only to shrink again like a landscape in the dark; but they saturate themselves into every part of the body and live always."

"Not in these fields, God's wilds, will you ever hear the sad moan of disappointment, 'All is vanity.' No, we are overpaid a thousand times for all our toil, and a single day in so divine an atmosphere of beauty and love would be well worth living for, and at its close, should death come, without any hope of another life, we could still say, 'Thank you, God, for the glorious gift!' and pass on. Indeed, some of the days I have spent alone in the depths of the wilderness have shown me that immortal life beyond the grave is not essential to perfect happiness, for these diverse days were so complete there was no sense of time in them, they had no definite beginning or ending, and formed a kind of terrestrial immortality. After days like these we are ready for any fate—pain, grief, death or oblivion—with grateful heart for all the glorious gift as long as hearts shall endure."

It is noteworthy that Muir's claim that exposure to the natural world, especially mountains, is transformative for humans has no requirement for any particular "belief" or "faith" on the part of the recipient of this transformation. That is, humans are transformed not by being aware of seeing the beauty and love of God in the natural world, and certainly not by "believing" any assertions about the nature of God, but wholly and simply by their *presence* in the natural world. *Being there* is enough, so long as you simply open your eyes and ears. "Few are altogether blind and deaf to the sweet looks and voices of nature."

9

Gaiacentrism: "Lord Man" overthrown

"The universe would be incomplete without man; but it would
also be incomplete without the smallest transmicroscopic creature
that dwells beyond our conceitful eyes."

Until he walked over the bridge spanning the Ohio River and began his thousand-mile walk to Florida, Muir had been surrounded by the traditional Christian version of the classic Western view that humans were special, set apart to rule over the earth and exploit it—*anthropocentrism.* The Bible was entrenched as the source of ultimate knowledge of man and the world in Muir's Scotch Calvinist home. Genesis told him that alone of all the earth's creatures, man had been created in God's own image, and charged by God to have dominion over the earth.

The Wisconsin frontier in which Muir lived from his 12th to 22nd year was a graphic example of exploiting the earth, with Muir taking an active part in the process 12 or more hours a day—as long as there was light—transforming the Midwest woodlands into farm, homestead, and wells. Always Muir was under the scrutinizing eye of his father, Daniel, looking up from his day-long Bible study in his favorite window chair to check young John's work pace. Muir's two years at the University of Wisconsin exposed him to the larger world, and people who were thinking new thoughts, but they were very busy years, crowded with both classes and working hard to support himself, as he did for several years after leaving the university.

But on his thousand-mile walk to the Gulf in 1867, Muir was finally alone and free to move, observe, and think. His journal reveals the quick and sure abandonment of the anthropocentric view of the world, and its replacement by a wider—much wider—view. It begins with the alligators of the southern swamps through which he slogged:

"Many good people believe that alligators were created by the Devil, thus accounting for their all-consuming appetite and ugliness. But doubtless these creatures are happy and fill the place assigned them by the great Creator of us all. Fierce and cruel they appear to us, but beautiful in the eyes of God. They, also, are his children, for He hears their cries, cares for them tenderly, and provides their daily bread...How narrow we selfish, conceited creatures are in our sympathies! how blind to the rights of all the rest of creation!...alligators, snakes...are part of God's family unfallen, undepraved, and cared for with the same species of tenderness and love as is bestowed on angels in heaven or saints on earth."

Note here the interesting suggestion that alligators, snakes, and presumably other creatures are distinguished from humans by being "unfallen, undepraved." The inference is that only humans have fallen from God's original grace and require saving; the rest of creation retains the original glow of creation. Muir seems to be suggesting that the salvation of humans merely restores us to that status that the other creatures have never lost—not a doctrine commonly emphasized in Calvinism or Catholicism!

Nor is this singular suggestion confined to his early and first ramble. On his eleven-day solitary sled trip on Muir Glacier in Alaska two decades later, Muir pens the previously-quoted comment that "In God's wilderness lies the hope of the world—the great fresh unblighted, unredeemed wilderness." God's wilderness is "unredeemed" precisely because it has never fallen and required the redemption needed by humans.

Somewhat later in the journal chronicling his thousand-mile walk, Muir's thinking switches from the glories of alligators to the folly of humans: "The world, we are told, was made especially for man—a presumption not supported by all the facts...He (God) is regarded as a civilized, law-abiding gentleman in favor either of a republican form of government or of a limited monarchy; believes in the literature and language of England; is a warm supporter of the English constitution and Sunday schools and missionary societies; and is purely a manufactured article as any puppet of a half-penny theater.

"With such views of the Creator it is, of course, not surprising that erroneous views should be entertained of the creation...Now, it never seems to occur to these far-seeing teachers that Nature's object in making animals and plants might possibly be first of all the happiness of each one of them, not the creation of all for the happiness of one. Why should man value himself as more than a small part of the one great unit of creation? And what creature of all that the Lord has taken the pains to make is not essential to the completeness of that unit—the cosmos? The universe would be incomplete without man; but it would also be incomplete without the smallest transmicroscopic creature that dwells beyond our conceitful eyes and knowledge."

Muir not long after enlarged his view even further, adding the time dimension and sketching in his journal a vision of creation breathtaking in its breadth and sophistication: "This star, our own good earth, made many a successful journey around the heavens ere man was made, and whole kingdoms of creatures enjoyed existence and returned to dust ere man appeared to claim them. After human beings have also played their part in Creation's plan, they too may disappear without any general burning or extraordinary commotion whatever."

It is conventional among Muir biographers to call this a shift to *biocentrism*. If we confine our view to the journal of the thousand-mile walk, that may be accurate. But Muir soon saw the Sierra Nevada in California, and quickly the "Range of Light" led him to further broaden his vision, to include not just plants and animals, but rocks and water as entities also bursting with spiritual life, as revealed in journal entries from 1869 and 1870:

"(The waters of Yosemite Falls) moved over the brink with songs that go farther into the substance of our being than ever was touched by man-made harmonies—songs that bear pure heaven in every note. The fleecy, spiritualized waters take the form of mashed and woven comets, going with a grace that casts poor mortals into an agony of joy."

"Yonder stands the South (Half) Dome, its crown high above our camp, though its base is four thousand feet below us; a most noble rock, it seems full of thought, clothed with living light, no sense of dead stone about it, all spiritualized, neither heavy looking nor light, steadfast in serene strength like a god."

Muir's radical shift of view from anthropocentrism, then, goes beyond biocentrism to include the whole planet. *Everything*, the entire immanent world, is alive. We may call his view, then, *Gaiacentrism*, an outlook that decisively dethrones what Muir time and again refers to as "Lord Man." This view, that all of our created world has beauty, wonder, and status, that no one part of that wondrous whole has the right to hold dominion over the rest, remains contentious today. The struggle between anthropocentrism and Gaiacentrism is far from being decided.

Muir's ground-breaking and eloquent espousal of an earth-centered, immanent worldview continues to inspire, continues to serve as one of the most challenging aspects of Muir's thinking. As we shall see in Chapter 26, upon our ability to make this shift may hinge the future of human civilization on the planet.

10

Death: no longer the great enemy

"…a change from one form of beauty to another."

Just as he came to espouse the immanent realm—actual, physical, experienced natural phenomena—as the "heart of the world," liberating himself from the transcendent Christian view of the superior place of humans in the world, so Muir quickly articulated his own view of death. On his long walk to the Gulf, the 29-year-old Muir wrote thus in his journal:

"On no subject are our ideas more warped and pitiable than on death. Instead of the sympathy, the friendly union, of life and death so apparent in Nature, we are taught that death is an accident, a deplorable punishment for the oldest sin, the arch-enemy of life, etc. Town children, especially, are steeped in this death orthodoxy, for the natural beauties of death are seldom seen or taught in towns…But let children walk with Nature, let them see the beautiful blendings and communions of death and life, their joyous inseparable unity, as taught in woods and meadows, plains and mountains and streams of our blessed star (earth), and they will learn that death is stingless indeed, and as beautiful as life, and that the grave has no victory, for it never fights. All is divine harmony."

These sentences reveal that not only has Muir thoroughly disenfranchised himself from the Christian "death orthodoxy" as punishment for human sin (or, more specifically, Eve's sin in the Garden of Eden), but that Muir has a low regard for established religion and its teachings. Indeed, his low regard for organized religion is matched only by that for cities and the hectic life lived therein.

Muir returns to his own view of death during his first summer in the Sierra Nevada, tending to a flock of sheep driven up to Tuolumne Meadows. Of the landscapes he traverses, he observes that "One is constantly reminded of the infinite lavishness and fertility of Nature, inexhaustible abundance amid what seems enormous waste. And yet when we look into any of her operations that lie within reach of our minds, we learn that no particle of her material is wasted or worn out. It is eternally flowing from use to use, beauty to yet higher beauty; and we soon cease to lament waste and death, and rather rejoice and exult in the imperishable, unspendable wealth of the universe, and faithfully watch and wait the reappearance of everything that melts and fades and dies about us, feeling sure that its next appearance will be better and more beautiful than the last."

Viewing the drying foothill fields of formerly gleaming gold flowers in late spring, Muir comments that "The death of flowers in this garden is only a change from one form of beauty to another."

These views are those of the young Muir. Did experience of life and its losses change them? Not really. As he ages, Muir speaks of his own future death calmly. While still living in Yosemite Valley, a year after the Inyo Earthquake had sent great rockslides tumbling into the valley from the high surrounding walls, Muir writes in his journal on March 11, 1873: "Last night I dreamed I stood with a friend on the edge of a precipice shaken by an earthquake. The rocks started to fall. I said: 'Let us die calmly. This is a noble death.' But it settled and we escaped…"

The same calm acceptance of death is revealed on his birthday two decades later, living now in the Alhambra Valley with Louie and their young daughters Helen and Wanda. Muir writes in his journal: "April 21, 1895. Alhambra Valley. My birthday—I am told the fifty-seventh, and yet I feel only a boy. Must make haste to get my work done ere the night falls. Made an excursion with the babes (daughters) to Mount Wanda." Death is only an approaching nightfall, and the prospect in no way clouds his daily excursion with his children to the flower-studded hill near his home.

Of course Muir experiences grief at the death of those he loves. Death is a return to our ancient home, but still humans miss their colleagues and mourn their departure to that home, particularly the illness and suffering involved. Muir twice mentions this attendant sadness. After the death of Louie's mother in the fall of 1897, he writes to Harvard botanist Charles Sargent that "This death, disease and pain business of our nature is horrible amid the joy and harmony of our blessed world, and we can only hope and trust that there is a still better world beyond this."

In the ensuing decade, Muir saw the death of Louie (which left him dazed with grief for a year, "deadly, stunningly tired" amidst a "mental barrenness" that made any writing impossible) and nearly all his closest friends—Edward Harriman, William Keith, John Swett, and others. Muir wistfully remarks in a letter to his daughter Helen in 1911, as yet another several friends pass away: "I wonder if leaves feel lonely when they see their neighbors falling."

Neither of these two comments is a renunciation of his larger views on death, of course. They are merely an old man's tired admission of the toll of losing those you love.

Near the end of his life, with so many deaths behind him and his own looming, Muir reaffirms his lifelong vision of death as but the final of life's transformations in a long and eloquent journal entry. The entry is undated, but journal editor and Muir biographer Wolfe places it at the very end of the journal, persuaded it was penned within a year or two of his own death:

"*Death*. The rugged old Norsemen spoke of death as *Heimgang*—home-going. So the snow-flowers (snowflakes) go home when they melt and flow to the sea, and the rock ferns, after unrolling their fronds to the light and beautifying the rocks, roll them up close again in the autumn and blend with the soil.

"Myriads of rejoicing living creatures, daily, hourly, perhaps every moment sink into death's arms, dust to dust, spirit to spirit—waited on, watched over, noticed only by their Maker, each arriving at its own heaven-dealt destiny.

"All the merry dwellers of the trees and streams, and the myriad swarms of the air, called into life by the sunbeam of a summer morning, go home through death, wings folded perhaps in the last red rays of sunset of the day they were first tried. Trees towering in the sky, braving storms of centuries, flowers turning faces to the light for a single day or hour, having enjoyed their share of life's feast—all alike pass on and away under the law of death and love. Yet all are our brothers, and enjoy life as we do, share heaven's blessings with us, die and are buried in hallowed ground, come with us out of eternity and return into eternity. 'Our little lives are rounded with a sleep'…

"Death is a kind nurse saying 'Come, children, to bed and get up in the morning'—a gracious Mother calling her children home."

The "death" that Muir refers to in all the references above is, of course, death of the natural variety, death as the culmination of a lifetime, whether it be the day of a mayfly or the Psalm's "three score and ten" of a human. Violent, senseless death was another matter. In Alaska he roundly chastises one of his Tlingit guides for shooting a bird as target-practice. The man's response: "Being around Boston-men (Euro-Americans) so much, we become careless of life." Even when his guides were shooting birds or seals for food from the canoe, Muir so frequently rocked the craft as they shot (thus skewing their aim) that it became a matter of humorous comment.

Though not a vegetarian, Muir was not keen on the eating of meat, both from ethical considerations and, tellingly for Muir, practical considerations: "Some people miss flesh as a drunkard misses his dram. This depraved appetite stands greatly in the way of free days on the mountains, for meat of any kind is hard to carry, and makes a repulsive mess when jammed in a pack."

Perhaps the best summary of Muir's views was penned by him in a letter to the children of the Harriman family he had befriended on the 1899 expedition of scientists to Alaska sponsored by railway tycoon Edward Harriman. "Remember your penitential promises," he writes. "Kill as few of your fellow beings as possible and pursue some branch of natural history at least far enough to see Nature's harmony. Don't forget me. God bless you. Good-bye. Ever your friend—John Muir."

Is Muir's unorthodox and radical acceptance of death predicated on his anticipation of resurrection and the eternal life of his spirit after death? Not at all. Beyond the very occasional and conventional mention of hope for "a still better world beyond this" one, Muir hardly ever speaks of resurrection of the body or survival of a soul after death. When he does mention "immortality" it is, rather, to claim that the joys of a day in the beauty of the natural world constitute true immortality, and that the "life after death" variety is superfluous—thus intimating that he holds no store in it. Losing track of time and being wholly absorbed in the beauty and vitality of the natural world—this is Muir's vision of "immortality."

On his first summer in the Sierra Nevada, for example, Muir writes in his journal: "June 13 (1869).—Another glorious Sierra day in which one seems to be dissolved and absorbed and sent pulsing onward we know not where. Life seems neither long nor short, and we take no more heed to save time or make haste than do the trees and stars. This is true freedom, a good practical sort of immortality." He reiterates the point on August 10: "Another of those charming exhilarating days that makes the blood dance and excites nerve currents that render one unweariable and well-nigh immortal."

Two decades later, during his 1890 trip to Alaska, Muir writes these already-quoted lines in his journal: "Not in these fields, God's wilds, will you ever hear the sad moan of disappointment, 'All is vanity.' No, we are overpaid a thousand times for all our toil, and a single day in so divine an atmosphere of beauty and love would be well worth living for, and at its close, should death come, without any hope of another life, we could still say, 'Thank you, God, for the glorious gift!' and pass on.

"Indeed, some of the days I have spent alone in the depths of the wilderness have shown me that immortal life beyond the grave is not essential to perfect happiness, for these diverse days were so complete there was no sense of time in them, they had no definite beginning or ending, and formed a kind of terrestrial immortality. After days like these we are ready for any fate—pain, grief, death or oblivion—with grateful heart for all the glorious gifts as long as hearts shall endure."

At the end Muir faced his own death calmly, almost eagerly. Now 76 years of age, he was pushing himself hard to get his *Travels in Alaska* finished before the end, working from seven in the morning until ten at night in the now-empty Victorian home in the Alhambra Valley, assisted by the widow of a friend. That summer of 1914 saw the beginning of World War I, which he pronounced "monstrous" and "horrible" to his daughter Wanda, who lived with her husband and sons in the historic adobe just north of the old house. Work on the O'Shaughnessy dam destroying his beloved Hetch Hetchy Valley at the mouth of the Tuolumne River was begun at the same time, a calamity so painful to Muir that he could not even speak of it.

In the midst of the war and the destruction of Hetch Hetchy, Muir pressed on with the Alaska book, taking time off only to shuffle to the nearby adobe and his daily play time with Wanda's four sons. "So flourisheth the boy undergrowth," he wrote. "Interesting mugginses and as lively as chipmunks."

Knowing he had very little time left, Muir reversed his long refusal to modernize the old Victorian home and amazed his daughters by having electricity installed, carting away old furniture, installing new bookcases, and requesting the assistance of the wife of another old friend on "a buying orgy" in San Francisco for velvets, rugs, and all manner of new furnishings. Clearly he was readying the home for new occupants.

By early December, Muir's long-weak lungs were filling with liquid. He instructed Wanda that he should be buried beside Louie in the Alhambra Valley, and asked for her to arrange a trip to visit his other daughter Helen and her three sons in the Mohave Desert town of Dagget. Taking the typed manuscript of his Alaska book on the train with him, he arrived two days before Christmas and took walks with Helen and his grandsons at their ranch. At night he sat by the fire and made changes in the manuscript.

Still his lungs filled. He staggered as he rose the second night, and an alarmed Helen sent for Wanda, and had her husband rush Muir to the California Hospital in Los Angeles. Muir insisted on taking the manuscript with him. At the hospital, after his son-in-law had returned home, he joked feebly with nurses and doctors, and asked for his Alaska pages to be put on the bed. Muir biographers ascribe this request to a desire to finish his changes to the book. I think not. Muir always hated writing, to the end.

When the nurse walked into the room after a brief absence that Christmas Eve, John Muir was dead, parts of the Alaska manuscript scattered about the bed. Muir had made his bed a shrine, and the piles of paper were not to revise, but rather were sacred relics of his adventures in that beautiful northern land.

Here was Muir Glacier and his eleven mystical days alone on it with his sled. There was Hugh Miller Fiord, where he had narrowly escaped the crunching bergs bearing down upon his canoe. Here was Brady Glacier, Muir desperately hitching himself along the narrow ice bridge over a seventy-foot crevasse in pelting snow, the dog Stickeen behind him. And there was the boulder-strewn shore of Glacier Bay, where Muir whiled away the precious night enraptured by prismatic bars of light marching across the vast sky above.

Muir had surrounded himself with mementos of the glorious immanent world.

The bed, now a gleaming altar containing Muir's body, studded with piles of icy beauty and adventures, sailed west with quickening pace into the gathering darkness and cold.

Going home.

11

How Nature Works: Muir the scientist

"How lavish is Nature building, pulling down, creating, destroying chasing every material particle from form to form, ever changing, ever beautiful."

As with his spiritual roots, the scientific work of Muir is not commonly remembered today. Yet he was a competent and widely-recognized scientist, investigating the workings of the immanent world with all the tools of scientists then as now: keen observation, patient work, the use of the equipment and techniques available at the time, a grasp of the current literature, and companionship with other scientists.

As a scientist, Muir was unusual in several respects, however. First, he made a scientific mark in two fields, botany and geology. In both disciplines he attracted the attention of already-established leaders in the field, communicated and often met with them for joint fieldwork, and earned their respect and friendship. Second, Muir possessed the ability to see not just the narrow picture, but the broad picture as well. His remarkable insights into the pervasive presence and importance of great interlocking cycles in the natural world were far ahead of his time. Let us examine the field of botany first.

In the Sierra Nevada, Muir remained an inveterate collector of new plants long after his thousand-mile walk, and became the companion of choice for visiting botanists from the East. Soon he was sending collected plants to the eminent Asa Gray at the Arnold Arboretum at Harvard, and accompanying Gray and the great English botanist (and Darwin confidante) Joseph Hooker through the Sierra Nevada and to Mount Shasta.

So impressed was Gray with Muir that he named two plants after him, the Sierra Nevada mousetail plant *Ivesia muirii* (like Muir himself, found on rocky slopes and cliffs in the High Sierra) and the Alaskan compositae *Erigeron muirii*, both discovered by Muir. Other prominent botanists with whom Muir worked include the California Academy of Science's Albert Kellog (his companion on the 1873 traverse of the Sierra Nevada range) and Charles S. Sargent, Director of the Arnold Arboretum and head of the National Forest Commission.

Muir's expertise in geology was equal to that in botany, but more controversial, initially. When he arrived in Yosemite Valley in 1869, the accepted explanation of the valley's distinctive geology was that of California's official state geologist, the imposing Josiah Whitney, who proclaimed that the valley floor had dropped in a violent cataclysm. Whitney's protege, Clarence King, had noted evidence of glaciation in the region, but dared not contradict his esteemed mentor.

Muir's keen eyes quickly noted the ubiquitous signs of extensive glaciation, and by the end of his first season in the valley Muir was propounding to all he met the glacial sculpturing of not just the valley but much of the Sierra Nevada. He convinced geology professor Joseph LeConte, visiting with students from the University of California campus, as well as John Daniel Runkle, the visiting president of MIT, who urged him to write up his ideas so that they could be published in the proceedings of the Boston Academy of Science. The visiting John Tyndall, reigning glaciologist of England, like Runkle sent Muir many books and much equipment afterwards to aid and enhance his work.

Spurred perhaps by Whitney's dismissive response that he was no more than an ignorant shepherd and his views unworthy of consideration, Muir spent the early 1870s amassing evidence for the glaciation of the range, and published an extensive seven-part account in *The Overland Monthly* in 1874, in which he displayed "close observation, brilliant inference, and equally brilliant induction" in the words of Muir biographer Thurman Wilkins.

Modern geologists have accepted Muir's findings on the role of glaciation, as well as his understanding of the critical role of cleavage in the shaping of Yosemite's granite slabs. Muir delineated five different types of cleavage planes in granite (termed "jointing" today), showing how each responds to the pressure of glacial ice. "Glaciers do not so much mold and shape, as disinter forms already conceived and ripe," Muir accurately claimed.

Beyond the thousands of plants collected, the discovery of plants new to science, the evidence amassed of glaciation's role in the Sierra Nevada, and the importance of cleavage planes in granite, it was Muir's formulation and elegiac description of the importance of great interlocking cycles in the natural world, to my mind, that must stand as his greatest scientific achievement. Consider these journal descriptions tying together the ocean, storms, snow, glaciers, landscape, soil, meadows and forests (clarifying material within parentheses by author):

March 1873, Yosemite: "Vapor from the sea; rain, snow, and ice on the summits; glaciers and rivers—these form a wheel that grinds the mountains thin and sharp, sculptures deeply the flanks, and furrows them into ridge and canyon, and crushes the rocks (under glacial paths) into soils on which the forests and meadows and gardens and fruitful vine and tree and grain are growing."

1890, Alaska: "When I look on a glacier, I see the immeasurable sunbeams pouring faithfully on the outspread oceans, and the streaming, up-rising vapors entering cool mountain basins and taking their places in the divinely beautiful six-rayed daisies of snow that go sifting, glinting to their appointed places on the sky-piercing mountains, joining ray to ray (as they are compressed into ice), forming glaciers amid the boom and thunder of avalanches, and at last flowing serenely back to the sea."

Intermediate and essential in these grand cycles are Muir's beloved glaciers. In his 1890 Alaska trip he muses lyrically upon them:

"Ice-sheet brooding with supreme dominion over the coming land-scape, clasping a thousand mountains in its crystal embrace; and to think that all this mighty glacial geological engine shaping the world, bringing out the face-features of the landscape, is made up of tiny and frail frost-flowers (snow), like children on a frolic with hands joined, children of the sea and the sun...What songs they sing as they gather and go to their pre-destined work, every one of the infinite multitude building better than they know, fields and orchards and flowers and birds and happy people, lakes and rejoicing rivers breaking forth into glad existence at their approach!"

Just as Muir had the talent to gaze from a height at a range of peaks and delineate in his mind's eye the various watersheds formed and the flow of rivers in these watersheds, so he possessed the talent to view a landscape and see in his mind's eye the *past* flows of rivers and glaciers which had sculpted the land, laid down its topography, gouged out the basins of lakes, ground up bedrock and deposited it here and there as soils giving rise to meadows and forests, as well as the insects, birds, and mammals adapted to live there. All in a glance, though a highly informed glance honed by years in the wilderness.

Perhaps Muir's favorite spot in Yosemite Valley was a prominent ledge of granite some 500 feet up the north wall just east of Yosemite Falls, which he named Sunnyside Bench (the same name it has among rock-climbers today, 150 years later). This was his special place, the spot too rugged for visitors or well-wishers to access, his own chunk of Yosemite from whence he had a panoramic view of the entire valley spread before him—and all in the precious sunshine, the north wall facing nearly due south.

Muir would sit on his Sunnyside Bench and with his almost-magical mind's eye "see" into the deep past, realizing how the forested portions of the valley took their present form as a result of the never-ending dualistic interplay of sun and shadow, as recorded in a portion of his 1873 journal entitled "Sunnyside Observations":

"Shadows. Sitting in my Sunnyside Camp, with the valley outspread before me like a map, it is interesting to watch the movements of the lights and shadows on the floor. The main masses of shade mark the boundaries and locations of the residual glaciers that lay in the shadows protected by them long after the main trunk glacier of the valley was melted. The residual glaciers, of course, formed terminal moraines, and it is upon these terminals moraines (and the soil created and stored by them) that the principal groves (of trees) are planted. This explains the relationship they bear to the shadows, the shadows controlling the glaciers, the glaciers controlling the position of the moraines, and the moraines (and their soil) governing the position of the groves.

"Some of the rocky slopes which have furnished ground for the principal groves are almost wholly the results of earthquake shocks…Many of the groves are growing upon soils that have no direct relation to moraines, such as that one which runs out into the meadow in front of the Yosemite Fall. This one is growing upon a rocky slope that was formed by Yosemite Creek during some great flood, the material having been derived from an earthquake talus, the result of an avalanche that was shaken from the cliff on the west side of the falls…And all around the walls on both sides of the valley, the width of the forest border is seen to depend upon the amount of wash of floods, excepting the moraine groves, which, as we have seen, depend on shadows."

Muir then sums up the keys to the distribution of forest on the valley floor: "All the high ground in the bottom of the valley is rocky and has been formed by floods, earthquakes, and glaciers, and all, without exception is more or less clothed with forest trees, such as firs, pines, cedars, and a few oaks."

Even the course of the Merced River in the valley can be read by Muir from his sunny perch: "It will now be easy to account for the meandering course of the river through the valley. It is jostled from side to side by the rocky slopes upon which the groves are growing. The first great bend at the head of the valley is evidently measured by the moraine slope of the residual Illilouette and Glacier Point glacier. Then the wash from Indian Canyon shoves the river back against the south wall. There it is shoved north again by the wash from the Sentinel Rocks. Then south again by the wash from the canyon between El Capitan and Three Brothers, with minor bends between these main bends due to minor taluses, moraines, and flood washes."

He concludes in a typical Muir elegy: "Thus it appears that everything here is marching to music, and the harmonies are all so simple and young they are easily apprehended by those who will keep still and listen and look: however far these harmonies may extend beyond our powers, they are simple enough on the surface."

Muir of course is also unusual in that he successfully combines science with a spiritual appreciation of the natural world. Both are valid and important, he claims. Consider this entry from his journal, penned in the last year or so of his life:

"On the rim of the Yosemite I once heard a man say: 'How was this tremendous old rocky gorge formed?' 'Oh, stop your science,' said another of the party. 'Hush! stand still and behold the glory of God!'

"I suppose silent wonder would have been better, more natural at first. Still, as the warmth and beauty of fire is more enjoyed by those who, knowing something of the origin of wood and coal, see the dancing flames and are able to contemplate the grand show as having come from the sun ages ago, and slowly garnered in cells (as the products of photosynthesis), so also are those Yosemite temples the more enjoyed by those who have traced, however dimly, the working of the Divine Mind in their making, who know why domes are here, and how sheer precipitous walls like El Capitan were predetermined by the crystallization of the granite (into cleavage planes) in the dark, thousands of centuries before development, and who know how in the fullness of time the sun was called to lift water out of the sea in vapor which was carried by the winds to the mountains, crystallized into snow among the clouds, to fall on the summits, form glaciers, and bring Yosemite Valley and all the other Sierra features to the light. In offering us such vistas, thereby increasing our pleasure and admiration, Science is divine!"

In saying "Science is divine!" Muir is asserting that scientific understanding of the natural world permits us to better appreciate its marvelous complexity and beauty. Far from being opposed to the spiritual appreciation of nature, science fosters and enhances it, for Muir. As we shall soon examine further, Muir in this respect echoes an insight arising millennia earlier in China: "The highest degree of the spiritual is to know clearly the ten thousand creatures," was how 7th century BCE Taoist Guan Zhong had put it.

As these quotes indicate, Muir saw the natural world as consisting of broad interlocking cycles bringing together the all-encompassing water cycle and a variety of geological processes. Often these processes are seen dualistically, as the dynamic interplay of sun and shade, light and dark, water and rocks, an essential feature of how nature "works."

These observations led Muir to appreciate that the natural world was pulsing with massive flows of energy in the waters, rocks, and wind, an orderly maelstrom of energy. Just as he pioneered the articulation of the water cycle and its interlocking with the glacial cycles of landscape sculpting and soil formation, so Muir foreshadowed (though in very general terms, here) the later work of physicists describing the intimate interacting flow of matter and energy reflected in the Laws of Thermodynamics.

Consider these thoughts from his 1869 journal entries, gathered in *My First Summer in the Sierra*: "Contemplating the lace-like fabric of streams outspread over the mountains, we are reminded that everything is flowing—going somewhere, animals and so-called lifeless rocks as well as water. Thus the snow flows fast or slow in grand beauty-making glaciers and avalanches; the air in majestic floods carrying minerals, plant leaves, seeds, spores, with streams of music and fragrance; water streams carrying rocks both in solution and in the form of mud particles, sand, pebbles, and boulders. Rocks flow from volcanoes like water from springs, and animals flock together and flow in currents modified by stepping, leaping, gliding, flying, swimming, etc. While the stars go streaming through space pulsed on and on forever like blood globules in Nature's warm heart."

A few pages later, Muir observes "How lavish is Nature building, pulling down, creating, destroying chasing every material particle from form to form, ever changing, ever beautiful."

The throbbing energy of nature is seen not just in stars streaming through space but in individual creatures: "Magnificent bears of the Sierra are worthy of their magnificent homes. They are not companions of men, but children of God, and His charity is broad enough for bears. They are the objects of His tender keeping...Bears are made of the same dust as we, and breathe the same winds and drink of the same waters...his life turns and ebbs with heart-pulsings like ours, and was poured from the same First Fountain."

Though he can observe and describe the pulse-beats of Nature, Muir is keenly aware how difficult it is to fully grasp and understand this cosmic feature. Viewing a spectacular valley along the Kings River on September 10, 1875 (or perhaps 1876), he writes in his journal: "From the Middle and North Forks' divide glorious views are obtained of all the Kings River Kingdom—the wideness of the valleys grassed with pines, the grandeur of their architecture on canyon-edges and all along their fountains, and the sweet, gentle beauty of their meads and gardens. I have yet to see the man who has caught the rhythm of the big, slow pulse-beats of Nature."

Muir, then, was a remarkable scientist in several respects. He gained the recognition (and friendship) of leading scientists in both botany and geology, and contributed to these fields in the collecting of distribution data on existing plants and the discovery of new species, as well as establishing the role of glaciation in forming the Sierra Nevada range and the importance of cleavage planes in geomorphology. Beyond this, he discerned and described in a scientific manner how seemingly disparate phenomena are linked in great interlocking cycles in the natural world, cycles often resulting from dualistic interplay of light and dark, sun and shade, rock and water. This accomplishment marks him as perhaps the first systems ecologist. And finally, he insisted that all immanent phenomena have spiritual dimension to them.

Some accomplishments—for a tramp!

Taken singly, any of the distinctive understandings Muir articulated about the world he sauntered through would be remarkable, as these chapters indicate. Taken together, though, Muir's worldview must be acknowledged as an unorthodox, radical expression of "the way things are" without precedent in the Western tradition. Consider the breadth of his view: his impassioned recognition of the beauty and love of the Creator blazing forth in every corner of the world, spiritualizing plants, animals, rocks and water. His experience of this charged immanent world healing the most care-worn and distracted human with a transforming, warming physical glow of terrestrial immortality. His overthrow of "Lord Man" by a clear-eyed recognition that all the creatures of the earth are kin, and contribute their key parts to the glorious whole, leaving no room for misguided notions of human superiority. His vision of death as but one step in the cycle of life, a blessed "coming home" to the awesome source of all creation. And his original contributions to the scientific understanding of botany, geology, and the grand dualistic, ecological cycles creating landscape—all this comes together to form a coherent worldview new to the Western tradition.

If we had to name Muir's new understanding of "the way things are," perhaps *Earth Wisdom* would be most appropriate. To be sure, others have realized pieces of Muir's Earth Wisdom: Heraclitus, St. Francis of Assisi, Alexander von Humboldt, Albert Schweitzer. None before him, though, articulated the same stunning breadth and depth of insight to create a seamless whole, a way of approaching the world—of living in the world—as exuberantly and prodigiously as Muir.

None in the Western tradition, that is. Because as I read Muir's life and writings, time and again a thought tugs at the corner of my mind. This sounds strangely like…That reminds me of…Unbidden, as a distraction, Muir's thoughts and actions constantly pull me eastward. Far eastward. Across North America, across the Atlantic, across Eurasia, to a land and culture thousands of years old when Muir immigrated to America. Muir's Earth Wisdom, new as a coherent whole to the West, is in fact old—in the East.

Part II
The Tao of Muir:
Earth Wisdom, East

"We lay down on the innocent mountain
The earth for pillow, the stars for cover."

—Li Po

You would think that John Muir is sufficiently fascinating and complex to command our complete attention, on his own. Surely that is the case. But given this, I find it intriguing—uncanny, even—that as I read Muir's writings and the various biographies of Muir, I am often reminded of experiences I've had in China, and of passages from Taoist writings.

John Muir was by no means the first or most prominent espouser of mountains as restorers of health and vitality. In the summer of 1985 my mountaineer friend Kyle and I were trudging up steep stone steps cut a thousand years ago into the granite of *Huang Shan* (Yellow Mountain) in Anhui Province, central China.

We were not alone.

Crowds of Chinese of all ages were passing us by, chattering and joking, unencumbered by the packs we carried. Not only were we the only westerners on the mountain, we were the only people carrying their own possessions, everyone else having hired local eleven- and twelve-year-old girls to pack their gear to the hostel at the top for them. On several occasions more than gear was being carried up the mountain: wrinkled old ladies passed us also, slouched down in palanquins weighing far more than the ladies themselves. The palanquins were carried by teams of stout peasant lads, though, rather than girls.

Our company on Huang Shan was a consequence of mountains having been considered sources of health and vitality for several millennia in China, cosmic pillars where the *qi* energy of earth contacts that of heaven, thus creating nodes of power. Being on a mountain permits you to connect with this qi energy, to your practical (not just "spiritual") physical and mental benefit.

While this is a somewhat different explanation than Muir offered, the essentials are the same: mountains possess an extraordinary power, which you connect with while there, and are healed and revitalized. As a theme, "travelers among the mountains" has been a major genre in Chinese art for a thousand years; see, for example, *Traveling Among Streams and Mountains*, from the 12th century Jin dynasty, or *Festival of the Peaches of Longevity*, from 14th century Ming dynasty, both at the Nelson-Atkins Museum of Art in Kansas City.

Dawn is held to be an especially powerful time for the flow of qi energy, so Kyle and I joined hundreds of others atop the mountain an hour before sunrise the next morning, donning the bulky "Mao coats" hanging on hooks on the hostel doors. Thus muffled against the chill, we joined the throngs making their way in utter darkness to the vista point looking east. Like the climb up the mountain, the dawn viewing was a festive occasion, marked by chatter and laughter. As the sky lightened, then was pierced with first mauve, then purple, then red bolts streaking through the clouds, the crowd quieted, awestruck. The clouds rendered the dawn ambiguous and rather anticlimactic—but no matter. Everyone quickly dropped into a qi-heightened celebratory mood again, and made for the refectory for hot tea, rice congee, and pickled vegetables.

Although we had slept on the mountain in a hostel that night, sleeping Muir-style on the ground was not unknown. Atop this very mountain a thousand years earlier, the T'ang dynasty poet Li Po (also known as Li Bai) recounted his experience:

To refresh our sorrow-laden souls
We drink wine deep into the splendid night,
Its moonlight charm far too precious for sleep.
But at last the wine overtakes us
And we lay down on the innocent mountain
The earth for pillow, the stars for cover. (Barnett translation)

Muir's writings contain passages eerily reminiscent of those by Taoist-inclined poets in ancient China. Consider this journal entry: "The Merced river is now at earnest work with all the beauty and poetry of unmarred nature. In the middle of the stream are immense rock islands hewn from the grandly sculptured walls. *I wished to camp in midstream on a flat, smooth rock.*" How this entry echoes the poem *A Green Stream* by Wang Wei, written also in the T'ang dynasty, which also describes a stream, and ends with "*Oh to remain on a broad, flat rock, casting a fishing line forever.*" (italics mine; the character translated as "to remain" might just as correctly be translated "to camp.")

Indeed, Muir's journal entries often have the distinct feel of Chinese poetry. Consider this from October 1871, reflecting Muir's euphoria after just discovering the Black Mountain glacier: "I walk down from the canyon to the lake, and around the lake to gather wood. Warm lappings of Scotland memory. Distant mountains dim in storm. Lake, mountain, sky, all one black at last...The drip, drip of water on my bed of cedar fragments. Slant snowflakes in light of fire...must sleep and wake."

Compare the evocative setting and feel of Muir's moment at his Sierra lake, with the slanting fall of snowflakes in the firelight, to the famous and oft-quoted lines by the Song dynasty poet Lin Bu, describing a plum tree beside a pond in his garden: "Its sparse shadows are horizontal and slanted—the water is clear and shallow / Its hidden fragrance wafts and moves—the moon is hazy and dim."

These similarities between Muir and Taoist aspects of China, including even similarities with the phrases and mood of poems from a thousand years ago, are intriguing. Muir had never been to China, and apparently not even given a moment's thought to that country or its culture, to judge from his journals and conversations with friends. To compound the puzzle, even those reasonably versed about China in the mid-19th century knew virtually nothing about the religion of Taoism, which was repudiated (when it wasn't, in fact, ignored) by educated, polite society in China, the strata comprised of Confucians or newly-minted Christians who regarded Taoism as the rankest of medieval superstition.

Yet the echoes sketched here merely presage an astonishing similarity between Muir's Earth Wisdom and the Taoist tradition of ancient China. What can be termed "the Tao of Muir" extends to mountains, water, cycles, transformation, humans, death, and the dance of yin and yang, as we shall see. But first: a few caveats regarding Taoism are in order.

First, what we term Taoism in the West (Daoism in the modern pinyin romanization) is in fact not so much a religion as a loosely-allied group of approaches to understanding reality. Those approaches include philosophical Taoism (intellectuals who focus on the *Daodejing* and *Zhuangzi*, formerly *Tao Te Ching* and *Chuang Tse*); reclusive Taoism (hermits who take to the mountains); priestly Taoism (the "high Taoism" of rituals); and China's folk religion ("low Taoism," famously eclectic and superstitious).

Second, Taoism is not only diverse, but in fact the oldest continuous philosophy (or religion) on the planet, having arisen in the Neolithic from shamanic roots, and adding layers of development and complexity uninterrupted to the present day. Because of this long, five-thousand-year history, the expected diversity of beliefs and practices in any major religion is considerably amplified in Taoism. To locate any *core* aspects of Taoism is thus difficult and, to some degree, arbitrary.

Third, Taoism has always been an underground movement, with respect to the reigning government of China. As the religion of the people, it has always been viewed with suspicion by autocratic rulers, then as now. Moreover, Taoism's stance toward the world is so starkly antithetical to that of the patriarchal, Confucian ruling elite of China that it has been deemed an ongoing threat to the central authorities, and rightly so, to judge by its frequent involvement in peasant revolts through the millennia.

Last, and by no means least, all levels of Taoism distrust verbal articulation of any sort, which makes it extraordinarily difficult to (verbally) describe the essence of Taoism. Any philosophy or religion whose central text (the *Daodejing*) begins with "The Tao that can be described is not the true Tao" is going to be challenging to describe.

A few key terms are central to our discussion of the Tao of Muir. One of the great insights of Chinese civilization is the recognition of an over-arching pattern to natural phenomena, a pattern resulting from inherent properties of matter and energy. The Chinese call the pattern-generating force the Tao (or Dao). And qi (formerly ch'i) denotes the energy that flows along the pathways set by the Tao, with yin and yang being the two general aspects of this energy flow.

13

Mountains: the Two Perfected Lords

"The Two Perfected Lords climbed the mountain and perched and rested together. The day now grew late; a pure breeze came softly; a bright moon stood in the void. The Two Perfected settled in the shade of a pine and chatted and laughed, forgetting to sleep."

—*VERITABLE RECORD*

China is a mountainous country, from the imposing western peaks of Szechuan and the Tibetan Plateau, to the numerous generally north-south ranges of southeastern China, to the east-west Qin-ling chain separating the dry northern plains from the wet southern marshes.

The Chinese view of mountains has progressed through three phases. In the Neolithic, Bronze, and early Iron Ages (from 10,000 to 221 BCE) the mountains were regarded as sacred but dangerous places, on which no human dare set foot. In the Kunlun Mountains of the far west (mythical peaks in the Tian Shan range) lived the ancient shamanic *Hsi Wang Mu*, the Queen mother of the West, "her appearance like that of a human, (but) with a leopard's tail and tiger's teeth. Moreover, she is skilled at whistling. In her disheveled hair she wears a jade clasp. She administers Heaven's calamities and five punishments."

All mountains in this phase were considered the residence of such half-human, half-animal totem ancestors of the great clans, terrifying creatures before whom humans could only bow and keep their proper (that is, great) distance. If the totem ancestors were pleased with the respect shown to them, they would send clouds laden with life-giving rain from the mountains onto the agricultural plains where humans dwelt. Zoomorphic representations of these totem ancestors appear very early, on Neolithic pottery from the Yangshao culture, and persist into the bronze creations of the Shang dynasty of 1750-1040 BCE.

This acute fear of mountains and their inhabitants gradually waned through the Qin and Han dynasties of early imperial China (221 BCE to 220 CE). By the end of the Han dynasty and for five centuries thereafter, Taoist holy men sufficiently skilled and reckless might venture onto mountains to gain spiritual power—if they survived. The mountains were now, in this second phase, considered cosmic pillars connecting the yang of heaven with the yin of earth, and thus sources of potent qi energy which exceptional humans might survive and master.

By the T'ang dynasty (618 to 907 CE), the image of mountains had further softened to the point where ordinary mortals began to visit them to benefit from their inherent abundance of qi energy—the third phase. Thus began a thousand-year tradition of pilgrimages to China's mountains, in which I participated with my travel buddies Kyle and AJ during the 1980s on visits to Huang Shan in Anhwei province and Emei Shan deep in Szechuan. (*Shan* denotes a mountain, quite graphically.)

shān

Thus there is a long and rich history in China of men (and occasionally women) taking to the mountains like Muir, and like him extolling the beauty and power of the rugged peaks. These mountain ramblers include the Taoist sages who search for immortality, full immersion in the Tao that imbues all the world but especially in mountains. The character for a

Taoist Immortal, *xian* (formerly *hsien*), in fact is comprised of two elements: "human being" on the left, and "mountain" on the right. An Immortal is a human of the mountains, or perhaps a human-mountain. The eminent Taoist scholar Kristofer Schipper comments further that "phonologically, the word *hsien* derives from the root meaning 'to change, evolve, go up,' or even 'to dance.' This recalls the theme of transformation." We recall that such transformation was vividly sketched by Muir in his descriptions of the relations among water, glaciers, and landscape.

xiān

Such Muir-like mountain ramblers were The Two Perfected Lords, Wang and Kuo, first mentioned in inscriptions of the 8th century CE, and described in the early Song dynasty *Veritable Record of the Two Perfected Lords* two centuries later. Wang and Kuo are seeking a mountain described to them by their teacher, and "made no excuse of distance, but took up their calabashes, put on bamboo hats, and made straight for Chiang-nan (the southeastern region)." They follow a winding path, traversing 34 mountains, gathering medicinal plants as they go. Observe how Muir-like their journey sounds in the *Veritable Record*:

"The Two Perfected Lords went to a place called Ch'i-li Mountain, uniquely grand in shape. They looked at each other and said: 'This mountain is auspiciously fine in scenery, truly a spot for divine immortals' cultivation and refinement.' Then they continued five li, to where the mountains were tall and hard; they saluted left and bowed right. The fine streams faced forward like family branches, spanning a hundred li. The thousand hills saluted in rings, like tigers crouching or dragons coiling.

"The Two Perfected climbed the mountain and perched and rested together. The day now grew late; a pure breeze came softly; a bright moon stood in the void. The Two Perfected settled in the shade of a pine and chatted and laughed, forgetting to sleep. With first dawn, they looked off to the south at the mountain's summit and made their obeisances and inquiries toward the three peaks of (Mt.) Hua-kai. When they were finished, the mists suddenly cleared, and right before their faces stood the three peaks themselves, like a cliff, thrusting out far beyond the skies. The Two Perfected rejoiced."

How many ways this journey of the Two Perfected Lords a thousand years ago reminds us of John Muir! Wang and Kuo are as oblivious as Muir to daunting distances, whether a thousand miles to the Gulf or four hundred miles to Mt. Whitney or two hundred miles on the Merced and San Joaquin Rivers. Like Muir, they travel extraordinarily light: "took up their calabashes, put on bamboo hats, and made straight for Chiang-nan." Amid "tall and hard" mountains they see things in terms of watersheds, Muir-like: "The fine streams faced forward like family branches, spanning a hundred li." Their ecstasy of being in the mountains is so complete that they chat and laugh through the night, "its moonlight charm far too precious for sleep," as Li Po put it about the same era.

Muir also mentions nights too precious for sleep. Consider 1869 in the Sierra Nevada: "After dark, when the camp was at rest, I groped my way back to the altar boulder (in the midst of a stream) and passed the night on it,—above the water, beneath the leaves and stars…precious night." Or 1879 in Alaska: "After sleeping a few hours, I stole quietly out of the camp, and climbed the mountain that stands between the two glaciers…the views over the icy bay, sparkling beneath the stars, were enchanting. It seemed then a sad thing that any part of so precious a night had been lost in sleep."

Or 1890 in Alaska again: "My bed was two boulders, and as I lay wedged and bent on their up-bulging sides, beguiling the hard, cold time in gazing into the starry sky and across the sparkling bay, magnificent upright bars of light in bright prismatic colors suddenly appeared…How long these glad, eager soldiers of light held on their way I cannot tell; for sense of time was charmed out of mind and the blessed night circled away in measureless rejoicing enthusiasm."

To complete the catalog of striking similarities, the Two Perfected Lords are also botanists, like Muir gathering plants as they ramble.

Today Mt. Hua-kai and surrounding mountains are dotted with shrines and altars to the Two Perfected Lords and to their teacher. Pilgrims climb to the shrines and light cedar incense to pay their respects to the Two Perfected Lords, recounting tales and legends of Wang and Kuo to their children and friends.

Indeed, something akin to such a cult surrounds Muir amongst those who frequent the glacier-bound bays of Alaska and the high country of the Sierra Nevada. His name is evoked around campfires as stars are being admired and exploits recounted, whether by park rangers, grizzled backpackers, or eager young boys and girls on their first trip into the back country. I have often heard Muir mentioned with spiritual awe by climbers and outdoors men and women in my company in the Sierras.

At a recent winter solstice celebration, my backpacking buddy Bill described to me his recent ascent of the rugged boulder-strewn Tenaya Canyon above Yosemite Valley, reminding me with gleaming eyes that Muir was the first man of European ancestry to accomplish the brutal six mile scramble (six miles as the raven flies; treble that as the human goes). With relish my friend recounted that it was one of the very few places where Muir's seemingly supernatural mountaineering savvy had failed him, leading to a serious fall that ended with the unconscious Muir tangled in *spirea* and scrub oak less than a yard from a further precipitous thousand-foot drop into surging Tenaya Creek below.

Beyond these intriguing similarities, specific thoughts and experiences of Muir in the mountains are uncannily replicated in the Taoist tradition. *Spirit flight* is a frequent phenomenon in Chinese literature about Taoist masters, where a sleeping Taoist's spirit leaves his body and soars abroad into far realms. Here is Muir, after a strenuous day in Hetch Hetchy and the Tuolumne River canyon-rim above it:

"No sane man in the hands of Nature can doubt the doubleness of his life. Soul and body receive separate nourishment and separate exercise, and speedily reach a stage of development wherein each is easily known apart from the other...My legs sometimes transport me to camp, in the darkness, over cliffs and through bogs and forests that seem inaccessible to civilized legs in the daylight. In like manner the soul sets forth at times upon rambles of its own. Our bodies, though meanwhile out of sight and forgotten, blend into the rest of nature, blind to the boundaries of individuals.

"But it is after both the body and soul of a mountaineer have worked hard, and enjoyed hard, that they are most palpably separate. Our weary limbs, lying at rest on the pine needles, make no attempt to follow after or sympathize with the nimble spirit that, apparently glad of the opportunity, wanders alone down gorges, along beetling cliffs, or away among the peaks and glaciers of the farthest landscapes, or into realms that eye hath not seen, nor ear heard; and when at length we are ready to return home to our flesh-and-bone tabernacle, we scarcely for a moment or two know in what direction to seek for it."

Scarcely knowing where to return from these spirit flights was not a problem only for Muir. One of the fabled Eight Immortals of Taoist tradition returned from a spirit flight and was completely unable to find his body—a disciple had burned it, thinking the Master was dead! The Master had to commandeer the body of a recently-deceased lame beggar to return to: thus Li T'ieh-kuai is the rough-looking Immortal with the iron crutch under his arm, his calabash strung about his neck. He is depicted in Huang Shen's Qing dynasty *Portrait of the Immortal Li T'ieh-kuai*, and Shang Hsi's Ming dynasty *Four Immortals Conveying Longevity*, both in Taipei's National Palace Museum.

The Muir reference to spirit flight quoted above is not the only instance of it we hear from him. In a letter to Jeanne Carr, upon her urging him to leave the mountains and return to Oakland to write, he proclaims "I will not be done here for years. I am in no hurry...My horse and bread are ready for upward...I will fuse in spirit skies!" At the meadow below Cathedral Peak, Muir writes in his journal, "Altitude 9820 feet. Night of August 17, 1872. In full moon, all the horizon is lettered and lifed. I want immortality to read this terrestrial language. This good and tough mountain-climbing flesh is not my final home, and I'll creep out of it and fly free and grow!"

Though spirit flight is definitely an ecstatic phenomenon, the Tao and qi of Taoist tradition are not what we Westerners think of as spiritual, but rather very physical and concrete, as befits a religion classified as "immanent" by scholars of religious studies. The hundreds of folks climbing Huang Shan with Kyle and me, and later Emei Shan when my buddy AJ joined us, were adherents of China's folk religion, intent not at all on a spiritual experience, but rather aiming to improve their physical and mental health on mountains. The mood was not the least reverent and spiritual, but, rather, brimming with boisterous good cheer and the enjoyment of life.

Their mood reflects an important point about Taoism, as recounted by the British sinologist Joseph Needham in his magisterial *Science and Civilization in China*. In the Taoist view, the stuff comprising physical reality is made of substances of varying degrees of "density," ranging along a continuum from gross and heavy at one end, to light and nearly (but not) insubstantial at the other. Mud and rocks might be towards the former end of the continuum, and the "spirit" of humans at the other. But even rocks have their light, spiritual component, which Muir saw and celebrated.

When Muir or Taoists speak of a person's (or animal's or rock's) "spirit," therefore, they are by no means implying something separate from and intrisically different than the heavier components of that entity's being. Spirit is part and parcel of a human (or animal or rock), not something opposed to the "body." That is why, in spirit flights, the spirit-part of Muir and Taoist immortals must always *return* to the body. How could it completely break free and have an independent existence? It is an integral part of the body, merely the lighter element of it.

This view of spirit as merely one end of a continuum of elements of a creature's body is, of course, quite different than the view found in transcendent religions, from Christianity to Buddhism, in which the soul is an independent element, fundamentally different than and opposed to the physical body, which it is only temporarily—and uneasily—occupying.

The laughter and cheerfulness of the crowds on Huang Shan and Emei Shan would be completely understandable to Muir. As noted earlier, Muir's view of the benefits of mountain dwelling included generous doses of physical affects, a whole-body experience. "The Sierra. Mountains holy as Sinai…Wonderful how completely everything in wild nature fits into us, as if truly part and parent of us. The sun shines not on us but in us. The rivers flow not past, but through us, thrilling, tingling, vibrating every fiber and cell of the substance of our bodies, making them glide and sing."

"We are now in the mountains, and they are in us, kindling enthusiasm, making every nerve quiver, filling very pore and cell of us. Our flesh-and-bone tabernacle seems transparent as glass to the beauty about us, as if truly an inseparable part of it, thrilling with the air and trees, streams and rocks, in the waves of the sun,—a part of all nature, neither old nor young, sick nor well, but immortal."

So like the millennia of Taoist mountain ramblers in China, exemplified by the Two Perfected Lords of Mt. Hua-kai, Muir took to the mountains: from Hoffman, Half Dome, and Whitney in the Sierra Nevada; to Lassen, Shasta, and Rainier in the Cascades; to the great peaks of Alaska later. Like the Taoist sages, Muir reveled in the life-giving, care-healing power of mountains. He enjoined his fellows to travel to mountains regularly and absorb their power, just as China's folk religion spurs the crowds surrounding Kyle, AJ and myself on Huang Shan and Emei Shan. Indeed, going to the mountains is going home, wherever it happens.

When it comes to mountains, Muir is at one with the Taoist tradition of China.

14

Water: the Black Dragon King

*"Through the (Tuolumne) canyon flows a river clear as crystal...
Nature's best gardens are here in deepest repose, fountains of wild
ever-playing water falling in every form—the endless song of
Creation shaking the devout listener into newness of life."*

John Muir spends fully as much time limning the wonder of water as
he does of mountains. Water as liquid flowing with pleasing sound in
mountain meadows, water as vapor rising from the Pacific to waft over valleys to the Sierra Nevada, and water as solid drifting down onto mountain
clefts to be pressed age by age into glaciers—all phases of water delight and
interest him. How does the Taoist tradition treat water?

Water (*shui*, formerly *schwei*) is considered a central element in the
flow of the Tao in the world, and is mentioned throughout Taoist writings.
According to the *Daodejing*, "The highest good is like water...Water gives
life to the ten thousand things (all of life) and does not strive. It flows in
places men reject and so is like the Tao." Indeed, water is at times compared
to the Tao itself: "Tao in the world is like a river flowing home to the sea."

shuǐ

92

In Chinese folk religion, many shrines and temples are located at sacred springs, and dedicated to the dragon kings which are held to reside in the water of streams and ocean. Here (and perhaps originally) a water god, the dragon's later transformation into a sky god was still water-related: the dragon kings bring rainfall from the sky to the land. Temples dedicated to the water-god Black Dragon King (*Heilongdawang*) are located throughout China, from the dry plains of northern Shaanxi province in the north, to the mountainous outskirts of Kunming in Yunnan province far to the south.

One of the largest folk religion festivals of Shaanxi Province for the past century up to the present has been held at the temple of the Black Dragon King in the Shaanbei region's Dragon King Valley (*Longwanggou*). In this dry part of China, the rain-bringing dragon kings are the paramount agrarian deities. Local legend has a village maiden in the deep past washing clothes in the local Wuding River when a large peach comes floating by. She takes a bite of the peach and is magically impregnated, soon giving birth to five dragon kings of varying color, including the Black Dragon King. Beside the main hall (*Zhengdian*) of the temple is another hall, the Dragons' Mother's Palace, where the village girl washing clothes in the river is revered as a fertility goddess to this day.

During the week-long festival beginning the ninth day of the sixth lunar month, roughly mid-summer, hundreds of thousands of people swarm into the valley every day to pay their respects to the water god, obtain samples of the Black Dragon King's magical water, and—this being an expression of the Taoist outlook—generally have an exuberant good time.

Hundreds of stalls line the entrance way to the Zhengdian hall, offering noodles and many other foods, candies, watermelon, beer, magical talismans, and the services of tooth-pullers, fortune-tellers, and gambling-mats, with plentiful beggars and prostitutes included in the crowds (as well as pick-pockets). Entertainment includes, besides the entire spectacle itself, tents featuring song and dance, circus acts, freak shows, and most importantly and popularly, four opera troupes offering classical Chinese opera from six in the morning until midnight at an open-air stage fronting the Zhengdian.

Certainly the festival's draw is the raucous, sensation-rich experience of all this, what anthropologist and contemporary chronicler of the festival Adam Yuet Chao of Cambridge University terms "red-hot sociality" (*honghuo*). But the heart of the festival for most visitors is a trip into the Zhengdian to bow before the nine-foot high statue of the Black Dragon King, passing paired columns inscribed with the couplet describing his importance: "Out he comes from his dragon palace, the winds gentle and the rains timely / Back he goes hiding in the sea, the country peaceful and the people without troubles."

Inside the Zhengdian, the worshiper tosses the joss sticks and receives his or her fortune; if there is an illness to be cured, the visitor also receives a yellow packet of magical medicine. Then the all-important visit to the spring at the cliff behind the Zhengdian. The opening in the rocks from which the water emerges is called Ocean's Eye (*Haiyan*) and is said to connect to the rivers and the ocean; the Black Dragon King himself lives here!

The water from the Ocean's Eye is collected in a trough at the foot of the cliff, where the pilgrims collect it in bottles to enrich their lives and ward off illness. "This miraculous divine water (*shenshui*) is arguably the strongest selling point of the temple," claims Dr. Chau, who estimates attendance nearing a million for this week-long festival honoring the god of water.

This central importance of water in many levels of Taoism, from the core texts of the *Daodejing* to the folk religion at Shaanxi's Black Dragon King temple, is amply mirrored in John Muir's estimation of the substance. Muir devotes considerable space, in his life and his writings, to water in all its forms, from raindrops to creeks to frozen glaciers. Consider his paean to the Tuolumne River flowing through his beloved Hetch Hetchy canyon:

"Snatch a pan of bread and run to the Tuolumne. In whatever mood the lover of wilderness enters the Canyon, he speedily yields to the spell of the falling, singing river, and listens and looks with ever-growing enthusiasm until all the world beside is forgotten…Through the canyon flows a river clear as crystal, bordered with trees, Cassiope, fairest of shrubs, and sunny meadows here and there. Nature's best gardens are here in deepest repose, fountains of wild ever-playing water falling in every form—the endless song of Creation shaking the devout listener into newness of life."

We have already referred to Muir lovingly tracing the journey of a raindrop from a Sierra storm: "How interesting to trace the history of a single raindrop…Happy the showers that fall on so fair a wilderness,— scarce a single drop can fail to find a beautiful spot…lake and river, garden and grove…God's messenger, angel of love sent on its way with majesty and pomp and display of power that make man's greatest shows ridiculous…From form to form, beauty to beauty, ever changing, never resting, all (the raindrops) are speeding on with love's enthusiasm, singing with the stars the eternal song of creation."

Again and again Muir speaks of the songs of moving water: "(The waters of Yosemite Falls) moved over the brink with songs that go farther into the substance of our being than ever was touched by man-made harmonies—songs that bear pure heaven in every note. The fleecy, spiritualized waters take the form of mashed and woven comets, going with a grace that casts poor mortals into an agony of joy."

And we have seen that Muir's love of water encompasses its gas and solid forms as well: "Vapor from the sea; rain, snow, and ice on the summits; glaciers and rivers—these form a wheel that grinds the mountains thin and sharp…and crushes the rocks into soils on which the forests and meadows and gardens and fruitful vine and tree and grain are growing."

This elegiac formulation encapsulates Muir's vision of water in all three physical forms at the very center of the planet's functioning, and seems an altogether fitting counterpart to the *Daodejing's* "Water gives life to the ten thousand things…Tao in the world is like a river flowing home to the sea."

The veneration of water in Taoism and Muir extends all the way to physical immersion in the element. When Mao Zedong was about to launch his Cultural Revolution in the summer of 1966, he kicked it off by taking a much-publicized and photographed swim in the Yangtze River at Wuhan in central China on July 16. Western press treatment (summarized in *Time Magazine* Sept. 27, 1999) centered on the 73-year-old Mao's demonstration of vigor, but completely missed what the Chinese (particularly

Mao's peasant masses) saw: a human avatar of the dragon-king sporting in his river home, a being pulsing with qi energy, participating in the flow of the Tao—which is futile to resist.

We have already recounted John Muir's fall 1877 epic float trip down the Sacramento River from Chico to Sacramento, all 195 water miles, followed by the 250-mile trip down the Merced and San Joaquin rivers from Hopeton to Suisun Bay. This was a man who loved to be on the water.

While he does not often mention bathing in Sierra Nevada streams during his many summertime rambles, I attribute this to his Scotch modesty, and am confident that in his solitary jaunts Muir frequently refreshed himself with creek dips. I crossed five creeks along the Middle Fork of the Kaweah River (Hamilton, Buck, Mehrten, Panther, Moro) returning to civilization from a recent saunter to a back country Giant Sequoia grove in Sequoia National Park, an area with which Muir was well-acquainted, and was unable to resist the pleasure of immersion in any of the five; I cannot imagine any more restraint in Muir.

15

Cycles, Flow, Transformation

"Life and death, profit and loss, failure and success, poverty and wealth, value and worthlessness, praise and blame, hunger and thirst, cold and heat—these are natural changes in the order of things. They alternate with one another like day and night."

—ZHUANGZI

The pulsing flow of the Tao in the world and the resultant ceaseless transformations that characterize existence are a constant theme of the classic Taoist texts.

From the *Daodejing*, various stanzas: "The ten thousand things (all of creation) rise and fall without cease…They grow and flourish and then return to the source. Returning to the source is stillness, which is the way of nature…Something mysteriously formed… Ever present and in motion, perhaps it is the mother of ten thousand things. I do not know its name. Call it Tao…Being great, it flows. It flows far away. Having gone far, it returns…*Returning is the motion of the Tao*." (italics mine)

The *Zhuangzi* places humans squarely in the midst of the unending flow of transformation: "You were born in human form, and you find joy in it. Yet there are ten thousand other forms endlessly transforming that are equally good, and the joy in these is untold. The wise man dwells among those things which can never be lost, and so he lives forever. He willingly accepts early death, old age, the beginning and the end, and serves as an example for everyone. How much more should we emulate the creator of the ten thousand things, on whom the great flow depends!"

According to many stanzas in the *Zhuangzi*, even death is but another of the transformations that characterize life. Tsu Lai and Tsu Li became friends. "Shortly thereafter, Tsu Lai fell ill. He lay gasping for life while his wife and children gathered around, crying. Tsu Li came to see him and said, 'Shhh! Get away from him! Do not disturb the transformation!' Leaning casually against the door, he said to Tsu Lai, 'Great is the Maker! What will he use you for now? Where will he send you? Will he make you into a rat's gizzard or a snake's leg?'…Tsu Lai replied…'Now, if I regard heaven and earth as a great melting pot of creation, and transformation as a master smith, then where can I be sent (by the Maker of Things) and not find it fitting? Thus, calmly I sleep and freshly I awaken.'"

Accepting the reality of "heaven and earth as a great melting pot of creation, and transformation as a master smith" confers upon humans a life of freedom and harmony, claim the Taoists. In the following selection, the *Zhuangzi* makes even the obtuse, stuffy Confucius into a Taoist to express this truth:

"Confucius said, 'Life and death, profit and loss, failure and success, poverty and wealth, value and worthlessness, praise and blame, hunger and thirst, cold and heat—these are natural changes in the order of things. They alternate with one another like day and night. No one knows where one ends and the other begins. Therefore, they should not disturb our peace or enter into our souls. Live so that you are at ease, in harmony with the world, and full of joy. Day and night, share the springtime with all things, thus creating the seasons in your own heart. This is called achieving full harmony.'"

How much this Taoist prescription of humans "achieving full harmony" reminds us of Muir in the mountains! Listen to Muir's description of his jaunts: "In September, 1871, I began a careful exploration of all the basins whose waters pass through the Yosemite Valley. Having health so good I knew nothing about it, unmeasured time, and perfect independence, I rejoiced over the rich wilderness that lay before me…This was my 'meth-od of study'; I drifted about from rock to rock, from stream to stream, from grove to grove. Where night found me, there I camped. When I discovered a new plant, I sat down beside it for a minute or a day, to make its acquain-tance and try to hear what it had to say.

"It is astonishing how high and far we can climb in mountains that we love, and how little we require food and clothing. Weary at times, with only the birds and squirrels to compare notes with, I rested beneath the spicy pines, among the needles and burrs, or upon the plushy sod of a glacier meadow, touching my cheek to its gentians and daisies. No evil consequences from 'waste of time,' concerning which good people who accomplish nothing make such a sermonizing, has fallen me."

This description of days rambling in the mountains amply explains Muir's decision after his eye-piercing accident in the Indianapolis carriage factory: "I could have been a millionaire, but choose instead to be a tramp."

We have seen above that Muir distinguished himself as a scientist by his recognition and articulation of the great interlocking cycles of flow, by which water rises as vapor from the sea, is deposited as rain in the moun-tains to begin its flow back to the sea ("Returning is the motion of the Tao"), or as snow to be compressed into ice and form the great glaciers which themselves flow, but more ponderously and powerfully, back to the sea, shaping valleys and grinding stone to soil as they go.

Everywhere Muir, like the Taoists, saw flow and movement. From his journal of his first summer in the Sierra, already quoted but now con-sidered in the light of Taoism's emphasis on flow and transformation: "Contemplating the lace-like fabric of streams outspread over the moun-tains, we are reminded that everything is flowing—going somewhere, ani-mals and so-called lifeless rocks as well as water. Thus the snow flows fast or slow in grand beauty-making glaciers and avalanches; the air in majestic floods carrying minerals, plant leaves, seeds, spores, with streams of mu-sic and fragrance; water streams carrying rocks both in solution and in the form of mud particles, sand, pebbles, and boulders. Rocks flow from volcanoes like water from springs, and animals flock together and flow in currents modified by stepping, leaping, gliding, flying, swimming, etc. While the stars go streaming through space pulsed on and on forever like blood globules in Nature's warm heart."

A few pages later in the journal, Muir summarizes the pulse of existence: "How lavish is Nature building, pulling down, creating, destroying chasing every material particle from form to form, ever changing, ever beautiful."

Both in the natural world as a whole, and in the lives of humans and especially himself, then, wandering through the mountains, Muir recognizes and celebrates the great cycles of existence, the ceaseless transformation and return, to which Taoism also gives a prominent role in its description of "the great flow" of the Tao.

16

Humans: one part of the spectacle

"You were born in a human form, and you find joy in it. Yet there are ten thousand other forms endlessly transforming that are equally good, and the joy in these is untold."

—*ZHUANGZI*

We have seen above that Muir very early, in his thousand-mile walk to the gulf, rejected the Christian version of the classic Western concept of humans as the center of the universe (anthropocentrism) and staked out his own biocentric view, which after experiencing the water and granite of the Sierras he quickly expanded into his Gaiacentric view that all creation—humans, plants, animals, stone, water—was imbued with precious beauty and love.

Throughout his adult life, Muir mocked what he termed "Lord Man" and that curious entity's unrelenting habit of assuming that all the rest of creation was made explicitly for his own use. Muir took a larger view: "This star, our own good earth, made many a successful journey around the heavens ere man was made, and whole kingdoms of creatures enjoyed existence and returned to dust ere man appeared to claim them. After human beings have also played their part in Creation's plan, they too may disappear without any general burning or extraordinary commotion whatever."

Muir was not the first to come to these conclusions; half a world and at least two millennia earlier, China's Taoist tradition had done the same. In the Taoist view, humans are "nothing extraordinary," in the words of Da Yuan Circle founder Liu Ming. We are simply one of the "ten thousand things" (*wan wu*). This uncompromising refusal to place humans on a pedestal is made clear throughout the Taoist source writings and in the distinctive Taoist approach to life.

"Everything has its own nature and its own function," says the *Zhuangzi*. "Nothing is without nature or function. Consider a small stalk or a great column, a leper or a beauty, things that are great or wicked, perverse, or strong. They are all one in the Tao."

And elsewhere, the *Zhuangzi* asks these pointed questions: "If a man sleeps in a damp place, his back will ache and he will be half-paralyzed. But does this happen to eels? If a man lives up in a tree, he will tremble with fright. But does this happen to monkeys? Of these three, who knows the right place to live? Mao Chiang and Li Chi are considered beautiful by men. But if fish saw them, they would dive to the bottom of the river. If birds saw them, they would fly off. If deer saw them, they would run away. Of these four, who recognizes real beauty?" The *Zhuangzi's* conclusion: "You were born in a human form, and you find joy in it. Yet there are ten thousand other forms endlessly transforming that are equally good, and the joy in these is untold."

Classical Chinese landscape painting illustrates the Taoist inclusion of humans into the landscape as modest, integrated elements of the overall scene. When humans are present in a painting of this genre, they are few, and occupy a small portion of the grand, mountain-and-cloud-dominated vision. Very often humans are absent altogether, and merely suggested by a bridge or a hut tucked away in a corner of the painting. The feeling one gets from the Nelson-Atkin Museum's *Fisherman's Evening Song* (Xu Daoning, 1049 CE), *Landscape after Zi Nan* (Dong Qichang, 1621 CE), and *Mountain on the other side of the River* (Shitao, 1703 CE) is not that humans are unimportant, but that they are merely one of many elements comprising a natural order, a totality whose structuring forces are overwhelmingly the qi energies of rock and water, and all the rest of the manifestations of the flow of the Tao.

So certainly, the Taoists do not imagine humans dominating the natural world. Muir's "Lord Man" is not in charge here; the flow of the Tao reigns supreme. As the *Daodejing* puts it: "Do you think you can take over and improve the universe? I do not believe it can be done. The universe is sacred. You cannot improve it. If you try to change it, you will ruin it. If you try to hold it, you will lose it."

Again: Muir and Taoism in accord.

17

Death: "A natural transformation"

Muir, we have seen, regarded the death of all creatures, humans included, as a homecoming shepherded by a loving Mother who is also the Creator of life. Death is not to be feared or hated, but is rather "as beautiful as life," a "return to eternity." Death is but a transformation: "Nature… is eternally flowing from use to use, beauty to yet higher beauty; and we soon cease to lament waste and death, and rather rejoice and exult in the imperishable, unspendable wealth of the universe, and faithfully watch and wait the reappearance of everything that melts and fades and dies about us, feeling sure that its next appearance will be better and more beautiful than the last."

Muir did not imagine that the human soul was immortal and thus granted a "pass" from the reality of death. He did envision immortality, but only "the practical sort" that involved complete absorption of the living into the experience of being in the natural world, during which experience time dissolves and freedom is complete. This type of "terrestrial immortality" he knew and cherished.

Not surprisingly, the diverse, multi-layered world of Taoist phenomena in China encompassed several distinct attitudes to death. The view expressed in the *Daodejing* and the *Zhuangzi* closely resembles Muir's view, seeing death as natural, a link in the great series of transformations through which all that exists is flowing. "Life arises from death, and death from life," author Zhuang zi claims. Elsewhere, he advises a cripple who has just been rebuffed by a clueless Confucius, "Why don't you simply make him (Confucius) see that life and death are one thread, the same line viewed from different sides—and thus free him from his cuffs and fetters."

One's own death was simply to be accepted. "The true men of old knew nothing about loving life or hating death," says the *Zhuangzi*. "When he was born, he felt no elation. When he entered death, there was no sorrow. Carefree he went. Carefree he came. That was all…He accepted what was given with delight, and when it was gone, he gave it no more thought."

Taoists are convinced that while death was the end of a human personality, it is not the end of the series of transformations of which it was a part. "When Lao Tsu died, Chin Shih went to the funeral," we read in the *Zhuangzi*. "He yelled three times and left. A disciple (of Lao Tsu) said, 'Were you not a friend of the Master?' 'Yes,' replied Chin shih. 'Then is it proper to mourn him in this way?' the offended disciple asked. 'The Master came because it was time,' replied Chin shih. 'He left because he followed the natural flow. Be content with the moment, and be willing to follow the flow; then there will be no room for grief or joy. In the old days this was called freedom from bondage. The wood is consumed but the fire burns on, and we do not know when it will come to an end.'"

Taoists enjoyed playfully guessing what the next stage of transformation might be. We have already mentioned Master Li entertaining the dying Master Lai with speculations that he might be transformed into a rat's liver or a bug's arm. In another deathbed scene, it is Zhuang zi himself who is dying—yet not losing his sense of humor. When his disciples talk of the grand coffin in which they will lower him into the ground at his funeral, Zhuang zi demurs.

"Why bother?" said Zhuang zi. "After I die, just use heaven and earth as my coffin; use the sun and moon as burial jades, the stars as jewels, and everything else around me as ritual wares. What funeral could be better than that?"

"But Master," the disciples gasp. "The crows and vultures will get you!"

"Above ground, the crows and vultures will get me," observed Zhuang zi. "Below ground, the worms and ants will get me. Why do you insist on taking food out of the mouths of crows and vultures and giving it to worms and ants? Death is a natural dispersion and transformation of the body, so why not let nature handle it?"

Being the realists that they were, Taoists were also not averse to admitting that no one could really know what transformation awaited them after death. "How can I tell if love of life is not a delusion," asks the *Zhuangzi*. "How can I tell whether a man who fears death is not like a man who has left home and dreads returning? Lady Li was the daughter of a border guard of Ai. When the Duke of Chin first took her captive, she wept until her dress was soaked with tears. But once she was living in the Duke's palace, sharing his bed, and eating delicious food, she wondered why she had ever cried. How can I tell whether the dead are not amazed that they ever clung to life?"

While Lao zi (formerly Lao Tsu) and Zhuang zi shared Muir's view of death, Taoism's priestly tradition, and the common folk practicing China's folk religion, have very different takes on death.

In priestly Taoism, there is a well-developed system by which every person's spirit (*shen*) while alive is composed of three lighter spirits (*hun*, or "cloud souls") in combination with seven heavier spirits (*p'o*, "bone souls"). Upon death, these scatter and disperse to their proper realms, with some of the former joining an amalgam of similar spirits of the individual's ancestors. Indeed, one of the most important functions of a Taoist priest at a traditional funeral is to successfully effect the transition of the deceased's various spirits onto their way, to propel their leave-taking from this world to the next.

Within the folk religion's welter of superstition, various temples display human souls suffering terrible punishments in a hellish afterlife, the consequence of immoral living. These displays, in large part the result of exposure to Buddhist and, later, Christian influence, strike one as almost playfully indulged, serving as a spur to virtuous behavior in order to escape the punishment gleefully depicted. Again, we are reminded that Taoism is a "big tent," with room for many different views.

But for a large swath of the Taoist tradition, the view that death is not an end, but merely a stage in the cosmic series of transformations, mirrors Muir's own convictions on the subject. Death, he observes, is "only a change from one form of beauty to another." As he penned in his journal as an old man: "The rugged old Norsemen spoke of death as *Heimgang*—home-going…Myriads of rejoicing living creatures, daily, hourly, perhaps every moment sink into death's arms, dust to dust, spirit to spirit—waited on, watched over, noticed only by their Maker, each arriving at its own heaven-dealt destiny."

18

The Yin and Yang of Muir

"Father was the biggest, jolliest child of us all."

—MUIR'S DAUGHTER WANDA

Though Muir never approached Taoism's sophisticated articulation of the dualism of reality and its two complementary constellations of patterns, he was certainly aware of it in his observations of the natural world, as well as in his own life. First, let us explore how the Taoists expressed it.

The Tao, properly understood, is both the *pattern* taken by reality (the "path"), and the *force* generating that pattern. The energy that courses along this path and conveys the flow of the Tao is qi. The Taoist tradition posits two very general groupings of related qi flows: the yin and the yang.

Yin is comprised of phenomena that tend to be dark, shady, receptive, accepting, curved, fecund, lunar, patient, nocturnal, liquid, female. These phenomena are by no means weak or passive. Like water, the favorite Taoist example, yin phenomena flow in places obscure or neglected, but can over time and in proper circumstances be immensely powerful—think of freezing water cracking great boulders, and the waves of typhoons destroying cities.

Yang, conversely, is comprised of phenomena that tend to be bright, sun-lit, demanding, aggressive, solar, impatient, diurnal, solid, male. These phenomena are active and forceful, characterized by overt strength and activity.

yīn   yáng

Reality for Taoists is the interaction of yin and yang, with every entity and situation having both elements within it. "The ten thousand things carry yin and embrace yang. They achieve harmony by combining these forces," says the *Daodejing*. The well-known "yin-yang circle" nicely illustrates this situation: reality is a circle containing both yin and yang, but in varying combinations. And crucially, each of the dual elements has a bit of the other right in the middle of it.

In the Taoist tradition, this is how reality is structured. Yin and yang are not mutually exclusive or battling with each other; they are not opposites. Rather, everything—including every person—is composed of *complementary* elements of yin and yang. To be sure, a "male" creature or the south-facing side of a hill (in the Northern hemisphere) has more yang than yin, and a "female" creature or the north-facing side of a hill has more yin than yang. But to the Taoist, a phenomenon or person composed entirely, or nearly so, of yin or of yang is monstrous, a dangerously imbalanced entity that will soon collapse into the more normal state containing elements of both.

How much of this is reflected in Muir's understanding of the structure of reality? His frequent description of the interaction of water and rocks in generating landscape and the plants and animals inhabiting it is a classic example of yin-yang interaction generating reality. Rocks are solid, with a brutal strength: yang. Water is flowing, with its own subtle strength: yin. Thus the following previously-quoted journal entry describes a yin-yang interaction:

March, 1873, Yosemite: "Vapor from the sea; rain, snow, and ice on the summits; glaciers and rivers—these form a wheel that grinds the mountains thin and sharp, sculptures deeply the flanks, and furrows them into ridge and canyon, and crushes the rocks (*under glacial paths*) into soils on which the forests and meadows and gardens and fruitful vine and tree and grain are growing."

Although Muir was clearly aware of the different properties that the Taoists describe as yin and yang, and their interactions to produce reality, we must admit that he did not have a nuanced overarching understanding of the relatedness of yin properties and yang properties, as the Taoists achieved over millennia in China.

What of Muir himself, Muir as a unique combination of yin and yang traits? Regarded with Taoist eyes, Muir was quite clearly a potent mix of both yin and yang, an extraordinary person whom others—male and female—regarded with fascination, awe, and occasionally unease.

The yang aspect of Muir is obvious to all, as recounted in our treatment of his wanderings in the natural world. The man was tough as nails, fearless, indefatigably strong, and apparently indestructible. Muir was equally at home in a howling snowstorm on a glacier as in the midst of an earthquake in a high-walled Yosemite Valley. He climbed jagged peaks beyond the strength and savvy of any others before him, and traversed rugged, boulder-strewn canyons declared "inaccessible" by other mountain men.

Surprisingly, this yang-charged man was also filled to brimming with yin traits as well. Let us recount what we might term the "soft side" of Muir, beyond his already-established admiration for the role of water in the world. To begin, he loved flowers and plants. Muir was perfectly happy to patiently key out and learn from a new plant; "I sat down beside it for a minute or a day, to make its acquaintance and try to hear what it had to say." One of the highlights of his long and eventful life, Muir always claimed, was the moment he discovered a patch of rare orchids in the wild bogs of Canada as a young man, described by his first biographer, Wolfe:

"Late one afternoon he was wearily trudging through a tangled mass of underbrush and fallen trees, looking for a tree where like a monkey he could make his nest for the night. Suddenly he saw ahead of him on a mossy bank of a stream the beautiful orchid Calypso. Long he had sought in vain for the shy and lovely 'hider of the north,' which retreated as fast as human settlement advanced. Now in the midst of this dismal swamp, rising white from a bed of yellow mosses, she bloomed for him alone." Muir, upon reaching the elusive orchids, wrote: "I sat down beside them and wept for joy." Hardly the experience of a macho male.

Muir was famously fond of children, and much beloved of them for his humor and antics. He took personal and long-lasting interest in the children of all the families with whom he stayed: the Carrs in Madison, the Peltons in Prairie du Chien, the Trouts in Canada, the Merrills in Indianapolis, the Swetts in San Francisco. Only a passing acquaintance was needed. During the several weeks aboard the railroad magnate Edward Harriman's ship in his 1899 scientific expedition to Alaska, Muir became a favorite of Harriman's children aboard. He dubbed Harriman's three daughters and their cousin "The Big Four" and regaled them with tales of his own "Big Two" (Wanda and Helen) at home in the Alhambra Valley. Harriman's two sons were "The Little Two" to Muir.

Muir's rapport with children was earned; he told endless silly stories, cavorted with them, and was always ready to listen to their stories in turn. When the older Muir writes in his journal, "My birthday—I am told the fifty-seventh, and yet I feel only a boy," it is not a poetic conceit; Muir always possessed a strong "inner boy," which he revered and frequently gave free rein.

We know from recollections and letters that Muir took a very active part in the rearing of his two daughters—when he was at home and not off on an adventure, at least. Meal times in the Victorian home in the Alhambra Valley were typically light-hearted, "periods of relaxation, story-telling, and often uproarious fun led by the naturalist (Muir) himself," according to one visitor. Regardless of the prominence of the frequent dinner guests, daughters Wanda and Helen demanded and were given the latest install- ment of Muir's long "Paddy Grogan" adventures—"an original tale of an Irish youth and his kangaroo steed." He routinely pressed his daughters to join him in improvising doggerel verses for general entertainment.

His daughter Wanda's judgment as an adult was spot-on: "Father was the biggest, jolliest child of us all."

As is true of genuinely amiable humorists, Muir was as willing to be on the receiving end of antics. In a letter to Wanda he describes a fall 1898 outing in New York City with Robert Underwood Johnson, editor of *The Century Magazine*, and Nikola Tesla, Serbian-American inventor and elec- trical engineer, the original prototype of the "mad scientist":

"Johnson is well and as funny as ever. He marched me through the wildest maddest parts of the town (New York City) last night, pretending he was taking me to jail for vagrancy—stopping now and then to ask little ragged boys the way to the police station—took me out into the middle of the streets among the whirl of cars and pretended he was afraid he would be run over to frighten me—showed me the moon and minutely told me how to know it among the million electric lights etc. and the way he fooled with Tesla was too funny for anything."

By virtue of this strongly-developed soft side—the yin aspect—of his character, complementing the more obvious yang aspect, Muir was a compel- ling, charismatic fellow to men and women alike. Among men, he had a very wide, diverse collection of friends and admirers. His closest friends were, like him, strong personalities who had carved successful careers. Among them one would list the painter William Keith, writer John Burroughs, editor Robert Underwood Johnson, Harvard Botanist Asa Gray, Kew Gardens director Josiah Hooker, railroad magnate Edward Harriman, *The Dial* poetry maga- zine editor Francis Fisher Brown, Bay Area poet and ornithologist Charles Keeler, and California State Superintendent of Education John Swett.

Intriguingly, and possibly due at least in part to his strongly-developed yin aspect complementing his obvious masculinity, Muir was enormously attractive to virtually every female he encountered. While he was never accused of outright seduction or sexual impropriety, at least one man charged Muir with alienating the affections of his wife, and probably not without foundation—the attraction of many men would pale before that of Muir.

Jeanne Carr, wife of Muir's chemistry and geology professor at the University of Wisconsin, was the first to fall under Muir's allure. She invited him to many dinners with her family, initiated a voluminous correspondence with the young Muir that lasted three decades, and arranged for Muir to meet any number of prominent visitors to her eventual Bay Area home. Though there has long been speculation about the propriety of their relationship, most Muir scholars conclude that she was merely utterly fascinated with the man and the two exchanged their deepest confidences in the course of their long correspondence.

At the end of his thousand-mile walk to the Gulf of Mexico, Muir worked three days at a sawmill in Cedar Keys, Florida before collapsing with what was probably malaria. Extraordinarily, the wife of the mill's owner promptly brought the young Muir into their home and nursed him attentively for three months, which surely suggests that Muir had cast his spell over her as well. Three decades later, when Muir called upon this Sarah Hodgson during a tour of the southern U.S. with Harvard botanist Charles S. Sargent, the white-haired widow squealed with delight at seeing him again. Here is Muir's account from a letter to his wife: "I asked if she knew me. She answered no, and asked my name. I said Muir. '*John* Muir?' she almost screamed. '*My* California John Muir? My California John?' 'Why, yes,' (Muir stammered in response). 'I promised to come back and visit you in about twenty-five years, and though a little late I've come.'"

While at Yosemite Valley in the early 1870's, Muir would often go on long botanizing walks with the young wife of his employer, James Hutchings, owner of an early valley hostelry. Doubtless both Muir and Elvira Hutchings were lonely; certainly they both loved botany and took pleasure in discovering new plants. His wife's attraction to Muir soured Hutchings on his employee, and the employment was terminated to the relief of both sides. Later the Hutchings divorced.

As recounted earlier, it was also during those early Yosemite Valley years that Muir captivated the glamorous British adventuress, Therese Yelverton, Viscountess Avenmore, whose Irish husband had thrown her over for a richer wife, though not before the affair was resolved by the British House of Lords (in, of course, her noble husband's favor). Upon arrival at Yosemite Valley on a world tour, she relied heavily on the young Muir to show her the sights. In a subsequent novel, she described a charismatic "Kenmuir," whose "open blue eyes of honest questioning and glorious auburn hair might have stood as a portrait of the angel Raphael."

With only one of the many women attracted to him did Muir reciprocate, apparently. Jeanne Carr had introduced the Strentzel family of Martinez to Muir while he stayed in the Bay Area, hoping to kindle a romance between their daughter Louie and Muir. Louie Strentzel was 27 when Muir first met her, and had turned down several proposals of marriage. She was well-educated and a talented pianist, but also had a practical side which she exercised in helping her father manage his orchards and keep the books. After staying with them at the end of his 1877 float trip down the Merced and San Joaquin rivers, Muir began to visit frequently. He and Louie would walk in the surrounding hills and orchards, identifying flowers and doubtless sharing confidences. They were married in April of 1880, and had two daughters.

Reading Muir's correspondence with his many female friends, and descriptions of his interactions with them, one becomes convinced that in addition to his well-developed "soft side," another trait appealing to females was his ability to unreservedly accept female individuals, to happily confer his complete attention upon them. Muir was authentically *present* to any female in whose company he found himself. He showered this presentness upon his male friends, also, of course—as well as upon Sierra flowers he encountered ("I sat down beside it for a minute or a day, to make its acquaintance and try to hear what it had to say"). But in the late nineteenth century, a male treating females and flowers with attention and respect equal to that he conferred upon males was unusual. And enormously appreciated by the females, one gathers.

The final evidence of Muir's "soft side" and his high regard of females was his surprising decision to be buried beside Louie in the Strentzel family cemetery in the Alhambra Valley. No doubt his friends and the public were shocked. The general expectation was that Muir's grave would be in Yosemite somewhere, perhaps in the little cemetery in the valley holding Galen Clark's grave. Or perhaps in Tuolumne Meadows. Or even some high mountain brooding over Muir Glacier in Alaska.

But no. Muir choose to rest for eternity beside the woman he loved and with whom he had mated and raised children. Her company was that congenial to him, his loyalty to her that complete.

Muir, then, was an extraordinary combination of strongly developed yang and yin traits. On one side were his indomitable strength, stamina, toughness, and lust for wilderness adventures. On the other side were his gentle love of water, plants, children, and laughter, and his devotion to his wife and family. The gift of his complete presence was freely conferred upon females as well as males. He was a fully-developed person, who had become nearly everything a human could be.

A Master, brimming with the exuberant flow of the Tao.

19

Muir's God and China's Tao

"Only the fingers of God are sufficiently gentle and tender for the folding and unfolding of petaled bundles of flowers…God's love covers all the earth as the sky covers it…No synonym for God is so perfect as Beauty."

We see from the previous seven chapters that in his mountain and glacial rambles, and the conclusions he drew from them, Muir fits remarkably well into the activities and worldview of China's Taoists, particularly the people's folk religion and the philosophical Taoist's *Daodejing* and *Zhuangzi*. Before we label Muir "a Taoist," though, we must ask whether the God that Muir saw creating the world is the same as the Tao that Taoists saw flowing through the world. Can we simply equate Muir's God and China's Tao?

To answer this question, we first must inquire what Muir meant by "God" when he used the term. Consider that the Christian God of the Bible thinks very highly of humans, having created them in his own image, alone of all his creation. After humans turn away from God in disobedience, he sends his only son to earth to be killed for the sake of the salvation of those humans who believe in him and his sacrifice, thus finding the way back to wholeness.

Very early, in his thousand-mile walk to the Gulf, Muir announces he doesn't believe any of this. Humans are not set apart from other creatures;

all creatures reflect God's beauty, enjoy his love, and have their essential and equally important place in the scheme of things. If humans are different, it is only in that they alone have fallen from their original godliness and require saving, unlike the rest of creation. Moreover, Muir remarks pointedly in his thousand-mile-walk journal how the human concept of God bears a remarkable resemblance to European males from the respectable ranks of society, and thinks this very strange.

Muir rarely mentions Christ in his writings once he has begun his rambles and thereafter. Certainly he does not depend on Christ and his sacrifice for a meaningful life. Immortality? Again, Muir nowhere refers to anticipation of that state by way of faith in Christ. Instead, he again and again avers that he has achieved a "practical, terrestrial" immortality by virtue of his mountain rambles exposing him to the beauty of God's creation.

If not a Christian concept of God, then, perhaps Muir's "God" is the Hebrew God. Certainly Muir quotes the Old Testament frequently, but does that mean he believes in the Judaic version of God? The God of the Old Testament, again, created humans in his own image, and is deeply involved in human history, intervening time after time to punish or assist his people. That is not Muir's "God" at all, who loves all his creation equally and seems not particularly interested in humans.

Regarding death, Muir's convictions are similarly divergent from the Western tradition. "On no subject are our ideas more warped and pitiable than on death. Instead of the sympathy, the friendly union, of life and death so apparent in Nature, we are taught that death is an accident, a deplorable punishment for the oldest sin, the arch-enemy of life"—the Biblical account, in other words.

Muir's concept of "God" is thus highly unorthodox. When his views are examined closely, it becomes obvious that Muir's approach cannot be described as either Christian or Judaic, so resolutely does he reject key tenets of those faith traditions. Muir's religion is couched in the *phrases* of Christianity and Judaism, but that is his only real point of contact with the religion of his father. For all his use of the term "God," what he means by the term is clearly worlds away from the orthodox view. All this leads us to ask: Does Muir's God have anything in common *at all* with the Biblical concept?

In only one aspect does Muir's God remotely resemble the God of either the Hebrews or Christians: God is the creator of the world and all its creatures. It is God who brings forth the world at the beginning of time, and daily brings forth the world fresh again and again. Muir's God is a loving God, moreover—not loving towards humans particularly, but loving to all his creatures, low and high.

In his early journal entries and the books drawn from them (*A Thousand Mile Walk to the Gulf, My First Summer in the Sierra*, and *Travels to Alaska*), Muir refers to "God" frequently, and uses a variety of associated terms to describe God and his actions. An examination of Muir's "god-talk" during these years reveals a surprising diversity in his conception of this creator God.

From *A Thousand Mile Walk to the Gulf* of 1867: "Now, it never seems to occur to these far-seeing teachers that Nature's object in making animals and plants might possibly be first of all the happiness of each one of them, not the creation of all for the happiness of one (humans). Why should man value himself as more than a small part of the one great unit of creation? And what creature of all that the Lord has taken the pains to make is not essential to the completeness of that unit—the cosmos?"

Notice here that at one point Muir has "Nature," capitalized, making the earth's creatures; then at another point has "the Lord" making those creatures. Clearly Muir is not a simplistic pantheist; throughout his writings it is abundantly clear that the creator is a force or entity separate from the creation, and manifested in the creation. Yet...here he pictures Nature doing what the Lord is doing.

Later on his walk he describes the unfolding of the cosmos in an impersonal view, as "Creation's plan," resulting from neither a God nor a Nature: "This star, our own good earth, made many a successful journey around the heavens ere man was made, and whole kingdoms of creatures enjoyed existence and returned to dust ere man appeared to claim them. After human beings have also played their part in Creation's plan, they too may disappear without any general burning or extraordinary commotion whatever."

Yet in addition to describing creation impersonally with no mention of God, Muir can also upon occasion intensely personalise God, as in this charming journal entry during the spring before his first summer in the Sierra: "*Nemophila maculata* (the Five-spot flower) came (bloomed) today. Its stigmas are small and black like spiders' eyes, and the corolla very delicate. Only the fingers of God are sufficiently gentle and tender for the folding and unfolding of petaled bundles of flowers."

And this entry describing Half Dome in Yosemite Valley: "The dome tissiack looks down the valley like the most living being of all the rocks and mountains; one would fancy that there were brains in that lofty brow…Surely the Lord loves this new creation, and His angels are now looking down at this new thing that His hands have wrought." Two years later, Muir puts it thusly: "God's love covers all the earth as the sky covers it."

Even the love embedded in creation is not always ascribed to God; sometimes it comes from "Heaven." Muir describes his first summer in the Sierra thusly: "…the greatest of all the months of my life, the most truly, divinely free, boundless like eternity, immortal, everything in it seems equally divine—one smooth, pure, wild glow of Heaven's love."

In addition to God and Heaven, the evidence of love Muir sees all around him sometimes comes from Nature itself. From a spring 1871 journal entry: "Nature loves man, beetles, and birds with the same love. With her storms of snow, hail, volcanic fire, and lightning, she seems to scatter firebrands, arrows, and death among her creatures, and so she does, but they are scattered as the stars are scattered in the heavens, each in its place, singing together in faithful harmony."

And later, in 1872: "To anyone who is in actual contact with the wilderness, these 'winter' storms are only emphatic words of Nature's love." And in August of 1875: "New flowers are already planted on the flood belts, showing Nature's modes of working towards beauty and joy."

Note here that Nature is feminine, while Muir elsewhere always refers to God as masculine. In these and many other passages, Muir speaks of Nature very much as he speaks elsewhere of God, as in this spring 1871 journal entry: "Nature, while urging to utmost efforts, leading us with work, presenting cause beyond cause in endless chains, lost in infinite distances, yet cheers us like a mother with tender prattle words of love, ministering to all our friendlessness and weariness."

Beyond referring to Nature as feminine ("like a mother") but as doing very much the same things that the masculine God does elsewhere in his writings, Muir employs other phrases to describe this creative force. From his journal in October of 1871, just after discovering the first Sierra glacier in the Merced river headwaters: "as we study and mingle with nature more, the pain caused by the melting of all beauties into one First Beauty disappears, because, after their first baptismal submergence in fountain God, they go again washed and clean into their individualisms, more clearly defined than ever, united yet separate."

The next day Muir encounters the dead body of a bear, and returns to the "fountain" metaphor as he muses upon the animal: "Bears are made of the same dust as we, and breathe the same winds and drink of the same waters…his life turns and ebbs with heart-pulsings like ours, and was poured from the same First Fountain."

The impact upon Muir of discovering the first Sierra glacier was evidently profound, for he soon adds another metaphor for God as he describes the aftermath of a storm at Lake Nevada: "It is as if the lake, mountain, trees had souls, formed one soul, which had died and gone before the throne of God, the great First Soul, and by direct creative act of God had all earthly purity deepened, refined, brightness brightened, spirituality spiritualized, countenance, gesture made wholly Godful!"

Finally, Muir forthrightly declares yet another description of the source of creation. From his journal of June 26, 1875: "No synonym for God is so perfect as Beauty. Whether as seen carving the lines of the mountains with glaciers, or gathering matter into stars, or planning the movements of water, or gardening—all is Beauty!"

We should not be surprised that the Muir who is so utterly unorthodox in his views of God, humans or death should have a richly-nuanced view of the creative force behind the natural world. We see that Muir variously refers to this creative force as a masculine God, a feminine (capitalized) Nature, Creation's plan, like a mother, Beauty, Heaven, First Soul, or First Fountain.

Clearly Muir is utterly convinced that the natural world is sacred, brilliantly reflects divinity, and is saturated with beauty and evidence of love. Beyond this conviction, though, Muir just as clearly must employ a wide and at times poetic variety of concepts in his attempts to describe what's behind all this endowment of beauty and love. The simple term "God" is clearly inadequate to the task. As Donald Worster puts it in his Muir biography, "'God' for Muir was a deliberately loose and imprecise term referring to an active, creative force dwelling, in, above, and around nature."

To judge by the variety of the concepts used, Muir is groping toward something very real, yet very difficult to pin down and describe. Something possibly beyond words. Something mysterious, yet also concrete in its myriad manifestations. Something perhaps beyond anything he has seen articulated in the Western tradition.

Which brings us to the Tao.

An enormous amount of ink has been spilled through the centuries—nay, through the millennia—attempting to elucidate the meaning of the term "Tao." To compare Muir's various conceptions of his Creator/God/Nature/Beauty/First Fountain to the Chinese tradition's "Tao," I will merely illustrate that Muir's conceptions are at least well represented within the realm of meanings ascribed to "the Tao."

The first English translator of the *Daodejing* was the Scotsman James Legge, who published his version in 1891. Legge translates Chapter 25 in this manner: "There was something undefined and complete, coming into existence before Heaven and Earth…It may be regarded as the Mother of all things. I do now know its name, and I give it the designation of The Tao."

In a 1972 translation by Jane English and Gia-fu Feng, they render Chapter 34 thusly: "The great Tao flows everywhere…The ten thousand things depend upon it…It nourishes the ten thousand things." In their translation of the other great Taoist classic, the *Zhuangzi*, English and Feng refer to the Tao in this way: "How much more should we emulate the creator of the ten thousand things, on whom the great flow depends." In their translation of the scene of Master Lai dying, Master Li visits him and comments: "Great is the Maker!" referring to the Tao. This last scene and remark is translated a bit differently by the American Burton Watson in his 1968 *Complete Works of Chuang Tzu*: "How marvelous the Creator Tao is!" In another sickbed scene, English and Feng describe the crippled Tsu Yu as remarking to his visitor Tsu Szu: "Great is the Maker of Things that he should make me as deformed as this!"

A comprehensive overview of the term Tao (also rendered Dao) is given by Donald J. Munro in his Afterward to Tsai Chih Chung's *Zhuangzi Speaks: the Music of Nature*: "The term Dao in the *Zhuangzi* has several meanings. One refers to that which simultaneously causes the ceaseless change in nature and also somehow integrates or unifies all things that participate in those changes. Zhuang zi (the person) used the expression 'maker and transformer' to convey this point. There is another meaning that the outside analyst can distinguish as separate from the one just given, though it would not have been separated by Zhuang zi. That is the orderly process or pattern of change itself. This meaning is present when our current text encourages us to 'follow the laws of nature, or the Dao.' This is also 'flowing with the Yin and Yang'."

Thus we see the Tao variously described by translators over the past century as "maker and transformer," "the Mother of all things," "the creator of the ten thousand things," "the Maker," "the Creator Tao," "the laws of nature," "the pattern of change," and "the Maker of Things." While this of course does not exhaust the possible ways in which the Tao has been described, the list does remind us very strongly of the various ways that Muir attempted to describe his Creator God and his Mother Nature, the source creating and nourishing all the creatures and materials comprising the natural world.

While I would not claim that Muir's "God" (or his "Mother Nature") is neatly synonymous with China's "Tao," it seems clear that *what Muir is getting at* when he uses the various terms examined above is well within the variety of concepts that have been advanced to describe "the Tao" of Taoism. And of course, just as importantly, we have seen above that Muir's life in the mountains and his approach to water, cycles, death, the place of humans, and the flow of yin and yang exhibit much this same congruency with that of Taoist philosophers and mountain ramblers.

Does all this make John Muir "a Taoist"? It would seem to, though I would prefer to highlight the vast historical and cultural gap between Muir and traditional China by use of a qualifying adjective for Muir. The Taoist tradition of China is extremely rich and varied, the result of millennia of development involving thousands of lives; Muir's Taoism is the fruit of one life, extraordinary though it may have been. This difference should not be minimized, regardless of the striking confluence of Muir's views with that of several aspects of China's Taoist tradition. So I would call Muir a Taoist, yes; but an American Taoist, to indicate his unique path to the worldview. Or better yet, an *accidental* Taoist, to indicate that he came to his own version of Taoism serendipitously, as it were.

What shall we term Muir's late 19th century worldview, so similar to China's Taoism? "American" or "Accidental" Taoism is descriptive and accurate, but it fails to fully acknowledge Muir's distinctive perspective, his own path to the worldview. Since Muir's worldview is rooted in his experiences as he rambled through mountains and glaciers, and hews closely to the earth and what he learned from it, I proposed in Chapter 11 to describe it as *Earth Wisdom*. China's version of the earth-centered, immanent philosophy of life is Taoism; Muir's version is Earth Wisdom.

That a 19th century Scotsman in America, raised in an evangelical Christian family, could independently stumble upon the same unusual, distinctive approach to life as that developed over the course of several thousand years half a world away in China, is astonishing. How could it have happened? Was it in fact wholly accidental?

20

Open Eyes, Open Mind, the Immanent

"By looking!"

—*DAODEJING*

Taoist traditions and texts suggest an explanation for the seeming accident of John Muir of 19th-century America formulating an Earth Wisdom so startlingly similar to ancient China's Taoism. As we have seen, for millennia Taoist adepts have taken to the mountains and traveled among them, observing the natural world keenly and closely. Numerous paintings in the Chinese landscape genre depict men (for the most part) simply sitting in the forest or at a lake, often in a crude shelter, looking at the scene before them. They are clearly not meditating, but rather just gazing at the scene and taking it all in, frequently drinking tea. The term by which Taoists designate their temples in China is *guan*, which has the connotation "to look."

This route to the Taoist understanding of life is summarized in stanza 54 of the *Daodejing*. English and Feng translate it thus: "How do I know the universe is like this? By looking!" James Legge translated it similarly a century earlier: "By the method of observation!"

By looking! By observing! At once the seeming "accident" becomes clear. Muir recapitulated in his rambling, clear-eyed life the method by which generations of Taoists in China arrived at their distinctive understanding of life. Both Muir and China's Taoists such as the Two Perfected Lords of

125

Mt. Hua-kai rambled far and wide, particularly in mountains. Both traveled through the natural world with eyes wide open, patiently investing time and full attention to what they saw.

And they both *saw* the same thing. A world in harmony, shot through with patterns, beauty, and the shimmering flow of transformation. A world in which humans belong as natural elements, if only they would relax their strivings and pretensions. A world generated by and suffused with a natural force both patently obvious in its manifestations, and exceedingly difficult to describe or fundamentally understand. Call it Creator God. Call it First Fountain. Call it Mother Nature. Call it the flow of yin and yang. Call it the Maker of Things. Call it the Tao.

Here, then, is the secret of the surprising similarity between Muir's Earth Wisdom and China's Taoism. The world, upon close and unbiased inspection by whomever is sauntering through it with fully open eyes and a mind free of prior bias, reveals itself in a *this-worldly, immanent* outlook fundamentally different than the *transcendent, other-worldly* views of the major religions, East or West.

(The philosophical term "immanent" here refers to a physically-manifest phenomenon rooted in the here and now of our experience. Its opposite is "transcendent," which refers to a phenomenon above or beyond everyday experience and the physical world.)

What is striking about the immanent worldview of Muir and Taoism is that it results not from the reading of books, nor systematic reflection upon philosophical principles. It *emerges* as the result of direct experience of the world. Earth Wisdom and Taoism are, at root, simply descriptions of experienced reality, "the way things are." Because reality is complex and enormously varied, this description is rich and wide ranging. The consequence is that both Earth Wisdom and Taoism are not neatly structured; you find no doctrines or creeds as in the Abrahamic religions, nor any tidy Four Noble Truths or Eightfold Path of Buddhism.

In order to summarize and discuss the worldview of Earth Wisdom and Taoism, then, we will here introduce some structure to their bewilderingly multifaceted outlook. What are the salient features of this immanent way of looking at the world? Three stand out, which we will term the *three pillars of the immanent worldview.*

First, this world is our true home. This world itself is awe inspiring, and is enough. The earth's mountains, rivers, plains, and creatures large and small present sufficient beauty, drama, challenge, and fulfillment to satisfy all human needs, to provide balm for every pain. There is no need to invent other, "better" worlds above or beyond this. No need to imagine that this earthly world is but a trial, or prelude—what nonsense! No need to pretend that death is not really death, that the joys and heartbreaks of living in this world are illusions, that something more fulfilling awaits us in a fantasy place in the future. Here and now is where we really live, and it is good, even in its pain and challenges.

We are already home.

Open your eyes, open your mind, saunter through enough of the world and life, and this first pillar of Earth Wisdom reveals itself with clarity and force. It was the uncanny, inherent ability of John Muir to free himself from the other-worldly orthodoxy of his Christian upbringing that permitted him to see the world as it really is: *home.* And then to tell us all what he saw.

The second pillar of the immanent view of Earth Wisdom and Taoism recognizes that in this world, humans are intimately related to every other living creature, and join other creatures in fully participating in the grand cycles of earthly existence. Like all life on the planet we come into existence through birth, grow, experience challenges and joys, then die, our bodies returning to the common storehouse of life in the soil and air. This second pillar may be described as a *kinship* view of human life: we are kin to all other life forms, and they to us.

The corollary to kinship, of course, is that humans are nothing extraordinary. We are not unique, certainly not uniquely molded in the image of a supernatural God (imagined to look and act suspiciously like ourselves, as Muir noted). Nor are we meant to hold dominion over the planet and exploit it. What a strange notion! No, our responsibility is to support and protect populations of our fellow creatures; they are our kin. We are all in this together; their health is linked to our own health. The second pillar of the immanent viewpoint, then, replaces the anthropocentric attitude with a planet-wide, Gaiacentric one.

The third pillar of the immanent worldview that Muir and the Taoists saw clearly in their sojourns in the world was the way certain clusters of phenomena work together to produce and support the whole; there is a *duality* to existence. Muir climbed to his Sunnyside Bench and saw how shadowed areas on the south side of Yosemite valley sheltered glaciers there and resulted in increased soil production and deposition. He noted how the soft flow of water in both its liquid and solid forms sculpted hard rock into mountains and valleys. The gentle and treasuring love of flowers, children, and moonlit streams were as important to Muir's well-lived life as the muscular feats of climbing high peaks and traversing glaciers.

The Taoists of China, noticing this for thousands of years, were able to perceive and describe these interactions more fully than John Muir in his one lifetime. Their sharp eyes noted the world's duality, and described it as yin and yang. The shady, nocturnal, yielding, nurturing, feminine phenomena interact with the sunny, diurnal, aggressive, destructive, masculine phenomena to produce reality, an interaction that is *complementary* rather than opposed. Both aspects are necessary in the flow of life; both contribute equally to life's abundance, in their own particular ways. Thus an ecosystem results from complementary interactions between soft and hard, cold and hot, water and rock, shade and sun, plant and animal.

The insight that yin and yang phenomena work together, that each has important roles to play in structuring reality, applies to the human sphere, of course. Both Muir and the Taoists recognized that a patriarchal, misogynistic society was unbalanced, displaying far too much competition, dominance, destruction, and masculine input. In a healthier, more productive society these yang traits would be balanced by greater input of cooperation, acceptance, nurturing, and feminine inputs.

In addition, at a practical level, the third pillar insists that human society is strengthened by emancipating its female members, and providing them the full participation that females and yin phenomena contribute in the rest of the world's living systems.

Muir's 19ᵗʰ century articulation of Earth Wisdom, the three-pillared immanent worldview in the West—earth is our home, we are kin to the rest of creation, and reality is generated by complementary interactions of dualistic phenomena—constitutes *his first legacy to the Western world*. Others in the West had broached one or another of the three pillars—Heraclitus, St. Francis of Assisi, Alexander von Humboldt, early feminists in England and America—but it was Muir who brought them all together, and introduced them to early modern Western society in his writings, particularly his journals, and his stirring life.

A third comprehensive articulation of the immanent worldview has flowered in the modern world since the appearance of Muir's Earth Wisdom and its preceding Taoism in China, of course: modern science. The corpus of knowledge resulting from a century and a half of the modern scientific enterprise fully shares the three pillars of Earth Wisdom and Taoism. This is not surprising, since the root of the scientific method—unbiased observation of the natural world—is also the foundation of Muir's and Taoism's worldview, as we have seen. The addition of controlled experimentation to the basic activity of observation has given modern science a much more detailed and quantified understanding of "the way things are." But the basic immanent worldview of modern science is strikingly similar to that of Muir and Taoism. Thus it is no coincidence that today's scientists are among the most important defenders of the integrity of the natural world.

If the articulation of Earth Wisdom in the modern West was Muir's first legacy, it would lead soon to a second legacy. The plans of a cabal of civic leaders in San Francisco, California to destroy Muir's beloved Hetch Hetchy Valley in Yosemite Park, by damming the waters of the Tuolumne River and channeling them to the growing metropolis, burst onto America's political stage in the early 20ᵗʰ century. The battle for Hetch Hetchy would galvanize the nation, from private citizens to great newspapers, reaching all the way into the halls of Congress and the inner rooms of the White House.

It was the battle to save the Hetch Hetchy Valley that began the transformation of Muir's Earth Wisdom into a formidable element in Western society. The battle failed, and led to Muir's premature death. But out of defeat rose a movement that today is worldwide, and of sufficient strength to threaten the power structure that has ruled throughout recorded human history, East and West. That environmental movement is Muir's second legacy, and it endures. Most importantly, it offers humanity the best hope for confronting its gravest challenge in its 200,000-year history on the planet. If the looming catastrophe of climate change is to be resolved, Muir's two legacies—Earth Wisdom and the environmental movement—must both play key roles.

Part III
A Blueprint for Human Survival

The Hetch Hetchy Battle (1909-1913)

"Dam Hetch Hetchy! As well dam for water-tanks the people's cathedrals and churches, for no holier temple has ever been consecrated by the hand of man."

John Muir came relatively late in life to what became, later, "the environmental cause." Full of love though he was for the natural world, it was not until 1889, when he was 51 years old, that he was finally persuaded by one determined friend to seriously take up cudgels, and battle to protect and preserve his beloved realm. Prior to this, his abundant energy had simply been directed to other areas. During the 1870s he was exploring California's Sierra Nevada and other wild areas; the 1880s saw him raising his family and working very hard at the Martinez orchard and ranch to secure their financial security.

Robert Underwood Johnson, editor of New York City's *The Century Magazine*, finally dragged Muir into decisive action. Johnson arrived in San Francisco in 1889 looking for articles about the West, especially about California, and especially by the John Muir that had piqued such interest with his writings in the 1870s—then disappeared from the public scene in the 1880s.

Muir promptly invited Johnson to join him in a trek to Yosemite, then a state-controlled reserve covering only the Valley and the Mariposa Grove of Giant Sequoias. There they were dismayed by the heavy hand of humans marring the valley. Traveling up to Tuolumne Meadows, it was no better.

Everywhere the pristine beauty of the area was being industriously destroyed by commercial interests. "Lord Man" was transforming the Sierras for his own profit, and California's state leaders were happy to let it happen.

Sitting around a campfire at Soda Springs on the edge of Tuolumne Meadows one warm evening, Johnson pushed Muir. It was possible to do something about the situation, he insisted. He had friends in Congress who would sponsor a bill to expand the current dysfunctional state-administered reserve to include a federal park encompassing the *whole watershed* draining into the valley, including Tuolumne Meadows through which the Tuolumne River flowed to the grand Hetch Hetchy Valley, one of Muir's favorite places in the Sierras. Would Muir contribute to the effort? Would Muir write two articles for *The Century Magazine*, extolling the grandeur of the Yosemite region and the need to protect it before the onslaught of Lord Man?

Muir agreed with alacrity; he had met a man whose enthusiasms matched his own. By the spring of 1890, the two articles were completed and sent to Johnson. While Johnson arranged for the introduction of the bill and the publication of the articles, Muir took off for his fourth trip to Alaska and his adventures on Muir Glacier. By the time he returned, the campaign was picking up serious steam, and by year's end, to Muir's surprise, the bill was passed and Yosemite National Park came into existence (to complement the continuing California state reserve in the valley and Mariposa Grove). Soon two more national parks were created: Sequoia and General Grant. Muir and Johnson had pioneered a wholly new phenomenon on the planet: environmental activism—and it had succeeded.

Johnson kept at Muir, who was increasingly receptive. You should create an organization to do more of this, he suggested. An organization of men and women who love the mountains and will fight to protect them from commercial exploitation. Muir knew many such people, throughout the nation but especially in the Bay Area. A year and a half later, in the spring of 1892, Muir and half a dozen friends founded the Sierra Club in the San Francisco office of attorney Warren Olney. Those present unanimously elected Muir its president, an office he held until his death 22 years later.

From its beginning, the Sierra Club took to heart the third pillar of Earth Wisdom, actively encouraging the full participation of women—a highly unusual stance at that time. Club histories note that "women established themselves at once as active participants in the club's activities." Three women were among its charter members. The first club High Trip outing was into Tuolumne Meadows in 1901. Muir brought along his daughters Wanda and Helen, who were joined by many of their friends and other women.

Describing that initial outing in the *Sierra Club Bulletin*, writer and photographer Edward Parsons commented that many of those ascending Mt. Dana (an imposing 13,061 feet high) above Tuolumne Meadows were "Berkeley or Stanford girls," whose "vigor and endurance were a revelation to all of us." The 1904 outing had among its usual crowd of young women a close friend of Wanda Muir, Marion Randall, whose vitality and cheerfulness captivated Parsons; they were wed soon thereafter, and Marion Randall Parsons served as a director of the Sierra Club from 1914 to 1938.

Another early participant of these outings was the young Chicago poet Harriet Monroe, founder of *Poetry* magazine, who recited a poem to the company on the 1904 outing, and wrote and produced a play performed at the 1908 outing. Indeed, the eighth president of the club was the California conservationist and educator Aurelia S. Harwood.

In the first decade after its 1892 founding, the Sierra Club initiated several environmental campaigns and supported those of others. But it was not until the early years of the new century that they sallied forth to do battle against the greatest threat to ever confront the High Sierras: the determination of San Francisco's elite to dam the Tuolumne River at Hetch Hetchy Valley and create a reservoir for the city's exclusive use—*within the new Yosemite National Park!*

James Phelan was elected mayor of San Francisco in 1897, and high on his list of priorities was assuring that the city would have plenty of water to grow far into the future. He dreamed of San Francisco as a world-class city, rivaling New York, London, and Paris. For that the city needed a secure and ready source of water—lots of water. And since they lacked funds to pay for it, the source ideally must be free of private claims.

U.S. Geological Survey (USGS) engineer John Lippincott pointed out to Phelan that the Tuolumne River was free of claims, surged year long with snow melt from the High Sierras, and was pushed all the way to the Bay Area by gravity. Best of all, the magnificent two-thousand-foot walls of the Hetch Hetchy Valley seemed preordained to anchor a dam for a magnificent reservoir. Neither the USGS nor Phelan were the least bit troubled by the minor fact that the valley was already part of a national park, and that the reservoir would flood a substantial part of the water-shed inside the park. True, there were multiple other sources for the water that San Francisco desired. Many such had been identified and explored; this was publicly acknowledged. But none of the other already-identified sources were as cheap and dependable as a Hetch Hetchy dam and reser-voir, which could as a bonus supply hydroelectric power.

In 1902 Lippincott filed a claim in the Department of the Interior for a permit to construct the dam at Hetch Hetchy, in the name of the city of San Francisco. Muir and the Sierra Club were alarmed, but not overly so. The claim was clearly and explicitly in violation of the Congressionally mandated regulations protecting Yosemite National Park (and other na-tional parks). Roosevelt's Secretary of the Interior, Ethan Hitchcock, did his duty and curtly denied the application.

End of story, Muir thought. He believed he had support in high places. President Roosevelt himself spent several days with Muir in the park in spring of 1903. They camped at the Mariposa Grove, and then at Glacier Point above Yosemite Valley, awakening with four inches of snow on their blankets—at which Roosevelt had exclaimed "Bully!" But then Hitchcock resigned as Interior Secretary in spring 1907, and was replaced by James Garfield, senator from Ohio and son of the assassinated President. Garfield soon announced he was opening hearings on the permit to dam the Tuolumne at Hetch Hetchy.

Now Muir and the Sierra Club were definitely alarmed. Muir wrote Roosevelt, suggesting that he instruct Garfield to do his job as Hitchcock had his. But Roosevelt was a lame-duck president in the summer of 1907, with little influence and less desire to initiate what could (and would) become a nasty fight. As the proposal advanced, Muir churned out letters and articles by the score. "Dam Hetch Hetchy! As well dam for water-tanks the people's cathedrals and churches, for no holier temple has ever been consecrated by the hand of man," he wrote in early 1908.

Muir's articles and Sierra Club protests in 1907 and 1908 were all for nought. The wealthy burghers of San Francisco brought enormous political pressures to bear on Garfield and Roosevelt. In May of 1908, Garfield reversed Hitchcock's former ruling on the matter, allowing San Francisco to tap the Tuolumne River for its water supply on two conditions. First, the citizens of San Francisco approve the funds to build the water system. And second, the actual dam at Hetch Hetchy not be built until, and if, the Tuolumne's waters at downstream Lake Eleanor were first depleted.

By now the 70-year-old Muir was exhausted and sick of the fight. As Roosevelt pointed out in a mollifying private letter to Muir, it would be a generation or more before Lake Eleanor was depleted. Another generation could then take up the battle anew, if needed. Wearily, Muir agreed that the fight seemed to be over, and persuaded himself that it would be far in the future before Lake Eleanor's capacity was overdrawn—if ever.

In November of 1908 Roosevelt's protege William Howard Taft was elected President, and was inaugurated in March 1909. Taft appointed Seattle attorney Richard Ballinger as his Secretary of the Interior. Then Phelan, still a force in San Francisco politics though no longer mayor, made a gamble. He persuaded the city leaders to request that Ballinger re-open the agreement, and change it to permit the city to *immediately* begin construction and utilization of a dam at Hetch Hetchy. San Francisco couldn't wait a generation for its free, unlimited Sierra water.

Muir and most of his Sierra Club colleagues were furious. At a pivotal meeting in the club's headquarters, a battle group was assembled, consisting of Muir, attorney William Colby (secretary of the club), the previously-mentioned Edward Parsons, and William Bade (professor of Old Testament at the Pacific Theological Seminary and editor of the club's *Bulletin*). This group and those who flocked to the cause created something unprecedented in American history: a nationwide, grassroots environmental campaign. The campaign mobilized nature lovers across America—many of them converted to Muir's Earth Wisdom worldview by three decades of his writings.

Women in and out of the Sierra Club were particularly active in this new experiment in political discourse, a development that cost Muir some support among the male population. The movement was caricatured by opponents as consisting of "short-haired women and long-haired men," an innuendo-laced charge that might today be equivalent to painting your opponents as perverts and hippies. A widely-disseminated cartoon caricatured Muir in a skirt wielding a broom in a vain attempt to sweep back Tuolumne River water.

Muir didn't care. He had won the admiration of women throughout his life, and called on them as well as his male friends to help the cause. He sought and won the support of the influential network of Women's Clubs in California. He persuaded Sierra Club member Harriet Monroe, by now a nationally prominent poet and scholar based in Chicago, to testify before the congressional committees that were holding hearings on the request.

The well-orchestrated outpouring of public support for preserving the integrity of Yosemite National Park surprised everyone, particularly Phelan and his party. Taft and Interior Secretary Ballinger were impressed. The latter asked the city of San Francisco to show cause why Hetch Hetchy should not be deleted outright from its petition for a municipal water supply. President Taft asked for a tour of Yosemite from Muir, who promptly agreed. Thus in October of 1909 Muir found himself hiking the valley and its surrounding heights with a second president (though this one did not camp overnight with him and awake covered by snow). A few weeks later Secretary Ballinger showed up, and Muir took him to Hetch Hetchy itself.

The congressional hearings dragged on throughout 1910 and 1911, the battle settling into a bitter stalemate. San Francisco's brute political and financial sway could not be defeated, but neither could the new grass-roots support pouring in to legislators from across the nation. The Hetch Hetchy defenders produced the first pamphlet containing a form letter for supporters to send to members of Congress—a tactic still in use a hundred years later. Even the resignation of Secretary Ballinger in March of 1911 due to the stress of fighting charges of corruption (later shown to be baseless, and politically motivated by Gifford Pinchot, Muir's long-time opponent) did not change the deadlock.

The strain of the seemingly endless battle took a heavy toll on Muir. In April of 1911, about to turn 73 years of age, he decided to embark on a year-long tour to escape the stress, and realize his youthful ambition to see the tropical plants of the Amazon Basin. Against the pleas of his daughters, physicians, and colleagues, he persisted in his plans for the solitary journey. The death of his old Scot friend William Keith on the eve of his departure was a blow. Arriving in New York City, Muir picked up Robert Underwood Johnson and together they visited Washington, D.C. to lobby yet more for the Hetch Hetchy cause before Muir's departure. As Muir related in a letter to his Sierra Club colleague William Colby:

"Had a long, hearty, telling talk with the President (Taft), three with Secretary (of Interior) Fisher, lunched with Champ Clark (Speaker of the House)...Saw lots of Senators and Representatives, and made an hour and a half speech on H.H. and parks at a grand dinner of the influential Boone and Crockett Club...Never imagined I could stand so much dining and late hours."

After receiving an honorary degree from Yale and staying awhile with the widow and daughters of railroad magnate Edward Harriman, and withstanding John Burrough's bellowed opinion that he was "gane gite, clean gite" for taking the journey alone, Muir finally set sail in August for Brazil. He soon realized his lifelong dream (at least since his thousand-mile walk of four decades earlier), boating a thousand miles up the Amazon to Manaus, and wandering the flooded forest in search of the giant water lily *Victoria regia* (which, unlike the rare orchid Calypso in the bogs of southern Canada, he could not find). He did succeed, however, in tracking down forests of the two South American species in the Mesozoic genus *Araucaria* (in Brazil and Argentina) before steaming across the Atlantic to introduce himself to the baobab tree (*Adansonia*) and others in Africa. After a brief time in Europe, he returned home, and recuperated from the rigors of the journey during the spring and summer of 1912 with daughter Helen and her family in southern California.

When Woodrow Wilson defeated Taft and the resurgent "Bull Moose" Roosevelt in November 1912, Muir and his colleagues were rightly apprehensive about the fate of Hetch Hetchy. Upon Wilson's appointment of his new Secretary of the Interior, their worst fears were realized: Hetch Hetchy's fate would be determined by Franklin Lane, former city attorney of San Francisco, and bosom friend of James Phelan. Shortly after Wilson's inauguration, the Raker Bill was introduced in Congress, which would allow San Francisco to immediately begin construction of a dam at Hetch Hetchy. Secretary Lane signaled his firm support for the proposal.

In despair, Muir and his new grassroots environmental movement once again rallied opposition to the bill, joined by the editorial boards of the *New York Times*, the *Boston Evening Transcript*, the Louisville *Courier-Journal*, Denver's *Rocky Mountain News*, and numerous other newspapers. Even California's Senator John Works opposed the dam, as did Helen Elliot, the president of the California Federation of Women's Clubs. Also joining the opposition to the dam were former Harvard president Charles Eliot, nature writer Enos Mills, and landscape architect Frederick Law Olmsted, Jr., among many influential men and women nationwide.

The work of the nascent environmental movement was impressive, and represented a new chapter in American, indeed world, history. But it was not enough. President Wilson, Secretary Lane, and political machines of San Francisco and beyond saw that the votes were delivered. The Raker Bill passed the House in September, the Senate in December, and was signed into law by President Wilson on December 19, 1913.

In a year the magnificent Hetch Hetchy valley was being surveyed by San Francisco engineers, its towering trees felled, its limpid streams buried under piles of mud.

And John Muir was dead.

Muir's first biographer, Linnie Marsh Wolfe, voiced the common opinion of those closest to Muir: the exhausting and tragic battle for Hetch Hetchy had brought the robust mountaineer to a relatively early death in December of 1914, at age 76.

The dam was finished in 1923, and the valley at the mouth of Muir's favorite Sierra canyon has been submerged under water ever since, the magical place of which he had written:

Snatch a pan of bread and run to the Tuolumne. In whatever mood the lover of wildness enters the Canyon, he speedily yields to the spell of the falling, singing river, and listens and looks with ever-growing enthusiasm until all the world beside is forgotten...Through the canyon flows a river clear as crystal, bordered with trees, Cassiope, fairest of shrubs, and sunny meadows here and there. Nature's best gardens are here in deepest repose, fountains of wild ever-playing water falling in every form—the endless song of Creation shaking the devout listener into newness of life. He who enters will hear a music which will never cease to vibrate in his life throughout all its blurring moil and soil.

22

Environmentalism's Flawed Model

"All the other torches were lighted from his."

—Robert Underwood Johnson

Considering the disastrous conclusion of Muir's last environmental battle, what can we say of his legacy? John Muir left dozens of national parks, national monuments, and forest preserves created by his efforts and those he inspired. He left his name on scores of mountains, glaciers, high passes, groves, and schools. And his articulation of the immanent, three-pillared Earth Wisdom, the first in the modern West, must count as his first legacy.

But a further, second legacy stands beside the first, a legacy that has changed world history. The scope, intensity, and tactics of the 1909-1913 battle to save Hetch Hetchy created the modern environmental movement, and John Muir, more than any other single person, marshaled that battle. As Robert Underwood Johnson put it in his eulogy to Muir: "To this (movement) many persons and organizations contributed, but Muir's writings and enthusiasm were the chief forces that inspired the movement. All the other torches were lighted from his."

Even before the battle over Hetch Hetchy was joined, Muir was clear about those who threatened the vast areas of exceptional natural beauty with which America was blessed. "These temple destroyers, devotees of a ravaging commercialism, seem to have a perfect contempt for Nature, and, instead of lifting their eyes to the God of the mountains, lift them to the Almighty Dollar."

He cast the struggle between profit-seeking commercial interests and the natural world in stark terms. A decade before Hetch Hetchy, he declared "The battle we have fought, and are still fighting for the forests, is a part of the eternal conflict between right and wrong, and we cannot expect to see the end of it." At the end, as Hetch Hetchy's trees were being felled and its waters polluted, Muir consoled himself with the comment to Robert Underwood Johnson that "the conscience of the whole country has been aroused from sleep, and from outrageous evil compensating good in some form must surely come."

In the two decades following its 1892 founding, Muir's Sierra Club had been joined by only one other national organization in its efforts to protect the natural world. The National Audubon Society was founded in Boston in 1905, and was in many ways the East Coast equivalent of the Sierra Club, focusing initially on one issue (the protection of birdlife), yet branching out to other closely related issues. The protracted struggle to save Hetch Hetchy in the first decade of the 20th century, however, propelled concern for the environment into the national consciousness, from the grassroots level of common citizens and groups such as Women's Clubs, to the halls of Congress.

Soon after Muir's death in 1914 other organizations appeared, focusing on various aspects of the struggle. In 1919 the National Parks Conservation Association was formed, to assist the growing national parks system Muir had done so much to create, and which openly acknowledged him as its "Father." In 1922 the Izaak Walton League appeared, the Wilderness society followed in 1935, and the National Wildlife Federation a year later. The Defenders of Wildlife was formed in 1946, The Nature Conservancy in 1951, and the World Wildlife Federation (U.S.) a decade later. Thus by the middle of the 20th century a healthy diversity of organizations had joined the Sierra Club in efforts to preserve the natural world from commercial exploitation, and to curb the worst excesses of human activity upon the environment.

An early decision regarding strategy by Muir and the Sierra Club in the Hetch-Hetchy battle proved critical in shaping the history and outlook of the burgeoning environmental movement, which has followed this lead for a century. Campaigns have emphasized preserving the beauty and vitality of the natural world, as well as its benefits to humans in recreation, health, and serenity—aspects of the first pillar of Earth Wisdom. In their steady inclusion of females in membership and activities (the early and influential Massachusetts Audubon Society, particularly, was dominated by females), Muir's third pillar was reflected.

But the second pillar of Earth Wisdom—Muir's ringing Gaiacentric claim that humans were kin with all creatures, not superior to them and certainly not destined to exert dominion over them—has been studiously avoided, from the Hetch Hetchy campaign to the present.

Several factors underlay this decision. One was simply the publishing history of Muir. Although he published five books during his lifetime, passages revealing the second pillar of Earth Wisdom are found almost exclusively in his journals—the private, uninhibited outbursts penned in the midst of his many adventures in the wilderness. These journals were largely unpublished during Muir's lifetime, though of course he utilized them as source material for his books.

It was only three years before his death that any journal material was directly published, 1911's *My First Summer in the Sierra*. Nothing more of the journals would appear before the public until two years after Muir's death, 1916's *A Thousand Mile Walk to the Gulf*, edited by his Sierra Club friend William Frederic Bade. It made hardly a ripple in the public perception of Muir, though it contains some of the most explicit, eye-opening claims of Muir's second-pillar convictions. Not until a full two decades later were most of the rest of his journals published, in biographer Linnie Marsh Wolfe's 1938 *John of the Mountains*.

Thus by virtue of his journals being published mainly after his death, and so rarely read by the public, Muir's great shift from anthropocentrism to Gaiacentrism was hidden, found in scattered writings known for the most part only to his several biographers. The general public, and probably most of his Sierra Club colleagues, were ignorant of the full claims of Earth Wisdom, and of the existence of this "hidden Muir."

In addition, however, Muir at the time of the Hetch Hetchy campaign—and environmental organizations since—shied away from publicizing the Gaiacentric, second-pillar aspect of his thought, because its radical new worldview of the place of humans in the universe is extraordinarily challenging. Environmental fundraising and campaigning is a delicate pursuit: you must alarm and inspire, but not alienate or unduly shock your potential supporters.

Bluntly put, it would likely be bad for business to trumpet Muir's view that "I have precious little sympathy for the selfish propriety of civilized man, and if a war of races should occur between the wild beasts and Lord Man, I would be tempted to sympathize with the bears." The hidden, robustly Gaiacentric Muir challenges the entire Western anthropocentric worldview, from the pre-Socratic Protagoras' "Man is the measure of all things" to the present. That challenge surely would be too much for early 20th century America to readily digest—and possibly in the 21st century as well. Best to keep the "hidden Muir" safely out of sight.

Or so Muir, the Sierra Club, and nearly every environmental organization since, judged. They extolled Muir's first pillar, the wonder and awe of the natural world, as they emphasized the benefits to humans of wilderness preservation, and the costs to humans of pollution. This approach might be termed "high, informed" anthropocentrism, as opposed to the "low, commercial" anthropocentrism exemplified by logging and sheep grazing. This model was viewed not as a betrayal of Muir's Earth Wisdom, but merely a strategic approach to secure what good could be realistically hoped for.

And it worked. Though the model was flawed by virtue of its exclusion of Muir's Gaiacentrism, it was still powerful enough to spark remarkable achievements in habitat preservation and pollution abatement. The flaw was acceptable for a century, and would not be revealed until the implacable threat of climate change began its transformation of the planet and posed an existential threat to human civilization. But in the intervening century, the flawed model produced tangible results.

The first half century of educating the American public and its leaders about the human benefits of environmental protection and preservation doubtless contributed to the nationwide reaction to Rachel Carson's 1962 *Silent Spring* and the 1969 Santa Barbara oil spill. The mounting environmental concerns culminated in the 1960s and 1970s with new organizations (The Environmental Defense Fund in 1967, Friends of the Earth in 1969, and Natural Resources Defense Council in 1970), and the first Earth Day in 1970.

But most spectacular was the ground-breaking array of federal legislation in the last half of the century: 1964's Wilderness Preservation system, 1968's Wild and Scenic Rivers Act, 1970's Clean Air Act, 1970's creation of the Environmental Protection Agency, 1972's Clean Water Act (amended in 1977), and 1973's Endangered Species Act.

These fruits of the 1960s and 1970s were monumental victories. They continue to affect the air, water, and public lands of America today, producing healthier cities and permitting millions of Americans to visit and enjoy the country's hundreds of preserved natural sites. It is a record and an achievement to be proud of. Building on these victories, America's mainline environmental organizations continued to flourish. Their lobbying efforts in state capitols and Washington, D.C. grew apace in scope and sophistication in the last decades of the 20th century. Clearly, the environmental cause in America was booming.

If any one man could illustrate this period of phenomenal growth, it would be Californian David Brower, who first established himself as an exceptional mountaineer. Brower and the legendary Norman Clyde spent much of the 1930s in epic climbing trips, establishing first ascents of scores of peaks in the Sierra Nevada and North America. When World War II began, Brower trained mountain brigades for several years, then himself led Allied troops in the mountains of Italy in the war's later stages.

After the war, Brower became associated with the Sierra Club in official capacities, editing its journal and directing its annual High Trips in the late 1940s. He was elected to the post of executive director in 1952, and held the position until 1969, during which time the influence and stature of the club skyrocketed. By 1960 the Sierra Club was active nationwide and an acknowledged leader in the environmental movement, helping create the groundwork for the incredible surge of environmental awareness and legislation during the 1960s and 1970s.

Brower constantly pushed the Sierra Club's board of directors to expand its environmental efforts well beyond wilderness preservation, which along with financial strains created tension between him and the board. In 1969 the board relieved Brower of his position. Brower soon founded Friends of the Earth, an organization that embraced a wide definition of environmental concerns, fighting against human overpopulation, the Alaska pipeline, the Supersonic Transport, Agent Orange in Vietnam, nuclear power, and Reagan appointee James Watts in the Department of the Interior.

By any number of measures the environmental movement seemed to be thriving in America in the 20th century's last decades. The earlier decision to ignore the Gaiacentric, hidden Muir seemed an acceptable one. But beneath the facade of success, roiling controversies rocked the movement. The high, informed anthropocentric model upon which the entire environmental enterprise was based was increasingly seen as fundamentally flawed, by members on both its left and right flanks.

In the 1970s three groups appeared which channeled the hidden Muir's Gaiacentric worldview, and whose activism earned them the term "radical environmentalism." Their aim was to protect the planet and its creatures, rather than making the planet a better place for humans to live. In 1971 a small group in Vancouver, Canada decided to adopt confrontational direct action to stop nuclear testing. Bob Hunter and his comrades hired a fishing boat to motor them directly into Aleutian waters near Amchitka, where a nuclear test was scheduled to detonate. The resulting publicity got that test postponed, and five months later the Amchitka tests as a whole were abandoned.

In 1972 the group coalesced around the name Greenpeace, and added direct action to stop the slaughter of marine mammals—whales and harp seal pups—to their antinuclear activities. Nearly half a century later, the same determination to thrust themselves into the midst of struggles continues, as shown in Seattle in the massive May and June 2015 gathering of Greenpeace "kayaktivists" blocking Shell Petroleum ships from embarking on drilling voyages to the Arctic. These harassing actions are widely acknowledged as contributing factors in Shell's stunning decision in October 2015 to abandon its plans for Arctic drilling, after having invested $7.5 billion in the project.

One of the early Greenpeace activists, Paul Watson, left the organization in 1977 to outfit a ship he christened *Sea Shepherd*, and the following year sailed to the ice floes of Eastern Canada to spray paint snow-white harp seal pups with an indelible dye, thus rendering them useless as commercial fur. From these flamboyant beginnings the Sea Shepherd Conservation Society has continued its direct action to stop illegal whaling and the destruction of marine creatures and habitat.

Sea Shepherd unabashedly proclaims its Gaiacentric stance. "Sea Shepherd operates outside the petty cultural chauvinism of the human species. Our clients are whales, dolphins, seals, turtles, sea-birds, and fish. We represent their interests," proclaims its website today. "We are pro-Ocean and work in the interests of all life on Earth."

Shortly after the appearance of Sea Shepherd, an even more explicitly Gaiacentric radical environmental group appeared: Earth First!, formed in 1979 (or 1980, in some accounts) by David Foreman and others. Inspired in part by Edward Abbey's *The Monkeywrench Gang*, Earth First! engages in civil disobedience, nonviolent sabotage, and "monkeywrenching" to interfere with commercial exploitation of the natural world. Preventing access to old-growth forests, tree-sitting, and tree-spiking were some early Earth First! activities, with undoubted influence on forest preservation in the Pacific Northwest.

The second and third pillars of the hidden Muir are front and center on its website: "Guided by a philosophy of deep ecology, Earth First! does not accept a human-centered worldview of 'nature for people's sake.' Instead, we believe that life exists for its own sake, that industrial civilization and its philosophy are anti-Earth, anti-woman and anti-liberty…To put it simply, the Earth must come first."

Greenpeace, Sea Shepherd, and Earth First! are still active today, attracting legions of devoted participants, though not the hundreds of thousand members of mainline environmental groups. And they continue to make their mark, particularly Greenpeace, which has active chapters in 40 countries. In India, for example, they lead the protests against the Mahan coal mine project, which would destroy a diversity-rich forest. When massive explosions rocked a chemical storage facility in Tianjin, China in 2015, it was Greenpeace who knew the range of materials stored there.

Yet for all their expertise, their daring, their courageous willingness to place themselves before bulldozers and oil tankers, somehow the radical environmental movements did not gain widespread support in the 1970s and 1980s. Perhaps radical environmentalism's actions and philosophy were simply ahead of the times in the 1970s and since, as Muir had judged would be the case in the early 1900s.

It was not just the radical environmentalists who viewed the mainline's high, informed anthropocentric model as flawed. Some in the mainline groups began to tire of the endless legal and legislative struggles to spot and challenge threats to the environment, the constant harassing of offending corporate and industrial entities. Surely it must be possible, they reasoned, to bring the corporations on board, to persuade them to tailor their activities to aid rather than threaten the environment. Thus was born the pro-business wing of the environmental movement.

Soon environmentalists were comfortably walking the corridors of power in Washington, D.C., commodifying pollution and cultivating "market opportunities" for environmentalism. As journalist Naomi Klein describes it, "Rather than advancing policies that treat greenhouse gases as dangerous pollutants demanding clear, enforceable regulations that would restrict emission and create the conditions for a full transition to renewables, these groups have pushed convoluted market-based schemes that have treated greenhouses gases as late-capitalist abstractions to be traded, bundled, speculated upon, and moved around the globe like currency or subprime debt."

The most notable and self-congratulatory of the pro-business Big Green groups was (and remains) the Environmental Defense Fund (EDF).

Back in its earliest days, the EDF was a collection of zealous lawyers operating under the slogan "Sue the bastards." They were instrumental in many of the striking achievements of the 1970s. But in 1986 Fred Krupp assumed the EDF's leadership and guided it in a different direction altogether, to much fanfare.

"The new environmentalism does not accept 'either-or' as inevitable" he grandly announced in a national advertisement. The EDF would form partnerships with corporations—"coalitions of former enemies"—and show them the financial benefits of going green. "Sue the bastards" now became "Create markets for the bastards." Soon the EDF was busily engaged with Walmart, McDonald's, FedEx, and AT&T creating profitable "solutions" to environmental degradation.

One can easily imagine what the hidden Muir would have thought of this peculiar strategy of engaging with those who lift their eyes "to the Almighty Dollar." So much for the eternal struggle between good and evil!

The collaborations between a few mainline environmental groups and Big Business consisted largely of corporations adopting practices marginally less destructive to the environment than in the past, which were then ballyhooed as "saving" the earth. An example is the saga of natural gas, which emerged in the 1990s and early 2000s as the "good" fossil fuel compared to coal. Natural gas would be a "bridge fuel" permitting less reliance on dirty energy sources, as a transition was imagined being made to sustainable sources such as wind and solar. Never mind that the transition always receded into the misty future.

Even the Sierra Club joined the trend, its then-director, Carl Pope, lobbying Congress with natural gas extractor Chesapeake Energy's CEO Aubrey McClendon. It was later revealed that Chesapeake Energy had funneled millions in donations to the Sierra Club. Meanwhile, Pope also partnered with the Clorox Company to lend the club's logo to a line of "green" cleaning products. All this as individual Sierra Club chapters (and other groups, often ad hoc) were engaged in pitched battles at the local level to prevent the increasingly favored method of extracting natural gas—hydraulic fracturing—from transforming their beloved countryside into an ugly patchwork of leaking wells, contaminated water supplies, and the constant screech of mammoth machinery.

All three wings of the environmental movement—mainline, radical, pro-business—marched steadily ahead in the latter decades of the 20th century, each secure in their distinct approach. Since the 1980s were the decade of Ronald Reagan and the glorification of free market capitalism, the pro-business wing seemed very much the wave of the future.

But in 1988 a climatologist presented testimony before a congressional hearing that called into question not just the importance and effectiveness of current environmental activities, but indeed the very model upon which the movement had operated for a century. James Hansen brought the subject of global warming to the national level, and everything changed—fundamentally and forever.

23

Ignoring Climate Change (1988-2012)

"Now, I make a point of never having any prejudices and of following docilely wherever fact may lead me."

—Sherlock Holmes

In June of 1988 the director of NASA's Goddard Institute for Space Studies, James Hansen, testified before a congressional hearing that the earth's climate was threatened by a buildup of heat-trapping "greenhouse gases" in the atmosphere. The phenomenon was not newly discovered; for several decades climatologists at Hawaii's Moana Loa Observatory had tracked steadily rising concentrations of carbon dioxide in the atmosphere, and many scientists had warned of its effect on atmospheric temperatures.

By 1988 sufficient data was available to make a credible case (to scientists, at least) that greenhouse gases resulting from the combustion of fossil fuels were changing earth's climate with serious, deleterious consequences to humanity. Early studies focused on the rise of sea levels, with consequent flooding of coastal cities; salinization of water supplies; and decline of crop yields due to heat stress of plants.

Four years later, a Union of Concerned Scientists letter signed by 1,700 senior scientists around the world, including the majority of Nobel laureates in the sciences, warned that "Human beings and the natural world are on a collision course" that "may so alter the living world that it will be unable to sustain life in the manner that we know…We must, for example, move away from fossil fuels to more benign, inexhaustible energy sources to cut greenhouse gas emissions."

While scientists were in Sherlock Holmes' habit of "following docile-ly wherever fact may lead," politicians and the fossil fuel industry were strongly prejudiced against the prospect of altering one of the bulwarks of the economy and modern life. The possibility proved impossible for them to contemplate, regardless of the scientific facts and the dire predicted consequences.

At least one of the major oil corporations, Exxon, had already been informed by its own staff scientists that such a threat to the planet's climate existed, even before Hansen's testimony. Records unearthed in fall 2015 by the *Los Angeles Times* and *Inside Climate News* indicate that Exxon executives decided to claim that the conclusions were uncertain, and to proceed full steam ahead with their extractive activities. This set the general trend of assertive denial of the evidence indicating climate change by Big Oil and Big Coal.

Soon a flood of funds from fossil fuel corporations, as well as various concerns controlled by the Koch brothers and other plutocrats, were washing into a host of hastily created centers and institutes questioning not only whether the earth was warming, but also the scientific consensus that combustion of fossil fuels was an important contributor to the phenomenon. The surge of money and its dramatic success is amply documented in Jane Mayer's 2016 *Dark Money: The Hidden History of the Billionaires Behind the Rise of the Radical Right.* Among many, perhaps the most active and effective climate-denying body was the Heartland Institute. This Chicago-based group had originally been funded by tobacco companies to spearhead the denial of any link between smoking and lung cancer.

Heartland used the same tactics for climate change they had used in the pro-smoking tobacco campaign: search exhaustively to ferret out a few scientists willing to express doubts about the data, put them on the payroll of Heartland or one of its many corporate sponsors, then trumpet their questioning of the science. Its annual climate conferences from 2008 to the present spotlighted denial of fossil fuel's connection to climate change from an impressive (and well-recompensed) range of policy officials, legislators, lawyers, and the occasional scientist—all of which confirmed Upton Sinclair's observation that "it is difficult to get a man to understand something, when his salary depends upon his not understanding it." Sherlock Holmes would have been dismayed.

For example, a Greenpeace investigation revealed a prominent speaker in the 2011 climate conference, astrophysicist Willie Soon, had for the eight previous years received 100 percent of his new research grants from fossil fuel interests. A 2012 leak of internal documents from Heartlands headquarters showed direct monthly payments from the institute to a range of climate skeptics: physicist Fred Singer ($5,000 plus expenses per month), geologist Robert M. Carter ($1,667 per month), founder of the climate-skeptic Center for the Study of Carbon Dioxide and Global Change Craig Idso ($11,600 per month), and a one-off $90,000 payment to blogger and one-time TV weatherman Anthony Watts.

As the scientific evidence for climate change caused primarily by fossil fuel combustion mounted, the climate deniers ramped up their well-oiled (and still well-paid) campaign casting doubt on the science. The result in the first years of the 21st century was widespread public confusion and doubt regarding not just the issue of climate change, but environmental issues in general. No matter that 97% of the world's climate scientists and thousands of their peer-reviewed studies agreed that combustion of fossil fuels was causing climate change threatening human civilization. Even among economic geologists, scientists employed by extractive industries to locate commercially exploitable fossil fuel deposits, surveys established that 47 percent believe the evidence points to human-caused climate change—an astonishingly high number, given Upton Sinclair's astute comments about the difficulty of assenting to something that threatens your income.

No matter. The economic and political power of the fossil fuel and mining corporations kept the simple solution—transitioning from fossil to renewable sources to generate power—off the table, by creating discord and confusion, even within the environmental movement. So successful was the Heartland Institute and its partners at discrediting the overwhelming scientific consensus that the United States in the first decade of the 21st century seemed to have reverted to a pre-scientific society, characterized by the ready belief in nonsensical assertions contrary to common sense and rational analysis. Not since the Salem Witch Trials had irrationality held such sway in America. The Heartlands Institute and the Koch brothers had dragged America four centuries into the past.

The Sierra Club and other mainline environmental organizations plugged doggedly away at their wonted habitat-saving and pollution-limiting tasks, but the sense was growing that such traditional activities were eclipsed by the issue of climate change. And on that issue, though individuals, cities, and some states (notably California and New York) were beginning to make credible responses, nothing of import was happening on the critical national or international levels. The century-old model undergirding the environmental movement was proving inadequate to the challenge of climate change.

In 2004, two persons long engaged in America's environmental mainstream reluctantly came to a startling conclusion. In an article provocatively entitled *The Death of Environmentalism*, Michael Shellenberger and Ted Nordhaus argued that although the century-old tactics of America's environmental organizations had achieved notable results, they were incapable of dealing with the great global challenges then facing the earth, such as climate change, biological diversity, and human overpopulation.

"Not one of America's environmental leaders is articulating a vision of the future commensurate with the magnitude of the crisis," they claimed. "Instead they are promoting technical policy fixes like pollution controls and higher vehicle mileage standards—proposals that provide neither the popular inspiration nor the political alliances the community needs to deal with the problem. By failing to question their most basic assumptions about the problem and the solution, environmental leaders are like generals fighting the last war—in particular the war they fought and won for basic environmental protections more than 30 years ago.

"Environmentalism is today more about protecting a supposed 'thing'—'the environment'—than advancing the worldview articulated by Sierra Club founder John Muir, who nearly a century ago observed, 'When we try to pick out anything by itself, we find it hitched to everything else in the Universe.'" Something more—something more fundamental—is required. "Environmentalists are in a culture war whether we like it or not. It's a war over our core values as Americans and over our vision for the future, and it won't be won by appealing to the rational consideration of our collective self-interest."

Without offering specifics, Shellenberger and Nordhaus suggested that "Environmentalists need to tap into the creative worlds of myth-making, even religion, not to better sell narrow and technical policy proposals but rather to figure out who we are and who we need to be." To my mind, it is telling that they quote John Muir, and specifically call out as problematic the appeal to human self-interest. For the first time in a century, the hidden Muir stirred. But the critique of environmentalism's ineffective model was not widely publicized outside the movement, and even there it caused only a temporary stir.

A low point came in 2009, when the United Nations climate summit in Copenhagen, billed as the last hope to address the crisis, failed miserably to agree to any binding emissions limits by any country. As before, in Rio de Janeiro in 1992 and Kyoto in 1997, nothing could be mustered beyond platitudes, and promises to try really, really hard to get close to unenforceable goals. Disappointed delegates to the conference wept. Big Oil and Big Coal had carried the day; one imagines champagne flutes clinking at the Heartland Institute.

The only notable accomplishment at Copenhagen was the agreement to mark 2°C as the maximum rise above pre-industrial average global temperature that could be tolerated by human civilization—with no mechanisms stipulated to achieve this goal. Even this, though, was fraught with controversy. Island nations, countries with significant low coastal regions, and many African nations already suffering from extended droughts protested vigorously, pushing instead for a goal of 1.5°C. They pointed out that even a 2°C rise would be a severe challenge, triggering salinization of much of civilization's fresh water supplies, frequent tidal inundation of great coastal cities and important delta agricultural areas, and decline in crop yields worldwide due to intensifying droughts. But in the end, 2°C was adopted—for the good that setting a goal with no plans to reach it might do.

By 2010, climatologists and other scientists had become sufficiently concerned at the lack of progress to sound the alarm more forcefully. "Why then are climatologists speaking out about the dangers of global warming?" asked Ohio State University's Lonnie G. Thompson. "The answer is that virtually all of us are now convinced that global warming poses a clear and present danger to civilization."

In 2011 the International Energy Agency indicated the planet was on track for 6°C warming by 2100. "Everybody, even the school children, know that this will have catastrophic implications for all of us," declared the report.

In 2012 the rush of data and predictions crested. A World Bank study indicated that a 4°C temperature rise by 2100 would result from current trends, "marked by extreme heat waves, declining global food stocks, loss of ecosystems and biodiversity, and life-threatening sea level rise...There is also no certainty that adaptation (by human civilization) to a 4°C world is possible."

Kevin Anderson, deputy director of Britain's Tyndall Centre for Climate Change Research, summarized that such a 4°C increase "is incompatible with any reasonable characterization of an organized, equitable and civilized global community."

A 2012 study by the international accounting and auditing firm PricewaterhouseCoopers concluded that the climate studies "mean, quite simply, that climate change has become an existential crisis for the human species." A manifesto issued that year by 21 past winners of the Blue Planet Prize, including James Hansen and former Norway prime minister Gro Harlem Brundtland, declared that "In the face of an absolutely unprecedented emergency, society has no choice but to take dramatic action to avert a collapse of civilization."

Together, the coalescing tide of studies made it clear that unacceptable consequences to human civilization would accompany any atmospheric temperature increase beyond 2°C: sea rise by 2100 of between 1 and 2 meters, rendering coastal cities uninhabitable (think New York City, Boston, Los Angeles, San Francisco, London, Vancouver, Mumbai, Hong Kong, Shanghai, among many others); vast inundation of broad coastal areas on many continents (Ecuador to Chile, and Brazil; the Netherlands; much of Florida, California, and New England; Bangladesh and India; the Philippines; and Vietnam); drastic declines in world production of grains due to floods, inundation of delta regions, drought, and heat stress; consequent widespread famines, particularly in tropical and subtropical regions of Africa and South Asia; wide-ranging, frequent droughts and raging wildfires; pest and disease outbreaks as new pathogens follow the changed climate regimes; fisheries collapses as the oceans become warmer and more acidic (already occurring earlier than anticipated); and dramatic water shortages worldwide as wells are invaded by salt water (on the coast) or water tables plummet (inland, also already occurring in many areas).

Then there are increased frequencies and intensities of storms and hurricanes. Since every 0.6°C increase in temperature expands the atmosphere's capacity to hold water by 4 percent, a 3.5°C increase would represent a 5.8 expansion factor, or 23 percent more water in the atmosphere, contributing to the predicted increase in storms worldwide.

As if all this were not enough, scientists say that somewhere between a 2°C and 4°C rise in temperature, several catastrophic "tipping points" would likely occur. These would include the thawing of the permafrost in northern regions, releasing millions of tons of methane into the atmosphere (equivalent to 205 gigatons of carbon dioxide). Methane is 25 times more powerful a greenhouse gas than carbon dioxide; thus global warming would suddenly spike another 0.5°C higher. Other tipping points predicted in the 2012 World Bank Study included "disintegration of the

West Antarctic ice sheet, leading to more rapid sea-level rise; or large-scale Amazon dieback, drastically affecting ecosystems, rivers, agriculture, energy production, and livelihoods...and impact entire continents" worldwide.

Clearly the data indicated not just *challenges* to civilization, but its widespread *collapse* around the world as temperatures increased above 2°C, accompanied by horrific death rates from famine and disease, especially in the already-warm equatorial belt. How many will die? Studies of the impact of severe weather precipitated by volcanic eruptions indicate the toll would not be in the thousands, nor hundreds of thousands, but in the millions. The 1783 eruption of Iceland's Laki volcano, for example, produced death-tolls estimated between 1.5 million to 6 million worldwide, including drought and famine in Japan and India, and flooding with brutally cold winters in central and western Europe.

Momentarily lost in the catalogue of impending disasters was a factor foretold in the Union of Concerned Scientists' 1992 *Warning to Humanity*: "Environmental and economic instabilities will cause mass migrations with incalculable consequences for developed and undeveloped nations alike." Europe's 2015 struggles with a mere million refugees from Syria, Afghanistan, and Iraq foreshadow the political and economic disruptions of coping with climate refugees in the hundreds of millions worldwide.

Had meaningful responses to climate change begun to be gradually phased in shortly after the initial 1988 announcement by Hansen, the threat could have been handled relatively easily, and catastrophe averted. Three decades of refusal to seriously address the issue, however, due primarily to the very successful efforts of Big Oil, Big Coal, the Heartland Institute, and the pro-business environmental groups, had presented humanity with a very different scenario by 2012.

What was now required to avert the specter of civilization's collapse on the planet was wrenching change focused into a short window of time. Serious global warming and its consequences, many scientists said, had already locked in as a result of the utter failure to reduce emissions since 1988. Whether the increase was 3, 4, or 6°C, humanity's tenure on the planet was in serious jeopardy.

At the American Geophysical Union meeting in San Francisco in the fall of 2012, all this was graphically illustrated in the session by a young, pink-haired geophysicist and computer modeler named Brad Werner. His presentation, entitled "Is Earth F**ked?", delved into highly technical and complex systems theory, charting perturbations, bifurcations, systems boundaries, inputs, dissipations, and attractors. At the end, when asked by a light-headed journalist whether all this meant the earth was, indeed, "f**ked," Werner sighed, and nodded. "More or less," he answered.

Indeed. And many in the environmental movement, as a result, were uneasy. Confused. Dismayed at the lack of meaningful national or international response to the stark predictions of the scientists. Wondering whether they were doing the right things for the right reasons. Unsure whether, in spite of all their efforts, environmentalism wasn't dead, and the planet wasn't, after all, f**ked.

A new model of environmentalism was desperately needed—and would soon be called for by a prize-winning journalist and the 266th Pope of the Roman Catholic Church.

24

(2012-2015) Hope Dawns, Blossoms...

*"The task is to articulate not just an alternative set of policy pro-
posals but an alternative worldview to rival the one at the heart
of the ecological crisis."*

—NAOMI KLEIN

The dismay and sense of a challenge not being met by the established
model led to changes in the second decade of the 21st century. In Muir's
Sierra Club, a new executive director assumed the helm in 2010. Michael
Brune came from previous posts at Greenpeace and Rainforest Action
Network, bringing a decidedly activist leadership to the nation's oldest en-
vironmental group.

Within a year of Brune's appearance, the Sierra Club had secured a
$50 million gift from Michael Bloomberg Philanthropies to invigorate
their Beyond Coal Campaign, which doubled its staff to 200 and tripled
its number of states affected, to 45. Soon the Sierra Club was the bane of
the U.S. coal industry, eventually succeeding in retiring 170 coal plants in
the U.S. and preventing the construction of over 180 proposed new plants
since the campaign's beginnings. The club had gone from being an apolo-
gist for the natural gas industry to the fiercest enemy of the coal industry.

The Sierra Club had a long-established policy prohibiting its executive
director from engaging in civil disobedience (though individual members
had just as long engaged in such activity). Brune in 2013 persuaded the

club's board of directors to change that policy. On February 13, 2013 he was arrested in front of the White House protesting the Keystone XL pipeline, and was hauled off to a D.C. jail. He had distinguished company: James Hansen, the original sounder of the climate change alarm; Julian Bond, civil rights veteran first jailed during a 1960 sit-in at the Atlanta City Hall cafeteria; Bill McKibben, founder of 350.org; and Robert F. Kennedy Jr., environmental activist from the famous clan.

Thus by 2013 a new day was dawning for the Sierra Club, which was beginning to look—and act—a bit more like the radical environmentalist groups who had taken the hidden Muir to heart four decades earlier. The Sierra Club under Brune partnered with other groups in organizing the massive September 2014 People's Climate March in New York City, the largest environmental demonstration ever. Over 400,000 people clogged Central Park West to urge the following month's UN climate summit to more seriously address the crisis.

The sense of something different being required to deal with climate change led to the formation of new groups with new approaches. Among the most influential was 350.org. Middlebury College professor Bill McKibben had written the first best-selling book to describe the coming climate crisis, 1989's *The End of Nature*. In 2008 McKibben took James Hansen's recently declared maximum safe concentration of atmospheric carbon dioxide as the basis of the name for a new, social-media-savvy environmental organization, 350.org. The group of mainly college students specialized in organizing nation-wide, then world-wide demonstrations *via* the internet and social media.

The proposed Keystone XL pipeline to carry particularly dirty crude oil from the Alberta, Canada tar sands to the Gulf of Mexico, which Hansen had declared "game over for the climate," became the group's focus. In August of 2011, two weeks of 350.org protests against the pipeline at the White House resulted in the arrest of an impressive list of demonstrators, including not just McKibben, but long-time labor activist Gus Speth, actor Danny Glover, author Wendell Barry, James Hansen, and journalist Naomi Klein. Speth and McKibben were in the first day's group, who spent three days in jail.

In the fall of 2014 Naomi Klein's *This Changes Everything: Capitalism and the Climate* was published. Winner of the Weston Trust Prize, the book masterfully describes the challenge of climate change, the capitalist economic system blocking an effective response, and the urgent need for a fundamentally new model to guide the rescue of the planet. "The most momentous and contentious environmental book since *Silent Spring*," said *The New York Times Book Review*.

This Changes Everything despairs of the power-brokers and the mainline environmental groups saving us from the impending catastrophe. Klein is not completely despondent, though, for she sees a glimmer of hope in the gathering numbers of indigenous peoples and peasant folk standing up to the destructive plans of extractive corporations to drill and mine on their lands: the Blockadia movement.

Beyond their common-sense approach, their urgency, and the frequent female leadership, the participants of Blockadia are characterized by another commonality: a way of thinking about themselves and the earth distinctly at odds with that of the modern, urbanized culture surrounding them. One of the peasant leaders protesting the Eldorado open-pit gold and copper mine on Greece's Halkidiki peninsula, young mother Melachrini Liakou, told Klein: "I am part of the land. I respect it, I love it and I don't treat it as a useless object...Because I want to live here this year, next year, and to hand it down to the generations to come. In contrast, Eldorado and any other mining company, they want to devour the land, to plunder it, to take away what is most precious for themselves."

Of Texas-based SWN Resources' plans for gas fracking in New Brunswick, Canada, First Nation educator Lelanne Simpson of the Mississiauga Nishnaaberg tribe said: the extractive view is "stealing...taking things out of relationship." The Anishinaabe view is "a way of living designed to generate life, not just human life but the life of all living things... Our systems are designed to promote more life."

"The task," Klein reflects, "is to articulate not just an alternative set of policy proposals but an alternative worldview to rival the one at the heart of the ecological crisis—(an alternative) one embedded in interdependence rather than hyper-individualism, reciprocity rather than dominance." And critically, this new model must inspire a mass worldwide movement, similar to America's abolitionists in the 1850s and the Civil Rights campaigners in the 1960s.

All of this should sound familiar: these are expressions of the very same Earth Wisdom we have seen John Muir develop in his life of rambling over the land, the same immanent worldview espoused by the Taoists in China for over two thousand years. We have come full circle. Like Muir and Taoists, Blockadia's indigenous peoples and southeast Europe villagers insist on the centrality of respect and love for the earth, and resolutely reject the dominance of commercial interests plundering the natural world for profit.

Reviews of *This Changes Everything* articulated the challenge and the hope. Mason Inman wrote in the San Francisco Chronicle: "Naomi Klein's latest book may be the manifesto that the climate movement—and the planet—needs right now...For those with whom her message does resonate—and they are likely to be legion—her book could help catalyze the kind of mass movement she argues the world needs now." Indeed, the book was published the very month—September 2014—of the Peoples Climate March in New York City.

Alas, neither Klein's book nor the 2014 march precipitated the widespread adoption of an "alternative worldview," nor a mass populist movement. The book, thick physically and intellectually, capped by 58 pages of small-print references, was widely reviewed and debuted at number 10 on the *New York Times* nonfiction best-seller list on October 5. It slipped to number 12 the next week, number 17 the next, and dropped off the list by the end of the month. Meanwhile, *The Boys in the Boat* and *Unbroken* roared on month after month on the list, it evidently being more pleasant to read about others' triumphs over daunting challenges, than to actually make it happen yourself in your own time.

Soon yet another call for a new way of thinking to save the planet and its humans appeared. This summons garnered considerably more attention than any of its predecessors, coming from a devout member of the

West's oldest institution of power: the 266th Pope of the Roman Catholic Church, Francis I.

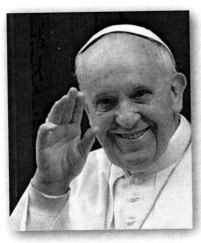

Pope Francis' encyclical on the environment, *Laudato Si'*, had been the subject of debate for months before its issuance. When the encyclical finally arrived in June 2015, it proved to be everything that had been hoped and feared—and more. Francis' analysis was thorough and in depth; the critique spared no institution or entrenched power. The radical document spawned a torrent of shocked criticism in America, exemplified by the fulminating right-wing radio ideologue Rush Limbaugh pronouncing the Pope "a Marxist," about the most damning adjective he could muster short of "the devil." "The Pope does seem to be enamored with solutions that are not pro-American in the slightest" declared a Philadelphia radio talk show host, perhaps a bit unclear on the Pope's job description.

Francis boldly states the problem. "The earth, our home, is beginning to look more and more like an immense pile of filth...the degree of human intervention (in the natural world), often in the service of business interests and consumerism, (is) actually making our earth less rich and beautiful, ever more limited and grey...We seem to think that we can substitute an irreplaceable and irretrievable beauty with something which we have created ourselves."

Francis sounds very much like Muir here, and even more so when he considers the world's cities, home to half of humanity. "Nowadays, for example, we are conscious of the disproportionate and unruly growth of many cities, which have become unhealthy to live in, not only because of pollution caused by toxic emissions but also as a result of urban chaos, poor transportation, and visual pollution and noise...We were not meant to be inundated by cement, asphalt, glass and metal, and deprived of physical contact with nature."

He adds his voice to those recognizing a key human input to global warming and frequent intense weather events: "Climate change is a global problem with grave implications...We know that technology based on the use of highly polluting fossil fuels—especially coal, but also oil and, to a lesser degree, gas—needs to be progressively replaced without delay."

Francis, of course, is a Jesuit, so he delves deep into two underlying factors bringing us to this point. In a brilliant section of the encyclical entitled *The Globalization of the technocratic paradigm*, Francis claims that "The basic problem goes even deeper; it is the way that humanity has taken up technology and its development according to an undifferentiated and one-dimensional paradigm…This (technocratic paradigm) has made it easy to accept the idea of infinite or unlimited growth, which proves so attractive to economists, financiers and experts in technology. It is based on the lie that there is an infinite supply of the earth's goods, and this leads to the planet being squeezed dry beyond every limit."

Though he nowhere uses the term "capitalism," it is clear that Francis, like Klein, is leveling a harsh critique of just that economic system, with its exaltation of profits and consumerism, "the lie" upon which it is based, and its "false notion... that the negative effects of the exploitation of the natural order can be easily absorbed."

For those who believe free-market capitalism is the final possible word in economic systems, Francis' analysis is deeply threatening. Un-American, yes, if America is defined by its economic system of the late 20th century. (Although the very notion that America could be defined by any particular economic system may, itself, seem rather "Un-American.")

Francis then proposes a second factor working in concert with the technocratic paradigm to create our present dilemma, a factor prominently remarked upon by John Muir a century earlier. "Modernity has been marked by an excessive anthropocentrism...An inadequate presentation of Christian anthropology gave rise to a wrong understanding of the relationship between human beings and the world. Often, what was handed on was a Promethean vision of mastery over the world, which gave the impression that the protection of nature was something that only the faint-hearted care about. Instead, our 'dominion' over the universe should be understood more properly in the case of responsible stewardship."

The solution? What is needed, Francis says, is a radical change in human culture, an overthrow of the technocratic paradigm and distorted anthropocentrism. "A great cultural, spiritual and educational challenge stands before us, and it will demand that we set out on the long path of renewal...Our efforts at education will be inadequate and ineffectual unless we strive to promote a new way of thinking about human beings, life, society and our relationship with nature." He later promotes conversion to "an integral ecology" paradigm.

At the end, then, Francis' solution to our current dilemma strongly resembles that sketched by Shellenberger and called for by Klein: the earth-centered worldview of southeast Europe villagers, indigenous peoples, and radical environmentalists, "a new way of thinking about human beings, life, society, and our relationship with nature."

Something very like the hidden Muir's Earth Wisdom, in other words.

Inspired by some combination of the scientific studies of 2010-2012, newly energized environmentalism exemplified by the Sierra Club and 350.org, and the writings of Shellenberger, Klein, and Pope Francis, the delegates to the December 2015 UN Conference on the Environment in Paris managed a feat none of the preceding 20 conferences had managed: an agreement to address human-caused climate change.

First, the good news. The 196 countries pledged to roll back their carbon emissions over the next decades, in INDCs (Intended Nationally Determined Contributions) vetted by the governments of each country. They reaffirmed the goal of a temperature rise of 2°C, with 1.5°C as an "aspiration." They would take stock of progress every 5 years, with expectations to ramp up efforts to achieve the 2°C goal at those assessments. Various developed nations pledged US $100 billion a year to the developing world to help it cope with climate change and direct its energy production to renewable forms.

Now the bad news. The INDC's pledged by the countries, upon scientific analysis, would bring the earth's temperature rise down to only 3°C—well above the goal of 2°C, and thus ensuring catastrophic events that would unravel human civilization.

Moreover, none of the agreed-upon provisions are legally binding, except the 5-year stock taking, largely because of the impossibility of getting them approved by the U.S. Senate as then constituted. As James Hansen pointed out in a caustic critique, there are no binding emissions reduction targets, nothing about specific decarbonisation measures to wean economies away from fossil fuels, and no firm date to achieve peak emissions and reduce them thereafter. And the only realistic path to prompt reduction in carbon emission, according to many economists—a tax or fee on carbon extraction and combustion—is neither mentioned nor encouraged by the agreement.

Leading environment groups were cautiously optimistic but clear-eyed. Greenpeace executive director Kumi Naidoo: "Today, the human race has joined in a common cause. The Paris agreement is only one step on a long road and there are parts of it that frustrate, that disappoint me, but it is progress. The deal alone won't dig us out of the hole that we're in, but it makes the sides less steep."

350.org spokesperson May Boeve: "Paris isn't the end of the story, but a conclusion of a particular chapter. Now, it's up to us to strengthen these promises, make sure they are kept, and then accelerate the transition away from fossil fuels and towards 100% renewable energy."

Bill McKibben of 350.org, in the center of the climate battle as long as Hansen, was impatient in the weeks after the conference. "The pistol has fired, so why aren't we running?" He detailed what had to stop immediately (new mining, drilling, fracking—anywhere) and what to start immediately (solar panels, windmills "at a breakneck pace—all over the world").

"At the moment, the world has no real plan to do any of those things. It continues to pretend that merely setting the goal has been work enough for the last two decades...They don't seem to quite get it: from this point on, if you're even slightly serious about meeting these targets, you have to do everything possible. There's no more compromises or trade-offs that can be made. You're no longer negotiating with a bunch of other countries around a conference table. You're negotiating with physics, and physics holds all the good cards."

All valid criticisms. Yet the dawning and blooming of hope in 2014 and 2015 was undeniable. The road map to save human civilization was drawn. Could we summon the will and discipline to follow it?

25

...and Falters (2016)

"This business of driving stakes through the heart of one project after another is exhausting. So many demonstrations, so many meetings. But for now, there's really no other way to kill a zombie."

—Bill McKibben

"We would need a much more aggressive approach than proposed at Paris (in December of 2015); it's not too late to do this, but the train is leaving the station as we speak."

—Toby Ault

In the months leading up to the Paris climate conference of December 2015, fossil fuel executives in Big Oil, Big Coal, and Big Mining recognized the momentum that was building to seriously address climate change. They responded by doubling down in stubborn efforts to protect their profits and continue their planet-wrecking activities for decades into the future, regardless of the cost to human civilization. Business was business; their high-flying lifestyles depended on high profits. And after all, why else had they paid all that money to politicians for 30 years, if not to see their will obeyed?

So the counter-offensive against the Paris agreement began even before the conference convened. As the first INDCs were being sent to Paris in late September 2015, Royal Dutch Shell announced that although it was discontinuing its Arctic exploratory projects, so effectively protested by Greenpeace, the corporation would press forward with its share of mines in Alberta's tar sands, a particularly dirty energy source, and its proposed buyout of England's BG Group.

"After 2050," Shell vice president Andy Norman loftily conceded, looking three and a half decades into the future, "we think that solar will be the single most dominant energy source in the global energy system, and we are working hard to understand where we can play a role in that transition and where opportunities might exist for us."

Nor was Royal Dutch Shell the only extractive corporation whose highly paid executives insisted on the continuation of their planet-altering practices. In October of 2015 the CEOs of ten oil and gas corporations (including BP Group, Saudi Aramco, Statoil, Pemex, and BP, as well as Royal Dutch Shell) met in Paris and pledged to "play their part" to limit global temperature rises to 2°C. They envisioned their "part," however, as merely switching from mainly coal and oil to more of the marginally cleaner fossil fuel of gas. "As a global community, we don't look for a total solution, which would be setting ourselves up for failure, we look for measures we can do," said BG Group CEO Helge Lund.

Greenpeace's Charlie Kronick promptly observed that "The oil companies behind this announcement have spent years lobbying to undermine effective climate action, each and every one of them has a business plan that would lead to dangerous global temperature rises, yet suddenly they expect us all to see them as the solution, not the problem. The world should thank them for their offer of advice but politely turn it down. Arsonists don't make good firefighters."

Also in October 2015, the *Los Angeles Times* and *InsideClimate News* published the explosive results of an investigation of ExxonMobile, based on hundreds of the oil behemoth's internal documents and interviews by Columbia University's Energy and Environmental Reporting Project.

Scientists employed by ExxonMobile knew of the disastrous effects of global warming as early as the 1980s, even before James Hansen publicly raised the alarm, and communicated these findings to the corporation's top executives—who decided to downplay and question the predictions as they vigorously continued with business (i.e. profits) as usual.

By late October 2015 the cutting-edge environmental group 350. org had gathered 49 prominent signatories to an open letter urging U.S. Attorney General Loretta Lynch to investigate. "As leaders of some of the nation's environmental, indigenous peoples, and civil rights groups, we're writing to ask that you initiate a federal probe into the conduct of ExxonMobile," the letter states.

Before any response emerged from the U.S. Attorney General to the petition, the New York state Attorney General's office announced in early November that it was investigating ExxonMobil for possible suppression of evidence of climate change's threat to humanity. "A major focus of the investigation is whether the company adequately warned investors about potential financial risks stemming from society's need to limit fossil-fuel use," according to the *New York Times*.

Kamala Harris, then California's Attorney General, soon announced a similar investigation into Exxon. Within months the Attorneys General of Massachusetts and the U.S. Virgin Islands joined New York and California in the investigation, with other states considering similar action. And U.S. Attorney General Loretta Lynch requested the FBI to begin a federal investigation.

ExxonMobile began to feel serious heat from all this attention. They turned, ironically, to the U.S. House of Representatives Committee on Science, Space, and Technology, 10 of whose 13 Republican members hail from Bible Belt southern states—not exactly bastions of science and technology. These 13 Representatives have received $3,411,173 in career contributions from the fossil fuel industry (defined as oil and gas, coal mining, and electric utilities industries). Chair Lamar Smith and Vice Chair Frank Lucas (both from Texas) have each received over $760,000 from fossil fuel corporations.

All those campaign contributions paid off. The 13 Republican committee members announced on May 18, 2016 that they had requested documents from 17 states' attorneys general and 8 environmental activist organizations (including 350.org, Greenpeace, and the Union of Concerned Scientists) related to their purported "coordinated efforts to deprive (fossil fuel) companies...of their First Amendment rights," claiming that the investigations into ExxonMobile's actions were "efforts to silence speech based on political theater rather than legal or scientific arguments." Greenpeace and 350.org defiantly refused to share their documents, leading to further threats from the distinguished committee and its $760,000 chair and vice chair.

Meanwhile, fossil-fuel corporation TransCanada on January 6 had announced it was invoking the North America Free Trade Agreement (NAFTA) to sue the U.S. government to recover $15 billion in damages over the Obama administration's November 2015 decision to cancel the Keystone XL pipeline. How was this possible? As detailed by Naomi Klein in *This Changes Everything*, NAFTA explicitly guarantees that transnational corporations cannot be deprived of their right to profits by local or national environmental regulations constraining their exploitative economic activities—a provision also reflected in the Trans-Pacific Partnership (TPP) negotiated by Obama, and the Transatlantic Trade and Investment Partnership (TTIP) currently being negotiated. The prospects of ratification for both are uncertain as of fall 2016.

The TransCanada suit will be decided by an arbitration process outside the American judicial system. Lori Wallach, director of Public Citizen's Global Trade Watch, and longtime critic of trade agreement provisions allowing corporations to seek damages, said that TransCanada was bringing its case at a time when panels that hear such disputes seem increasingly more willing to rule against governments. "We've really dodged the bullet to date," she commented.

The devastating consequences of coal-powered electricity-generating plants, highlighted by the Sierra Club, had already led to a discernible shift away from coal in the United States, with three of the four largest corporations (Peabody, Arch Coal, Alpha Natural Resources) declaring bankruptcy in recent years.

But it is a very different story with coal in Asia. In May of 2016, barely four months post-Paris, World Bank president Jim Yong Kim, in "an unusually stark warning," declared that planned coal-fired plants in South Asia would be "disaster for the planet." China has plans to build 150 gigawatts (GW) of such plants by 2020; India, 125 GW; Vietnam 40 GW; and Indonesia 25 GW. The construction of these plants "would make it highly unlikely that we would be able to get to 2°C" as envisioned in Paris, said World Bank senior climate official John Roome.

In the actions recounted above and others, Big Oil, Big Coal, and Big Mining have vigorously attempted to torpedo the resolutions hammered out in Paris in December of 2015. At the very least, they are striving to prolong their activities well into the second half of the 21st century—reaping their customary profits all the way. Quite clearly, profits are more compelling to them than the health of the planet or the fate of human civilization. In these efforts, they have plenty of well-paid allies in the halls of power in Washington, D.C. and other world capitals.

Big Oil, particularly, has continued to be startlingly forthright about its plans to continue the extraction and combustion of fossil fuels for at least the next three and a half decades, admitting only that it may somewhat increase the proportion of marginally-less-polluting natural gas. This despite the clear indications from every scientific panel of the world that the greenhouse gases emitted from combustion of *whatever* fossil fuel at the current rate will very soon lock in levels of global warming and associated climate changes in the 2 to 4°C range of increase, with consequences that will have devastating effects on human civilization.

We have seen that among these affects will be widespread drought, famine, severe-weather episodes, flooding of coastal areas, and creation of climate refugees in the hundreds of millions, which will together bring about the death of millions of people. These sobering conclusions are based on studies by numerous scientists, historians, and the International Energy

Agency (2011), the World Bank (2012), and the American Association for the Advancement of Science (2014).

Which inevitably brings up an interesting question. If the International Criminal Court and its associated specific Tribunals at The Hague can prosecute warlords from the Balkans and Africa for crimes against humanity resulting in the deaths of *thousands* of people, should the court not consider the prosecution of Big Oil executives for their actions which will lead to the deaths of *millions*?

Can this be anything but a crime against humanity?

Can crime on such a scale be ignored?

But we are getting ahead of the story. May of 2016 produced more discouraging developments. Shareholder meetings of Exxon and Chevron saw the lopsided defeat of resolutions presented by climate activist investors. Chevron CEO John Watson emphatically rejected a call to tax carbon emissions. "When people talk about a price on carbon, you're talking about raising the price of energy—you're talking about raising the price of everything," he declared, which he insisted would hurt the world's poor, hungry for affordable energy to improve their lives. The spectacle of a Big Oil executive piously claiming concern for the world's poor passed with nary a comment.

Some environmental organizations attempted to counter the fossil fuel corporations' well-organized and richly-financed offensive post-Paris. 350. org had tabbed May as the month for worldwide demonstrations against fossil fuel extraction, its *Break Free 2016* campaign. In dozens of countries, impressively passionate and disciplined protesters blocked and often occupied sites for days on end. Yet for all that, the actual numbers involved in each action were disappointing: more often in the dozens or hundreds than thousands. No event remotely approached the size of the fall 2014 New York City march on the United Nations. And certainly no extractionist activities were abandoned or even shut down for long.

At the end of the month, energy ministers from the world's largest economies met at a Clean Energy Ministerial in San Francisco to discuss how to transition to renewable energy, with clean-technology entrepreneurs from Silicon Valley amply represented. The *San Francisco Chronicle* noted the four-day conference came "at a time of immense promise and uncertainty." Yet no announcements of important developments emerged from the meetings. Though several international meetings were scheduled before the next UN Climate Conference in Morocco in November 2016, translating the Paris pledges and goals into reality was proving to be a daunting task.

The dawn of hope in 2014 and 2015, which had seemed to blossom in Paris, looked to have wilted in the ensuing months under the relentless and well-financed fossil fuel counter-offensive. Most of the mainline environmental groups were strangely silent. Even the Sierra Club seemed unable to mount a campaign commensurate with the gravity of the moment. The fatigue of the relatively few environmentalists battling in the trenches—350.org and Greenpeace principal among them—bordered on heart breaking. 350.org's Bill McKibben compared it to fighting the undead, in a January 19, 2016 column in the *Los Angeles Times*, just weeks after the conclusion of the Paris UN conference. The essay's title: "Can zombie fossil fuel be killed? Only by putting a stake through its heart, one project at a time."

McKibben describes how "local activists are making desperate stands to stop new fossil fuel projects, while the energy companies are making equally desperate attempts to build while they still can. The outcome of these thousands of fights, as much or more than the paper promises made at the UN climate conference in Paris in December, will determine whether we emerge from this century with a habitable planet...The protests are endless, and the protesters have to be endlessly resourceful...This business of driving stakes through the heart of one project after another is exhausting. So many demonstrations, so many meetings. But for now, there's really no other way to kill a zombie."

Aside from his weary confusing of vampire-vanquishing technique with zombie-vanquishing, McKibben was right-on. He continued to produce brilliant, hard-hitting depictions of the stakes involved, including an August 2016 piece in *The New Republic* likening the struggle to World

War III, and another chronicling the alarming decline in the health of the oceans. ("On an ocean planet, we are wrecking the ocean"!)

October of 2016 saw the release of a study revealing that climate change is producing a 70% chance of megadroughts lasting three to four decades ravaging the Southwest United States (centered in California, Arizona, Nevada, and New Mexico) before the end of the century, if current rainfall patterns continue. If rainfall in the region declines, as most climate-change models forecast, the odds of megadroughts increases to 90%. With groundwater tables already dropping precipitously throughout the region, these conditions would render dense urban centers such as Los Angles, Las Vegas, and Phoenix uninhabitable, and cripple agriculture throughout the region.

The study's lead author, Toby Ault of Cornell University, commented on what it would take to avoid these near-certain megadroughts. "We would need a much more aggressive approach than proposed at Paris (in December of 2015); it's not too late to do this, but the train is leaving the station as we speak."

The same month saw a report from the Global Commission on the Economy and Climate, co-chaired by leading climate change economist Lord Nicholas Stern. Noting that the world is expected to invest $90 trillion of infrastructure (power plants, roads, buildings, sanitation) in the next 15 years, including 1500 coal plants already in construction, Stern and the other authors called for an *urgent and immediate* shift to low-carbon projects, away from the current carbon-heavy plans.

"We cannot continue with business as usual, which will lock in high-carbon infrastructure and create further congestion and pollution while choking off development opportunities, particularly for poor people," he noted. "We can and should invest in and build cities where we can move and breathe and be productive, while protecting the natural world that underpins our livelihoods."

Several days later, World Bank President Jim Yong Kim, frustrated by the continuing lack of movement toward carbon-light investments that would give the Paris pledges a realistic hope of being met, reiterated his

May warning of the disastrous consequences of the planned South Asian coal-fired power plants (some already under construction). He pointed to Lord Stern's report, and seconded the urgent call for all infrastructure investments to be shifted from carbon-heavy to carbon-light.

Despite McKibben's drumbeat of articles, looming megadroughts in the U.S., and plaintive calls for urgent action from the World Bank president and economists such as Lord Stern, concrete steps from those with the power to confront the climate crisis remained woefully few. In the most critical moment of mankind's 200,000-year history on the planet, the forces of destruction seemed to have the upper hand.

Even with increasing droughts and extreme weather events, widespread fires, and relentless waves of refugees from southern countries, with the role of fossil fuel combustion clearly understood in bringing about the existential threat to human civilization on the planet—yet the greed of Big Oil, Big Coal, and Big Mining still ruled, and venal politicians dutifully blocked effective responses. The crushing inertia of a worldview solidly based on the notion that humans are the center of the world, superior to other life forms and not constrained by the laws governing the rest of life, was relentlessly preventing the necessary urgent responses to climate change.

If the human experiment on the planet were to escape catastrophe and survive, something had to change. Something fundamental. And quickly.

Here we must turn to John Muir and the Two Perfected Lords of Mt. Huakai. Doubtless they are now sauntering along a shaded path under tall pines and cedars on some lofty mountain slope, a clear stream gurgling beside them, amiably discussing the merits of various medicinal teas, and the evidence of glacial sculpturing at nearby high passes. We must interrupt them, courteously, and ask if we might borrow the Gaiacentric, immanent worldview from them, to offer to the world in its hour of great need.

They will hesitate. As we have seen, though vigorous and tough, they are not fond of controversy. Will this require that they descend to the dusty valleys and engage in argument with greedy, shouting men? No, we inform them. You have given us Taoism and Earth Wisdom, through your writings, your wanderings, your lives. We merely want to borrow your precious legacy, and present it to the world.

Hearing this, they smile shyly. Shrug their shoulders. Whatever. Good luck, they say, and turn back to their mountain rambles with sparkling eyes. Soon they are out of sight amongst the trees.

But we have their legacy. Surely this is the moment for the hidden Muir to emerge from its century-long obscurity, to offer the environmental movement and the rest of humanity a path to change the human relationship with the earth: Earth Wisdom, the Gaiacentric, immanent worldview it shares with Taoism and modern science.

26

The Immanent: how to kill a zombie

*"Our efforts at education will be inadequate and ineffectual un-
less we strive to promote a new way of thinking about human
beings, life, society and our relationship with nature...We do need
to slow down and look at reality in a different way."*

—POPE FRANCIS

We have seen in Parts One and Two of this volume that John Muir and
the Taoist tradition of China independently developed a common,
three-pillared worldview, rejecting anthropocentrism for Gaiacentrism.
Intrinsic to Earth Wisdom and Taoism is the *immanent* stance: an earth-
centered approach to understanding reality that focuses on the actual,
manifest world. A third worldview, the Darwinism of modern science,
also shares this stance and these pillars. (The immanent worldview contrasts with the human-centered, *transcendent* one of Western religions and
Buddhism, which focuses on a future state "beyond" the earth, whether
conceived of as Heaven or Nirvana.)

Part Three of this volume traces how civilization's very survival is
threatened by consequences of unbridled economic activity exploiting the
natural world, particularly the reliance on fossil fuels as an energy source.
We have seen that this destructive treatment of the earth is rooted in the
anthropocentric worldview, which sees humans as superior to the planet's

other life forms, and not constrained by the laws governing the rest of life. Indeed, the Judaeo-Christian perspective, upon which the modern West was founded, claims humans as uniquely created in the image of God, and explicitly commanded to have dominion over the planet and exploit it.

Thoughtful observers from various backgrounds—including Shellenberger from the environmental, Naomi Klein from the secularist, and Pope Francis from the religious—have recently come to the same startling conclusion: only the widespread adoption of a new way of thinking about the earth, and the place of humans on it, can provide the necessary impetus for the world's leaders to modify the governing economic system and avert the looming catastrophe. And this must occur within a decade, at most.

Working within the currently dominant anthropocentric worldview, an alliance of four decades among scientists, environmental organizations, and policy makers has consistently failed to adequately address the threat of climate change. Their best, indeed only noteworthy achievement, the December 2015 UN Climate Summit in Paris, produced nothing more than nonbinding pledges to reduce carbon emissions to 3°C, far short of the 2°C level necessary to avert disaster to human civilization.

Meeting even these pledges amid the inevitable changes in governments and renewed resistance of fossil fuel corporations will be difficult. Expanding these pledges to meet the 2°C benchmark will be highly unlikely—within the current anthropocentric worldview. The lack of meaningful movement toward even the minimal Paris goals in the ensuing year after Paris has clearly established this. The calls for an entirely new way of thinking must be heeded, then, and soon.

But the appeals of Shellenberger, Klein, and Pope Francis have fallen on deaf ears, it may be said. Why persist? Curiously, these three did a superb job of delineating the problem and its underlying causes, but gave their proposed solutions short shrift. Shellenberger barely sketched his suggestions in 2004, in a paragraph or two. Klein in 2014 devoted a dozen dense chapters to analyzing the problem—the capitalistic system and its drive for profits—with meticulous footnotes. Yet she devotes mere pages to the indigenous worldviews that might somehow inspire a mass movement, leaving the reader wishing for a treatment of the solution more on a scale with that of the problem.

The same with Pope Francis. His encyclical's trenchant analysis of the technologic paradigm and excessive anthropomorphism is lengthy and persuasive. Yet while he calls ringingly for a new way of thinking about the place of humans in nature, on the one hand, he insists in numerous places that humans are, indeed, still exceptional in the eyes of God. It is merely "distorted" anthropocentrism that underlies today's unprecedented crisis, he thinks. Beyond an emphasis on education, the rejection of the technocratic paradigm, and introducing the phrase "integrated ecology," he assays precious little description of his new way of thinking and how it might spread.

In this current volume, I have attempted to complement the efforts of Shellenberger, Klein, and Pope Francis by examining in considerable detail the experiences that give rise to the immanent worldview contained in Earth Wisdom, Taoism, and Darwinism; the most prominent principles and features of the new worldview; and how they contrast with the old anthropocentric stance.

So let us be clear. The root of the current existential crisis facing humanity is the old worldview that humans are the center of the universe, created uniquely in the image of a supernatural creator of the world, and enjoined by that creator to have dominion over the earth. This worldview engenders and supports the capitalistic economic system exploiting the resources of the natural world, emphasizing profits and growth as fundamental goals overriding all other concerns.

This archaic, mistaken anthropocentric stance must be replaced with an immanent, Gaiacentric one, if human civilization is to survive on the planet. Again, Pope Francis: "Our efforts at education will be inadequate and ineffectual unless we strive to promote a new way of thinking about human beings, life, society and our relationship with nature...We do need to slow down and look at reality in a different way." And as Naomi Klein states: "The task is to articulate not just an alternative set of policy proposals but an alternative worldview to rival the one at the heart of the ecological crisis."

We have three vigorous, coherent worldviews that satisfy these requirements. Earth Wisdom, Taoism, and Darwinism all share the three pillars of the immanent worldview. The earth is our home, the focus of our existence, the provider of all we need. We are related to all other life in kinship, one creature among many, and not marked for special privileges. And reality is generated by the complementary interplay of two clusters of phenomena, the yin and feminine being just as important as the yang and masculine.

These three pillars shared by these three worldviews will be the salvation of humanity on our planet—if we can but persuade enough of us to actively espouse the immanent worldview and demand that our rulers heed its demands. What will that take?

The Three A's. It will take, in the first instance, the frequent *articulation* and description of the new stance. One of the great puzzles of the last century of environmentalism in America has been the nearly complete absence of any articulation of the overarching worldview behind its concerns. The websites of dozens of mainline groups are brimming with beautiful photos of habitats and ugly photos of pollution, surrounded by numerous ways to send money to save the former and banish the latter. Yet mention of what's behind all this? The worldview that the groups stand for? Never mentioned. Rarely even alluded to.

The one exception to this is the radical environmentalist groups. The Gaiacentric stance they have taken is out of the cultural mainstream; it makes people uncomfortable. All right. People need to be made uncomfortable at this stage of an existential crisis, early and often (as Lyndon Baines Johnson said of the need to vote in his Texas elections).

So the first step is prominent articulation and description of the worldview and three pillars of Earth Wisdom or Taoism or Darwinism, whichever seems most persuasive. The immanent stance they all exemplify must be proclaimed, explained, and constantly placed before the peoples of the world.

The second step is *advocacy*. The current crisis threatening the human presence on earth, its creation by the anthropocentric worldview, and its resolution by the Gaiacentric, immanent worldview—this must be front and center always, must be analyzed and advocated in every public forum. How and why the new stance will resolve the crisis, which I explore below, should be a constant refrain.

And only then, when articulation and advocacy have laid the base, can meaningful **action** attract the overwhelming support needed for success. Only when masses of the world's population have been persuaded by articulation and advocacy for one of the immanent worldviews will they render the requisite action unavoidable, whether in a democracy or an authoritative regime.

The advocacy of any of the three versions of the immanent, Gaiacentric stance will highlight two great advantages resulting from its widespread adoption.

<u>Advantage of effectiveness</u>. First, the actions necessary to avert catastrophe will become markedly easier to gain support and more effective in their results. For the past four decades, all the efforts of scientists, environmentalists, and policy makers to curb the ravages of the extractionist, fossil-fuel corporations have been agonizingly difficult. So long as the anthropocentric worldview is dominant, advocating for the non-human world and for constraints on the comfort and profit of humans is an uphill slog, paddling against a strong upstream current, as it were. Like trying to kill zombies, as Bill McKibben of 350.org says.

Thus in the current anthropocentric society, environmental organizations have long been playing an exhausting game of "whack-a-mole," rushing about to preserve a critical habitat at one location, only to see ten more threats pop up as the one is being dealt with—sometimes successfully, often not. Untold hours of negotiation and threats are required to enact minimal policy changes to barely acceptable limits of toxins in air and water, or incremental increases in gasoline mileage.

In these never-ending, against-the-current efforts, success is never assured and often elusive. But as frequent articulation and advocacy of Earth Wisdom, Darwinism, and Taoism converts more of the world's peoples to the immanent, Gaiacentric worldview, the current will shift. Paddling against the current now becomes paddling *with* the current; efforts now have the wind at their back. The actions flowing from articulation and advocacy will now have widespread, insistent public support. From the Gaiacaentric viewpoint, actions to salvage human civilization become spontaneous and obvious, "no-brainers" to large segments of the population.

If earth is our true home, and provides all that we need if we but respect it, then *of course* we will desist from destroying the natural world upon which we depend. Of course we will promptly shift to power sources which do not spew greenhouse gases baking the planet. Whatever got into us, sticking with such polluting sources as coal, oil, and gas for so long?

Of course we will cease poisoning waters, atmosphere and soil, interfering with the ancient cleansing cycles of the planet. Of course we will respect the limits of photosynthesis and hence food production of the planet. How could we have ever imagined that humans alone of all species on the earth are immune from the restraint of carrying capacity and the other ecologic laws of the planet?

When the various versions of the immanent worldview are widely adopted, biodiversity will be assiduously cultivated rather than destroyed; other creatures are our kin! We depend upon them, from bacteria to benthic stream invertebrates to insect-devouring bats, to keep the planet's living systems balanced, productive, and healthy. *Of course* we will protect biodiversity and ensure its flourishing health. This is our home. If we hurt it, we hurt ourselves.

Widespread adoption of the immanent worldview in the coming years will provide exactly the "other way to kill a zombie" McKibben yearns for. Adamant, irresistible society-wide disapproval of habitat-exploitive projects will render them clearly outside the boundary of acceptable actions; they will no longer be seriously broached. Leaders will be compelled to actually lead where the world's people demand.

Advantage of truth. The second advantage of the immanent, Gaiacentric worldview as a basis for the new way of thinking urged by Pope Francis, Klein, and Shellenberger is simply that it represents the most accurate description of "the way things are" in the world. Put succinctly, *it is the truth*—at least our closest contemporary approximation to the actual state of reality.

Muir and Taoists such as the Two Perfected Lords came to the three pillars of Earth Wisdom and Taoism by critically and closely observing the world with open eyes and open mind. "By looking!" as the *Daodejing* puts it. They described what they saw. Thus their "method" (one translation of *tao*) of garnering input to their worldview was fundamentally similar to that of science. The accuracy of their vision has been amply established by modern science's several centuries of findings in numerous fields. Because of this, the immanent stance regards science as a friend, and is fully consistent with scientific findings. Consider the three pillars of the immanent stance.

<u>First-pillar evidence</u>. The first pillar notes that this world, the earth, is the proper focus of existence, the true home of all life. Science now has ample evidence that life evolved on the earth and responded to its changing conditions over the eons. The fossil record clearly shows all the planet's life forms coming into existence during this long process, including the mammals in the early Mesozoic era. After the demise of the dinosaurs in the late Mesozoic, mammals proliferated, including the tree-dwelling primate order. As the climate dried in the Cenozoic's Pliocene epoch, some primate apes ventured onto the spreading savannahs in Africa, and hominids appear in the fossil record. A series of hominid species proliferated in a bush-like evolutionary pattern; out of that constellation of upright, hands-free primates (including multiple species in the genera *Ardipithecus*, *Australopithecus*, and *Homo*) emerged *Homo erectus*, which gave rise to today's *Homo sapiens*.

Far from lowering the status of humans, this view incorporates us into a momentous, staggering spectacle. As Darwin ended his *Origin of Species* a century and a half ago: "There is grandeur in this view of life, with its several powers, having been originally breathed into a few forms or into one; and that, whilst this planet has gone cycling on according to the fixed law of gravity, from so simple a beginning endless forms most beautiful and most wonderful have been, and are being, evolved."

<u>Second pillar evidence</u>. Consider the judgment of science on the second pillar of immanence, the kinship of all creatures, humans merely one among many. The fossil evidence cited above, and everything else science has learned of humans, contradicts the notion of human "exceptionalism." Humans are composed of the same molecules as every other life form. The "plan" for humans is encoded in the same DNA with the same four nucleotides as the instructions for *Escherichia coli* bacteria, Giant Sequoia trees, Banana slugs, and all life in between.

One by one, all the old traits that we formerly regarded unique to humans have been identified in other animals. *Tool use* is widespread, occurring not just in primates such as chimpanzees, but also in elephants, and many birds including crows, Egyptian vultures, Green herons, and Galapagos finches. Even invertebrates use tools, defined broadly as objects put to a utilitarian use, as for example the coconut octopus (*Amphioctopus marginatus*) which carries a coconut shell into which it can hide when threatened.

Language (defined as meaningful communication between individuals, either verbal or nonverbal) occurs in chimpanzees and bonobos, elephants, bats, prairie dogs, dolphins, whales, and sea lions. Among invertebrates, language has been demonstrated in honey bees and reef squid (who use color, patterns, and flashing to send messages to other squid).

Even being *conscious* of one's self, perhaps the last bastion of supposed human uniqueness, has recently been shown (by experiments with mirrors, in which the subject recognizes that the reflection is, indeed, their own self) in not just our close cousins chimpanzees and bonobos, but also orangutans, elephants, dolphins, and even in a bird, the magpie (no surprise there; remember the old Heckle and Jeckle cartoon magpies from Terrytoons).

Nor are humans exceptional in their outsized influence on the planet; other groups in the past have dominated the planet much as we do today. The Trilobites were extraordinarily successful and plentiful marine arthropods for 270 million years in the Paleozoic era. They diversified into eleven orders, thousands of genera, many thousands of species, occupying nearly every ecological niche of the seas. *They are now extinct.*

The non-avian dinosaurs were extraordinarily successful and plentiful for 135 million years in the Mesozoic's Jurassic and Cretaceous periods, dominating the terrestrial vertebrate fauna. Over 500 genera have been identified, and over a thousand species, in virtually every terrestrial niche. *They are now extinct.*

Nothing indicates that humans might be exempt from this pattern. Science, as well as common sense, then, demonstrates quite conclusively that humans are not unique and specially favored, given the planet to do with as we please for all time by a God whose image we, alone, bear. The immanent view's second pillar recognizes this scientific fact, and the overwhelming evidence supporting a Gaiacentric view of reality, replacing the outdated and unsupported anthropocentric view.

<u>Third pillar evidence</u>. The third pillar of the immanent stance recognizes that a duality exists within a broad range of phenomenon on the planet. Sun and shade, light and dark, can be distinguished in landscapes and their distinctive effects noted, as Muir did looking at Yosemite Valley and its glacial past from the vantage point of his Sunnyside Bench. The same is true for fire and water, for heat and cold, for oxidative and reducing chemical reactions among molecules, for the right and left sides of the human brain—all signified by the yin-yang concept in Taoism.

The phenomenon of duality and its complementary mode of working applies for females and males among sexually-reproducing plants and animals, as science has established. Among a wide variety of species, each sex has been shown to have its own particular role and attributes which contribute importantly to the whole—at a minimum in reproduction, and often beyond that to other areas and activities as well, such as social organization.

For example, among mammals with social systems, those are most often led by females of the group, as shown by E.O. Wilson in his *Sociobiology*. At the same time, it is also true that the mammals exhibit a degree of plasticity in social systems; in some species, males are typically dominant over females. Our own species, along with our cousin species the chimpanzee (*Pan troglodytes*), represents an example of this latter arrangement. Though, interestingly enough, our other cousin species, the bonobo (*Pan paniscus*), is marked by the more common female leadership in society.

Many more examples could be adduced of the complementary interaction of dualities producing our shared existence on the planet, the insight of the third pillar of the immanent worldview.

A foundation of truth. We thus see that the three-pillared immanent, Gaiacaentric viewpoint of Earth Wisdom, Taoism, and Darwinism is in accordance with the nature of reality on the planet earth, as the careful observation of the scientific enterprise has established it. Immanence provides a firm, reliable foundation for Klein's and Pope Francis' new way of thinking about the relation of humans and the planet—a foundation that represents accurately the way the world works. Though it has perhaps not always been the case, having a foundation based upon truth bodes well for any enterprise.

For the widespread adoption of the immanent, Gaicentric worldview to occur—and promptly—the many individuals and groups struggling to save humanity from the impending climate change catastrophe must articulate and advocate their favored version of the immanent view prominently and frequently, whether Earth Wisdom, Taoism, or Darwinism. The varied voices must coalesce into one persuasive message that can change lives and societies, and provide the unstoppable impetus for world leaders to perform the difficult work that must be done.

But what about those actions that we foresee flowing from the immanent view's adoption? What will be the general outlines of a society based on the immanent, Gaiacentric worldview?

A Rough Map to the Immanent Society

"Awe in the face of mystery and majesty (of the natural world) has the power to transform behavior."

—D.M. YEAGER

Let us begin a description of what happens when the immanent worldview is widely adopted by noting an important point. Choosing the path of the immanent in human society will not "save the earth"—because the earth itself is not fundamentally threatened.

Continuing along the bleak path based upon the anthropocentric worldview and our current exploitive economic model will not, in fact, "destroy the earth." Changes will occur, to be sure. Individual plants and animals will die in the widespread droughts and fires. Many species will go extinct. Others will see their ranges shrink or expand. Many more habitats will be destroyed by continuing extractive activities. Coral reefs certainly will disappear, and shelled marine life become dramatically less important on the planet.

These sorts of things have happened before, many times. As early as 1982, David Raup and John Sepkoski showed in a famous *Science* article that major extinction episodes have occurred periodically throughout the history of life on the planet, roughly every 26 to 30 million years. And life, though changed, continues. New species appear, adapted to the new conditions.

So the earth will survive even if humanity chooses to continue its path to the unraveling of civilization. The tides will roll in and out, the moon above will wax and wane; seeds will germinate; birds will migrate in the spring and fall; the stars will rotate overhead throughout the night whether human eyes notice it or not.

All will be well, as the planet shrugs and moves on.

But will there be humans in functioning societies to participate in the planet's continuing cycles? That is the issue. What is fundamentally called into question by the present course of climate change is *viable human civilization* on the earth. It is humanity that is critically threatened in the anthropocentric scenario, because the only destination on this current path is misery leading to barbarism: overcrowded societies in narrow bands of habitable conditions, constantly fending off epidemics, and warring for diminishing resources—with extinction of the human species quite possible after several miserable centuries.

So the choice between the current anthropocentric situation and a possible earth-centered immanence will have enormous implications for humanity. But for the earth it will not be of any lasting importance. A blip of turbulence, then the ancient systems move on, another interesting and briefly dominant species left behind.

We humans, though, would prefer to persist much longer than another several dystopian centuries on the planet. To us it is, in fact, quite important to avoid the descent to barbarism and our possible early extinction. We have seen that the first step is to articulate and advocate for the various versions of the Gaiacentric, immanent worldview, resulting in the creation of an irresistible, worldwide popular movement. Leaders will be persuaded to make policy decisions and take actions in line with the immanent stance. But what does this new worldview lead to in society itself? What kind of life is lived in a Gaiacentric culture?

Let us begin by briefly outlining the overarching direction of changes in the move toward an immanent society, as reflected in the three pillars.

First: More Earth, living here and now;
Less Heaven, living in the future and elsewhere.
Second: More Kinship with all earth's creatures;
Less Human superiority and focus.
Third: More Yin traits expressed; Less Yang dominance.
(More cooperation, acceptance, nurturing, and feminine;
Less competition, dominance, destruction, and masculine)

These guidelines will inform all the changes in the transformation to an immanent society.

Experiencing the immanent. Some people will make the shift to the new worldview as a result of learning about the shared role of humans with our kin species in the evolution and ecology of the planet, and the dependence of humans upon the healthy functioning of the natural world. For them, a *cognitive* change is sufficient. But for most people, a fundamental shift in attitude or worldview requires an *affective* rather than a cognitive change.

"To perceive something as beautiful (or sublime) is to perceive it as worthy of care. We are not cruel to that which we perceive to be lovely. That which we treasure, we preserve and inspire others to preserve...Awe in the face of mystery and majesty (of the natural world) has the power to transform behavior," observes ethicist D.M. Yeager of Georgetown University.

It was lightly snowing as my wife, two children and I slushed up the slope of the Mariposa Grove in Yosemite Park on snowshoes one recent winter. The sound of our passage was the only noise in the snow-blanketed forest, other than the kids' occasional comment of how cold and wet they were. After some half hour we turned a corner, and there it was. An enormous Giant Sequoia tree towered in a clearing straight ahead. The "Grizzly Giant" already seemed huge, from fifty yards away, but as we snowshoed up to it, our disbelief grew apace. Soon we stood beside it: this creature clothed in shaggy red bark, marked by black fire scars, was 40 feet from side to side, and reached over 200 feet into the leaden sky. It had been two thousand years old when Columbus arrived in the Americas. We stood in stunned silence—even the kids.

Other times, awe in the face of the natural world evokes shouts. Several springs ago my wife and I were on a vessel in the middle of Monterey Bay in central California. For the past hour our group of 30 chilly eco-tourists had watched schools of California sea lions cruising the choppy waters, and packs of Risso's dolphins playfully coursing beside the bow of our boat. Then, not eighty feet to the left, a humpback whale erupted from the ocean, water cascading off its sides. Only half of its hundred-foot body arced above the surface, but that was plenty to provoke shouts and screams from all of us.

The massive spiraling body hung in the air for a second, looming beside us larger by far than a school bus, the barnacles encrusting its sides clearly visible. Then it submitted to gravity and crashed back to the ocean, sending huge waves in all directions and rocking our boat.

A brief, staggered silence, then the screams of wonder erupted from us again, and laughter, wave after wave of laughter as sheer joy somehow surged within us. As my oldest daughter described a similar experience later, "It was as if an angel had touched us!" Indeed.

Most people must *experience* the grandeur of the natural world and learn to love it before they will be moved to cherish and protect it. This means escaping more often and for longer durations into natural environments, where the touch of humans is but lightly felt. It does not have to be a "wilderness." Too much ink by far has been wasted on academic arguments about whether there is in today's world—or ever has been—a true wilderness. We do not require a strictly human-less "wilderness" to connect with the natural world and enter into an immanent relationship with it. All we require are places where humanity's eager hand has not extensively transformed the environment from its natural state of high species diversity, and subverted its wonted cycles.

Not many of us can, like John Muir, "throw some tea and bread into an old sack and jump over the back fence" to get into a patch of the natural world. This is possible for the fortunate amongst us who live next to a forest preserve in New England, or have a home along a coast or in the foothills of the Sierra Nevada. But for most of us, getting into the natural world in a serious way requires a bit of planning and gear. It is important to go to the trouble, though.

Much is made these days of having a healthy work-life balance. All to the good. But there is another balance which must be struck: *the human-earth balance*. Too many of us spend all our time in the world of human cares, concerns, controversies, and artifacts. We are hardly ever not in the midst of a city, negotiating the demands of life made by existence surrounded by "cement, asphalt, glass and metal," as Pope Francis put it. The "news" (composed of the struggles and difficulties of human activities) dominates our minds and hours—our lives.

Enough. We cannot exclude the larger whole and remain healthy and happy. A shift is required, instead, to a more realistic human-earth balance. We are not alien, independent creatures; we evolved in the natural world and our bodies and minds need its presence and input. The immanent worldview is not just the truth of our existence; it is the necessary ingredient to make us complete. To make us happy.

So being complete and happy means carving out opportunities in our busy lives to camp, bicycle, kayak or hike in natural areas. Here in the United States, we are fortunate to have (thanks to Muir and his movement) an abundance of national and state parks, seashores, monuments, marine sanctuaries, and yes, "wilderness" areas, in which we can reconnect with the natural world and nurture an immanent stance in the living of our lives.

And when we spend time in the natural world, we bring others along with us to experience the beauty and wonder: our friends, our children, our parents, our classmates, our workmates. The experience must be amenable to its visitors, which means we must be prepared to handle the challenges presented to us by the natural world. Tents with rain flies, and people with rain gear; sunscreen and protective hats to temper solar radiation; packs appropriately light for oldsters and youngsters; kayaks with "dry bags" to protect cameras and binoculars; walking shoes adequate for the trails. And plenty of guidebooks.

While several long summer or winter trips into the heart of the natu-ral world are key, shorter jaunts throughout the year will become a habit for us. A day in a forest or along a river or shoreline is plenty to remind ourselves of how beautiful, how vital, how important the natural world is, not just for us, but in its own right. We will all have a *rota* of day excursions within easy drive of our homes, and we will know them well. Nor must we leave the cities to experience the natural world. Most cities have parks and natural areas within their boundaries, in which elements of the natural world are present. We will be regular visitors in these spots.

Noticing the natural world even within the city means we're not star-ing at our smartphones. As Pope Francis observes, "When media and the digital world become omnipresent, their influence can stop people from learning how to live wisely, to think deeply and to love generously...a mere accumulation of data which eventually leads to overload and confusion, a sort of mental pollution."

So we turn our smartphones off, regularly and often; we put them away, out of our sight and hearing. We keep our kids from becoming ad-dicted to them, perhaps the most important (and difficult) task of modern parents. We look up at the clouds in the sky, and take a deep breath. Focus on our friends and family, the birds and insects in the photosynthesizing trees around us. The great cycling planet upon which we're privileged to exist, surrounded by the products of four billion years of life changing and adapting to geological processes and cycling seasons. *Be Here Now.*

If you're fortunate enough to have a backyard, spend time there. I have a habit of sleeping on a cot in my backyard on full-moon nights during the summer and fall, reminding me of what a miracle stars are, and how evoca-tive and beautiful the moon is, particularly when high clouds are soaring across it. The morning advance of light, and the awakening of bird and insect life in the towering oaks above me, are magical starts to the day.

If we are raising children, our highest parental privilege and duty is to expose them to the beauty and wonder of the natural world, to give them the precious gift of adventures (and occasional misadventures) in that world, and knowledge of the fascinating lives of its plant and animal inhabitants. A healthy human-earth balance will become an integral and valued aspect of their lives—and ours.

Spending time in the natural world, we come to love it. Loving it, we are moved to protect it. As we experience the natural world, the rightness of the immanent worldview becomes clear to us, and the integral ecology paradigm sinks its roots and spreads its limbs, whether we are most interested in Earth Wisdom, Taoism, or Darwinism.

<u>Educating about the immanent</u>. Pope Francis rightly emphasizes education as a key element in the process by which the immanent worldview and its integral ecology paradigm spreads. This education incorporates and refers to the scientific discoveries which so forcefully demonstrate the primacy of the natural world, how its intricately interlocking cycles and creatures provide the framework of all life and living on the planet, including human. And how the disruption or ignorance of "how the world works" results in impoverished human lives, and dysfunctional human societies. Ecology, energy flow in ecosystems, biogeochemical cycles, population dynamics, symbiotic partnerships, ocean chemistry and dynamics, the rudimentary taxonomy of life, and the biology of the planet's array of creatures will all be taught and learned in our schools, from the early to the later levels as appropriate, if viable human populations are to persist on the planet.

While science will be the foundation of education in integral ecology, history will also be important. As Jared Diamond so convincingly details in *Collapse: How Societies Choose to Fail or Succeed*, the record of human civilizations on the planet also demonstrates that viable human culture depends on the natural world. When you destroy elements of the natural world around you, you doom your human culture to dysfunction or extinction, whether it is today's Haitians on Hispaniola, or the past's Petra in Jordan, Easter Island in the Pacific, the Anasazi in the American Southwest, or the Mayans in central America, whose demise is succinctly related in a recent study: "Overpopulation, environmental degradations and drought, followed by famine and disease, created a 'perfect storm' to bring down the great lords and their kingdoms…Finally, only squatters eked out a subsistence living among the remains of the once-great cities." Our current worldwide civilization is in no way immune from such extinctions of societies chronicled in the past.

Both public and private school curricula will have week-long field trips to the many environmental camps now existing, and others that will appear. Here students will be immersed within a natural setting, and learn from knowledgeable teachers the interactions of soil, weather, and the plants and animals with which they share their local habitats. They will see what star-studded skies look like outside of cities, and learn about the great cycles of the natural world that Muir chronicled and rejoiced in.

On a recent jaunt to kayak the sea caves of Santa Cruz Island off the southern coast of California, we shared the camp site with 50 students from Santa Barbara's Anacapa School, who spent a day each kayaking, snorkeling the Giant kelp forests, and helping restore the sheep-disturbed island habitat. Perfect. The numerous existing natural history museums will be enjoyed throughout the year as frequent adjuncts to such field trips.

Incorporating the immanent in society's infrastructure. It is all very good to incorporate the experience of the natural world—which gives rise to the immanent viewpoint—in our personal lives and that of our families, and to structure an educational system that teaches our youth the critical scientific and historic knowledge of "the way things are," including our integral participation in that working. But beyond all that, important though it is, the successful transformation from the anthropocentric, technocratic paradigm to the Gaiacentric, integral ecology worldview will result in changes to the infrastructure of human societies reflecting the new paradigm. It is not possible to explore all that must happen, in this volume. But a few things can be highlighted here.

First, women will be permitted full participation in the life of society and its institutions. Many studies show that as females became emancipated and enter fully into the social compact, societies improve in infant survival, in life expectancy, in education, in income, and various other measures of prosperity. All this requires that women be allowed full access to education and to decision-making roles, throughout the economic, political, and social aspects of society.

This applies to religious institutions as well. Though it is the oldest continuous institution in the West, the Roman Catholic Church will shrivel and become irrelevant in human society if some courageous Pope does not, soon, boldly declare that female priests are not forbidden by the Bible, and are welcome to join their male colleagues in leading the church forward into the modern world of the immanent view. It would be a shame if the positive aspects of Roman Catholic tradition—its music, its rituals, its sense of community—were to disappear from human society; but it will surely happen if such changes are not made, and soon.

Cities will bring more of the natural world into their geography. That means more parks and green spaces, creeks liberated from their concrete channels and coursing merrily through urban areas, trees common everywhere, outdoor playgrounds liberally spaced, and plentiful funds devoted to the upkeep and security needed to permit all to enjoy the city's natural areas in safety. Even Los Angeles is currently searching for the funds (and the gumption) to liberate a small portion of the Los Angeles River from its long-channelized cement straitjacket. If Los Angles can contemplate such an action, there is surely hope for such measures everywhere.

Nor is it a given that today's cities are doomed to relentless increase in size, pollution, and gridlock. Matias Echanove and Rahul Srivastava of the Institute of Urbanology in Mumbai and Geneva point to India's emerging "circulatory urbanism," in which villages and small towns are themselves growing prudently into nodes of economic activity, connected to the distant megacities by India's widespread rail transportation system (which desperately needs upgrading) and prevalent smartphone and other wired systems.

A similar phenomenon has been noted in France, where in many areas, villages are now seeing an inflow of residents instead of the decades of outflow as youth fled to the cities. France's strong transportation system, and today's internet-fueled ability to work in any wired location, permits the so-called *neoruraux* to answer the call for a less frenetic environment where the natural world is closer in one's everyday living.

All of these changes are demanding. Yet it is in the economic sphere that most resistance will arise from the old order.

It's the Economy, Stupid: general traits

"Economic policy is about the facts and the circumstances."

—CHRYSTIA FREELAND

Of all the changes associated with the shift to an immanent, earth-friendly worldview, and the resulting transformed society, it is those involving the <u>economy</u> that seem most daunting to many. The fundamental transformation of the current capitalist economic model may seem unimaginable and highly threatening to many Americans, particularly the plutocrats who dominate the system. But throughout the wider world we see that most economies today are variations of a "mixed economy" that marries aspects of capitalism to highly regulated, sometimes centrally directed activities.

The rest of the world has long recognized that capitalism contains inherent contradictions that any functional economic system should avoid, not least its inexorable increase in debt and frequent financial crashes. Somehow, amidst the many alternatives and variations of economic organization, the sky has not fallen. As Canadian Trade Minister Chrystia Freeland commented after her Liberal Party's victory in the October 2015 elections, "It's really important that people not approach economic policy as ideology or with quasi-religious convictions. Economic policy is about the facts and the circumstances."

An Economy of Life. To begin, let us sketch the broad picture of what an immanent, earth-friendly economic order might look like. Because the general features of a given society's economic system are determined not by economists, but by the philosophical, political, and social outlooks prevalent in that society, we will draw on diverse sources, from Muir and Darwinism to Naomi Klein and Pope Francis, to sketch the outline of the immanent economy. There is an overarching theme that ties together all aspects: the immanent economy is one *in the service of life*—all life, human and nonhuman.

We can now see that, in too many ways, the economic order of the past several centuries has been in the service of death. Death of other species, and death of mountains and rivers defaced and poisoned, cannot serve humans in the long run. Now that we realize the earth is our home and its creatures our kin, we know that we only prosper as the planet and all its creatures prosper. So the immanent economy serves life.

Profit versus Employment. Profit as the most important gauge of economic activity will be eclipsed by a more fundamental goal: full, steady employment at a living wage. This proposition was advanced not only by Pope Francis in *Laudato Si'*, but by Franklin Delano Roosevelt in his 1944 State of the Union comments on a "Second Bill of Rights" for America. Outside of publicly subsidized enterprises, making a profit will of course still be important, but merely having costs met by income will suffice, so long as gainful and efficient employment is maintained. The days of outsiders taking over corporations and reorganizing them to extract an extra percent of profit for investors, at the expense of firing thousands of workers—those days are over. The successful company is one which meets expenses while providing steady employment, either in the production of quality goods or efficient services.

Automation. Technologies which automate tasks formerly performed by workers will receive long scrutiny. Only when the displaced workers can with certainty be trained for other, identified employment will such technologies be adopted. Today's increasingly common factories, rich with robots but poor with humans, will be a sign of failure, not progress.

Perhaps a wholesale revisioning of tasks constituting "employment" will be needed. Certainly government payments in lieu of steady jobs (described as a "basic income") is a step in exactly the wrong direction. Even *The Economist* recognizes these concerns, and in a June 25, 2016 leader recommended attention to Denmark's "flexicurity" system, which supports laid-off workers as they retrain and seek new employment. Again, Pope Francis and FDR are right: gainful employment in a meaningful task at a living wage is essential to a satisfying, meaningful life, not government handouts to those idled by a system worshiping profit at any and all cost.

Growth versus Steady State. Since the earth and its resources are finite and limited, and moreover play critical cycling and renewal roles in the planet's ecological functioning, the human economy cannot be predicated on infinite growth. The economy must be reconfigured as *a steady-state phenomenon*. And since the economy is steady state and not growing, then the population of humans incorporated into that economy must also be steady state. Population growth in humans, in other words, must level off promptly and, in fact, decline from its current rate. Certainly the 9.5 billion population predicted for 2050 will be unsustainable. The 12 billion predicted for 2100 is a fiction, a nightmare of dystopian societies which would quickly destroy themselves as they destroyed their environment.

David Brower, David Foreman, and Paul Ehrlich have been right all along: limiting human population is critical to a sustainable and healthy planet, as well as to a human "civilization" that fits the definition of the word. Recent population studies indicate that much of the world is, in fact, approaching a stable population: both Americas, Europe, and North Asia. It is in Africa and South Asia that populations continue to skyrocket and determine the unacceptable estimates for 2050 and 2100. Demographers will work with public officials to steadily dampen population growth in these areas. Populations there *will* decline; epidemics, famine, war, and migration will accomplish it, if careful policy planning does not. And economists will figure out how to best cope with the skewed demographic age distributions that result; there simply is no alternative.

<u>Corporate Charters</u>. Corporations originally were chartered with specific conditions permitting their formation and activity, as with the British East India Company. That practice, common until the 19th century, will again be practiced in the immanent economy. These charters will specify how large corporations will provide steady employment and reap sufficient profit to maintain themselves in an earth-friendly manner. Those corporations straying from the agreement and its stipulations will have charters revoked and dissolve—after remediating any destruction they may have caused. Small, entrepreneurial businesses will be exempt from the charter requirement, so long as they operate in an earth-friendly, sustainable manner.

The notion to resurrect the requirement that corporations "should be required to declare on incorporation their intention 'to deliver particular goods and services that serve a societal or economic need'" is explored in Will Hutton's 2015 *How Good We Can Be: Ending the Mercenary Society and Building a Great Country*, and echoed by Oxford management professor Colin Mayer in a 2015 lecture to the British Academy.

Corporations providing public services—energy and transportation, for example—may be nationalized so that any profits be applied to improvement of the services. Nationalization will not be a certainty, though. If private enterprises can provide the service at high quality and reasonable cost, that would be preferred. The return of charters, and detailed ones at that, may in effect create hybrid entities exhibiting aspects of both public and private companies. In any nationalized enterprise, features of the private sector should be incorporated, such as evaluation and rewards for high-performing employees, in order to minimize the too-frequent banes of public entities: poor service and sloppy management.

<u>The End of Extractionism: Fossil Fuels</u>. The most dramatic change in the transition to the new immanent economy will be the prompt and dramatic curtailment of extraction and combustion of fossil fuels. This decreased activity must be managed in a timeline of months and years rather than decades, given that severely challenging consequences are already locked in and steadily increasing every day our current system

persists. Here we are in emergency mode and must respond with all due haste. Current megaprojects, such as the Alberta tar sands dirty oil and Wyoming's Powder River Basin coal, must be shuttered, regardless of how much of the targeted resource remains to be extracted. "Keep it in the ground" must soon become official policy, as the Sierra Club and 350.org, most prominently, are demanding.

One long-suggested step in this direction is the imposition of a <u>carbon tax</u> (or fee) which dramatically increases the cost of fossil fuel extraction and combustion. This is a market-based solution, which has the disadvantage of simply passing on the cost of civilization-wrecking emissions onto the public, in the hopes that alternative energy sources will prove more attractive by virtue of lower cost, as the tax ripples through the system. Given the seriousness of the current situation and the great need for prompt action, the carbon tax may well fall into the category of "too little, too late" that has characterized four decades of failing to come to grips with our dire prospects. But it is a step in the right direction, at least, if adopted promptly and widely.

Such a carbon tax has been in effect since 2008 in Canada's British Columbia. The tax is relatively high ($24/ton), covers about 75% of the province's carbon sources, and has led to a drop in emissions between 5 and 15% since its adoption. Critically, it has done no perceptible harm to the region's economy as a whole—leading neighbor province Alberta to consider steps to strengthen its own carbon tax.

A 2008 study by Greenpeace, the World Wildlife Fund, and The Energy Foundation (*The True Cost of Coal*) urged that China, the world's largest producer and user of coal, increase the cost of its coal by 23% to reflect coal's true financial impacts on human health, water pollution, air pollution, and mining deaths, which cost the country a total 1.7 trillion yuan a year, more than 7% of the country's GDP.

As extraction of fossil fuels plummets (and the remediation of associated habitat destruction commences), renewable sources of energy must, of course, come online to replace those abandoned. The schedule, again, will be measured in months and years for the transition, rather than decades. As

Klein has documented, replacement technologies of solar, water, and wind energy have been available for over a decade. The huge subsidies given to the fossil fuel industries will now be freed up to apply to renewable energy. If the renewable replacement technologies cost more per unit of energy produced, compared to fossil fuels, then the subsidies switched from fossil fuels will cover much of that. Soon, once investors are convinced that renewables are the only energy producers "in business," research and experience will drive down the per-unit cost.

But let us remember: the current cost-per-unit-of-energy estimates for fossil fuel sources are deceptive and wildly inaccurate, because they do not include the costs associated with the health consequences of pollution, nor—more importantly—the costs associated with the looming and locked-in droughts, famines, storms, mass migrations, and sea-level rises at coastal cities. When these *actual* costs are taken into account, it becomes grimly evident that cost-per-unit-of-energy is dramatically higher for fossil fuels, even today, than for the renewables of solar, water, and wind.

In fact, measures of cost of fossil fuels versus renewables is immaterial. We are trying desperately to avoid the breakdown of human civilization on the planet, with the outcome still very much in doubt. When planet-wide barbarism and epic death tolls are looming, calculations of economic cost are swamped, and simply not relevant. We cannot lose sight of this fundamental, inexorable reality.

The End of Extractionism: Mining. In addition to fossil fuel extractive projects, large-scale mining of ores, chemicals, and other materials must also be promptly curtailed, for two reasons. First, these megaprojects always entail destruction and massive disruption of the natural world and its cycles. They are insults to what we now know is the source of human life and happiness. Whether envisioned as God's creation, the Tao, Mother Earth, or healthy ecosystems, we now know that mountains and rivers are too valuable—and too beloved—to desecrate for the enrichment of a few.

Secondly, the vast amounts of pollution and poisons inevitably produced by large-scale extractive mining projects (including mercury, arsenic, cadmium, lead, and other heavy metals) are no longer acceptable by-products of *any* economic activity, even were the habitat destruction not present. The average gold mine in the U.S. uses 1,900 tons of cyanide each year, which is sent to adjacent "holding" ponds along with all the other toxins. By-products so lethal to life—human as well as nonhuman—cannot be countenanced. Again: economic activity must be in the service of life, not death.

There are 161,000 abandoned mines in America's 12 Western states and Alaska alone, according to the Government Accounting Office (GAO). The Environmental Protection Agency (EPA) in the past 20 years has cleaned up only 18 of the 137 most-polluted sites in its Superfund program, and that at exorbitant cost. The Bureau of Land Management (BLM) lists 4,807 mines under its jurisdiction as active environmental hazards.

As a matter of fact, the scope of the abandoned pollution very often defies remedy, and the sites are merely monitored, until a hapless government functionary mistakenly sends the poisons into a nearby river (as in the August 2015 incident where EPA workers released water containing potent doses of arsenic, cadmium, and lead into the Animas river in Colorado) or a "holding" dam gives way (as in the November 2015 avalanche of mercury- and arsenic-carrying mud that swept away a village and left a dead zone in 500 km of the Doce River and the coastline in Brazil's Minas Gerais state). Such situations cannot be countenanced.

Step one is to promptly curtail large-scale mining; step two is to devote adequate resources to cleaning up abandoned mines. Legal processes must be created posthaste to insure that the mining corporations (and their highly paid executives personally) be required to remediate and resolve the poisons and pollution generated at the site with all due urgency, and restore the habitats to the fullest extent possible by current practices—*before* any legal chicanery such as bankruptcy is permitted. The plethora of abandoned mining sites choked with lethal pollutants around the world, the responsible individuals and corporations long beyond the reach of the legal system, is a scandal. As always in our current economic system, it is the public who end up paying for the crimes of the corporate executives.

Since, unlike renewable energy to replace fossil fuels, alternative sources of all the materials produced by mining are not yet readily available, some mining will be allowed in the immediate future, but only at much smaller scale and with stringent, vigorously enforced conditions. These conditions will include immediate, ongoing, on-site conversion of poisonous waste products to innocuous forms, and remediation of habitat alteration on the same timetable. No more "holding" ponds will be permitted. The costs associated with these conditions will be folded into the resultant product. Subsidies and encouragement of research into alternative, sustainable materials for products of mining operations will be promptly enacted and generously funded.

Clearly, today's products featuring refined metals from mining activity must become capable of extensive repair, reuse, updating, and recycling. Though not being able to replace last year's smartphone with this year's model may seem impossible for many to contemplate, we must always remember the true cost of such profligate use of metal-rich products: the unraveling of human civilization resulting from climate-induced famines, epidemics, and hordes of migrants from uninhabitable tropical countries besieging northern nations, putting impossible strains upon formerly stable societies.

29

The Immanent Economy: getting there

"The most important thing to understand about the energy transition is that it's not optional. Delay would be fatal. It's time to make a plan—however sketchy, however challenging—and run with it, revising it as we go."

—RICHARD HEINBERG

We have sketched the general features of an immanent economy above. The work of bringing this about will, without question, be enormously challenging. Progressive economists such as Lord Nicholas Stern and his colleagues at the London School of Economics' Grantham Research Institute on Climate Change and the Environment will help bring about the transformation from the current economy to the more earth-friendly version outlined here.

We must keep in mind, though, that we are not envisioning the bloody overthrow of modern capitalism, but rather its transformation into an economy not destructive to the planet and human civilization. Hopefully some of the positive features of modern capitalism can be largely retained in the newly transformed economy, and the negative features of centrally directed economies largely avoided. Here we rely on the competence and innovation of economists to lead the way.

In those countries with mixed economies already featuring extensive government control, such as China, the transition to an immanent, earth-friendly economy may be accomplished relatively smoothly. In countries with a mid-range of government control, such as found in Europe and South America, the transition may be bumpy, but not a huge challenge. Only in the few countries with little (or ineffective) government control of the private sectors, such as the United States, will the transition be quite challenging.

Many think tanks bulging with economists have already begun considering the specific steps involved in this transition, particularly in western Europe and the United States. Here we will briefly outline the scenario envisioned by Richard Heinberg of Silicon Valley's Post Carbon Institute and David Fridley of the nearby Lawrence Berkeley National Laboratory. They divide up the task (looking mainly at the United States) into three stages: easy, harder, and hardest.

Electricity Generation and Electrification. This relatively easy cluster of actions would reduce carbon emissions in the United States by an estimated 40%. The replacement of electricity generation by coal with solar, water, and wind processes is the most obvious and immediately achievable of the changes. This alone would transform nearly 25% of the energy use in the United States.

The electrification of personal transportation would be next, involving the widespread use of hybrid or all-electric cars; gasoline-powered vehicles would become rare and only permitted with extremely high efficiency. At the same time, urban design permitting more use of public transport, walking, and bicycling would also occur, with generous investments.

The production of food would change to dramatically curtail the use of fossil fuels in its growth (i.e. fertilizers, gas-powered machines), processing, and transportation. The result would be a food economy that is significantly more organic and local. Such an economy already exists in early stage, as attested by the prevalence of farmers' markets and the burgeoning organic and locavore movements; these will expand to become the norm.

Freight Shipping, Human Transport, Manufacturing. The second, harder stage of the transformation envisioned by Heinberg and Fridley will reduce carbon emissions in America by another 40%, and begins with shipping of freight. The use of trucks will decrease significantly, as rail shipping increases. This will entail investment in more rail tracks and associated infrastructure.

In addition, the volume of long-distance shipping of freight will decline in general, as a result of the localization of manufacturing and food production. Globalization, while it has conferred some economic advantages, simply requires an unacceptable degree of fossil fuel consumption on land, sea, and air. Regions and nations will become much more *self-sufficient* in every sphere of economic activity. The resulting drop in carbon emissions from long-distance transportation of products must occur.

Short- and medium-distance movement of humans will be accomplished by completing the electrification of public transport within cities, and by intercity and interstate rail lines. The Amtrak rail system will be renovated and expanded, bringing back the common state of affairs a century ago in America, when railroads connected virtually every town and city with frequent and dependable service. The dominance of personal vehicles which so thoroughly directed America's infrastructure and lifestyle after World War II will be substantially reduced, as the moving of products and people is transformed to an earlier, more earth-friendly state. A nation that can put a man on the moon can certainly accomplish this restoration of a transportation system that does not entail the destruction of human civilization on the planet.

Some manufacturing of products currently uses electricity, rather than fossil fuels; the proportion will increase substantially. Products currently utilizing fossil fuel components, such as fertilizers and plastics, will be replaced with organic, renewable precursors. Even now, Brazil's eucalyptus-based pulp industry is researching "green" substitutes for plastics, and investing in parallel research in Canada.

The production of metals and cement currently requires huge amounts of intense heat generated by fossil fuels. Even as the mining of metallic ores changes dramatically, alternate processing or alternative sources of heat for metals and concrete must be researched and promoted, including construction substitutes for concrete. As mentioned in the previous chapter, recycling, updating, repair, and reuse of materials requiring high energy inputs must come about for manufactured products in general.

Communications and Long-Distance Transport. Eliminating the last 20% of America's current carbon emissions will be the most challenging. In the area of communication, components such as phones, computers, and wiring use large amounts of fossil-fuel-powered materials and processes, particularly the metals from extractive mining. Again: our phones and computers must utilize as many renewable elements as possible, and must become less frequently and readily abandoned for new models.

Global transport must significantly decline, as localization burgeons. When the true costs of long-distance transport of food and materials are examined, our several decades of purportedly cheap electronics from overseas, and exotic, out-of-season foods from southern climes are, in fact, exorbitantly expensive—indefensible luxuries built on unconscionable suffering in the not-so-distant future.

The extensive aviation system built up since World War II is also a cruel luxury whose considerable contributions to climate change cannot be reconciled with either human decency or the continuation of civilization on the planet. Unfortunately, no substitute for fossil fuels to power airplanes seems currently feasible. Until this changes, frequent travel by airplanes will become a thing of the past, difficult though it may be to accept. Travel by rail, both short- and long-distance, will correspondingly increase many fold, along with improvements in the frequency and comfort of such travel, as was true before World War II.

Travel overseas will shift back to primarily by ship, as it was a century ago. Promising developments in wind-assisted technologies for our current seagoing vessels will be supported and refined, such as the wind-driven rotors for large cargo vessels currently being tested by Britain's Energy Technologies Institute. Considering that 90% of world trade travels by sea, harnessing the power of wind again to assist the moving of freight as well as people on continent-linking ships will become increasingly efficient and important.

These scenarios of a society weaned from the extraction of fossil fuels and mining products inevitably conjure a world much different than that which bloomed (or metastasized, more accurately) after World War II. *That world, our current world, so familiar, so comfortable, so convenient, in retrospect must be seen as a fool's paradise.* It was built on processes and products whose lethal consequences were invisible, and shoved to the future. Now those resultant costs are known to us, and are already exerting their inexorable effects. If we do not decisively and promptly dispel the hypnotic mist, our much-vaunted civilization will soon descend into famine, epidemics, and bloody southern borders clogged by never-ending waves of refugees from heat- and drought-ravaged tropical countries. Is such a nightmarish near future really worth an easy weekend flight to London or Paris? An avocado or banana in the middle of winter? Can we wrench ourselves out of the deadly dream we're in?

However wrenching, the change must be made, and quickly. As economist Heinberg points out, "The most important thing to understand about the energy transition is that it's not optional. Delay would be fatal. It's time to make a plan—however sketchy, however challenging—and run with it, revising it as we go."

The transformation outlined above may seem impossible to some. Yet our current capitalistic economic system in America is not set in stone, and never has been. In many ways, today's version of capitalism is already undergoing a transformation, so that the envisioned changes may not be as daunting as they seem.

Fluidity of Modern Capitalism. On the negative side, dissatisfaction with fundamental aspects of modern capitalism has been voiced by mainstream economists for several decades, and has grown apace since the Great Recession of 2008 and the faltering subsequent attempts at recovery. The tendency to accumulate untenable debt, at both the institutional and personal level; the short-term tyranny of quarterly corporate reports; and the long history of crashes in the system, are seen as inherent and serious defects. Concern has long been expressed at the cumbersome nature of the publicly-held corporation, with its maze of regulators and diffused centers of responsibility (stock-holders? fund managers? executives?).

On the positive side, the rapid proliferation of entrepreneurial start-ups, marked by clear, flexible, contract-guided ownership and control, promises to reconfigure the very model of business organization. Silicon Valley is creating a new way of doing capitalism. As *The Economist* said in October 2015: "Today they (start-ups) can expand very fast by buying in services as and when they need them. They can incorporate online for a few hundred dollars, raise money from crowdsourcing sites such as Kickstarter, hire programmers from Upwork, rent computer-processing power from Amazon, find manufacturers on Alibaba, arrange payments systems at Square, and immediately set about conquering the world."

All of which suggests that modern capitalism contains more fluidity and receptivity to change than right-wing plutocrats and their well-recompensed political servants would like to admit. The changes mandated in the pivot to an immanent economy of life may be considerably more feasible and less traumatic than might be imagined.

Or not. Either way, it must occur.

30

Who Will Lead?

"The life of the mind is a gift of God, and to deny the best of current knowledge is not using the gifts God has given you."

— EPISCOPAL BISHOP KATHARINE JEFFERTS SCHORI

As we have seen, it has been primarily the decades-old alliance between scientists and environmentalists, with important recent input from journalist Naomi Klein and Pope Francis, that led to the emission-reduction pledges of the 2015 Paris climate summit. Though a huge step in the right direction, these pledges would reduce global emissions from the current 4 or 6°C range to only 3°C—far short of the 2°C needed to avert catastrophic consequences.

Merely translating these anticipated steps from pledges to reality in the coming decades will be extraordinarily difficult, given the pressures in every country from extractive Big Oil, Big Coal, and Big Mining interests to temporize, fudge, and evade. To go beyond the Paris pledges and achieve the *further* emission reductions to achieve the 2°C goal (much less the aspiration of 1.5°C) will be even more difficult. It is post-Paris, 2015 that the serious heavy lifting to save human civilization will be demanded. For this to have any serious chance to happen, the science-environmentalist alliance will require new impetus, a new surge of support.

As Shellenberger, Klein and Pope Francis persuasively argue, these further steps can only succeed if a new way of thinking about the world and the place of humans sweeps the world in a social movement akin to America's Abolitionism of the mid-19th century and the Civil Rights Movement of the mid-20th. The various voices expressing such a new way of thinking are all sheltered within the expansive umbrella of the immanent worldview, which we saw develop from sources as diverse as the ancient Taoists of China, John Muir in America (his no-longer "hidden" views), indigenous peoples, and the scientific enterprise, which we may call Darwinism.

For a worldwide social movement based upon the critical new way of thinking to come into being, and compel the world's leaders post-Paris to what they must do to save human civilization, that immanent worldview and its various versions must be articulated and advocated prominently and frequently. Who will lead this articulation and this advocacy? Who will bring about what Pope Francis terms "the ecological conversion" of humanity?

Environmental Groups. Perhaps the most obvious candidates are the existing environmental groups. The pro-business ones busily forming "corporate partnerships," such as Environmental Defense Fund, are part of the problem, not the solution. They will be occupied, anyway, preparing their legal defenses with their Big Oil friends, for their appearance before the International Criminal Court at The Hague.

The most effective environmental organization in this concerted campaign for the immanent worldview will be Greenpeace. Its long experience, its expertise in numerous areas, its international scope, and its dedicated worldwide corps of activists have earned Greenpeace the right to lead. Of the several radical environmental groups, Greenpeace has credibility *par excellence*.

Partnering with newly focused mainline groups, Greenpeace is already an important part of the international mass movement pushing the world's leaders to make the hard decisions necessary to save humanity. But even Greenpeace must adopt a page from its fellow radical groups Sea Shepherds and EarthFirst!, and like them explicitly articulate the

Gaiacentric, immanent roots to its activism, and advocate for that foundation as well as the specific steps flowing from it.

Standing shoulder-to-shoulder with Greenpeace is Bill McKibben's 350.org, which has mushroomed worldwide in recent years, and now claims to be the world's largest grassroots climate campaign, with activists in every country save North Korea. It has proved remarkably effective in organizing focused rallies (15,000 in 189 countries—and counting) and the use of social media. 350.org's push for massive peoples' marches in the lead-up to the UN's December 2015 Paris climate summit was typically impressive. Among other groups who have been remarkably effective alongside Greenpeace and 350.org are Friends of the Earth, Rainforest Action Network, and Natural Resources Defense Council.

The mainstream organizations, preeminently the Sierra Club, can best contribute to the integral ecology conversion if they forthrightly discover the hidden Muir and proclaim the Gaiacentric component so central to the immanent worldview. The days of compromising and shrinking from a radical view and its activist espousal are over. What worked for the first century of the environmental movement—an "informed, high" anthropocentrism and a courteous decorum of conduct—is no longer adequate to the current crisis, not remotely adequate. The mainline environmental groups, and indeed "respectable" citizens worldwide, must overcome their unease over activist operations, realizing that without such activism the push for a new way of thinking cannot possibly succeed. Distaste for the confrontation involved in activism cannot trump the urgent need to transform to the immanent worldview; that way lies disaster.

Sierra Club and other mainline groups will also have to divert some of their considerable resources from the never ending, whack-a-mole rushing about to save this or that habitat. More and more they must focus, instead, on education (of adults as well as youth) on the rightness of the immanent worldview, the fundamental new way of thinking that alone can generate and sustain the push for the radical change necessary. Part of this educational focus will entail organizing a drumbeat of forums (talks, seminars, field trips, retreats) providing opportunities for the immanent view to be articulated, advocated, and experienced. These groups will judge whether they are more comfortable (and effective) highlighting a specific version of the immanent worldview (surely the Sierra Club would focus on the hidden Muir's Earth Wisdom) or the overarching philosophical stance itself.

Foundations and philanthropic organizations possess considerable resources, which should be directed particularly to this educational spread of the immanent worldview and the abundant evidence supporting it. Surely no better use could be found for these institutions of accumulated wealth than leading the push to rescue humanity from the greatest challenge it has faced in its 200,000 years on the planet.

Science itself must also step forward in articulating and advocating for the immanent view underlying science and revealed by its results. Traditionally, scientists have been reluctant to express personal values and take sides in social controversies, even those in which scientific knowledge provides critical input. The old view is that science is a method, a tool to obtain accurate knowledge of the natural world. What society does with that knowledge is another matter—or so the thinking went. "We are not given to theatrical rantings about falling skies," admits Ohio State climatologist Lonnie G. Thompson. "Most of us are far more comfortable in our laboratories or gathering data in the field than we are giving interviews to journalists."

Yet the gravity of the climate change debate and the infuriatingly willful ignorance and outright lies of climate deniers have persuaded many scientists to become more actively involved in the public discussion, as we have seen. This trend must be accelerated and broadened to include the articulation of the immanent view basic to the actual "doing" of science and revealed in the body of knowledge created by centuries of this activity.

This volume proposes "Darwinism" as a descriptive label for science's body of findings which illuminate and support the immanent worldview. The term can be thought of as science with a heart, or the marriage of science with passion. Darwinism is science as the basis of a way of life, beyond and distinct from its use as a tool to understand the natural world. Just as

Darwin himself was much more than a biologist, making important contributions to understanding geology, paleontology, and the genesis of coral reefs, so "Darwinism" incorporates not just the life sciences, but the earth sciences as well, all these disciplines contributing to the understanding of a healthy, sustainable way of living on the planet.

Which brings us to <u>religion</u>. Nearly two centuries into the modern scientific age, religions still hold remarkable influence upon people worldwide. Playing a positive role in the necessary transformation to an immanent, Gaiacentric stance and the integral ecology paradigm will be challenging for them, given their typical anthropocentric and patriarchal foundations, both in their texts and their histories. This is especially true for the Abrahamic religions of Judaism, Christianity, and Islam. Can the world's religions have any role at all in the transformation to the earth-centered, immanent worldview?

In fact, religions can and will have important roles to play. In general, religions will contribute to the saving of the earth and human civilization by moving their theology and practice in the direction of the immanent viewpoint—what may be termed the "immanentizing" of their faith traditions. Succinctly, this entails the same overarching changes as applied to society, patterned along the lines of the three pillars:

First: More Earth, living here and now;
    Less Heaven, living in the future and elsewhere.
Second: More Kinship with all earth's creatures;
    Less Human superiority and focus.
Third: More Yin traits expressed; Less Yang dominance.
    (More cooperation, acceptance, nurturing, and feminine;
    Less competition, dominance, destruction, and masculine)

(See Appendix 1 for a presentation of these changes, and the worldviews already incorporating them.)

Moving in the direction of these three changes will be easy for some religions, difficult for others. But the changes represent the key points in the transition from institutions estranging humans from their true home, to institutions connecting humans to their noble roots; the passage from the too-often misleading conceptions of the past to the truthful conceptions of the future.

We have already seen Pope Francis boldly reminding Roman Catholics of the importance of "Brother Sun and Sister Moon," and all the creatures on our planet reflecting the love and glory of their Creator—much as John Muir did a century ago. Francis' rejection of uncaring, exploitative "dominion," and his embrace of loving "stewardship" recognizing the integral ecology relationship among all of earth's creatures, is a large step in the right direction, though he retains the fundamental anthropocentric stance. Moses-like, he brings Roman Catholicism to the very border of the Promised Land of Gaiacentrism; he himself may not cross over, but perhaps others will.

If Pope Francis and the Roman Catholic Church fall short, currently, of a full embrace of the immanent viewpoint, the same cannot be said of some of the Protestant Christian denominations. The majority of these in the United States have in recent decades taken concrete strides in the immanent direction. The U.S.-based Episcopal Church, with over 2 million members, has admitted female priests and bishops for several decades, and elected its first female presiding bishop to head the church in 2006.

Presiding Bishop Katharine Jefferts Schori forthrightly said of those who deny the science behind climate change: "Episcopalians understand the life of the mind is a gift of God, and to deny the best of current knowledge is not using the gifts God has given you. In that sense, yes, it could be understood as a moral issue...It is in that sense much like the civil rights movement in this country, where we are attending to the rights of all people and the rights of the earth to continue to be a flourishing place."

The patriarchal and other-worldly language of the three-century old *Doxology* has been amended towards immanence in recent years by the Disciples of Christ and by the United Church of Christ, the new version proclaiming (*traditional version in parentheses*):

Praise God from whom all blessings flow; (*unchanged*)
Praise God, all creatures here below; (*Praise him, all creatures here below*)
Praise God for all that love has done; (*Praise him above, ye heavenly host*)
Creator, Christ, and Spirit, One. (*Praise Father, Son, and Holy Ghost*)

In the practical sphere of church finances, the United Methodist Church recently joined other Protestant denominations in the fossil fuel divestment movement, removing coal companies from its pension fund. Even Evangelical polities, on the far "conservative" side of the Protestant spectrum, have addressed themselves vigorously to the injustices which environmental pollution concentrates on the poor, and the mandate to love and protect God's creation.

Further movement of American Protestantism in the immanent direction rests, as with John Muir a century ago, in the full recognition of the inherent value of God's creation ("Then God looked over all he had made, and he saw that it was very good"), as well as the recognition that females are due full participation in the church's leadership. Former president and Southern Baptist Jimmy Carter's words are pertinent: "During the years of the early Christian church, women served as deacons, priests, bishops, apostles, teachers and prophets. It wasn't until the fourth century that dominant Christian leaders, all men, twisted and distorted Holy Scriptures to perpetuate their ascendant positions within the religious hierarchy.

"The truth is that male religious leaders have had—and still have—an option to interpret holy teachings either to exalt or subjugate women. They have, for their own selfish ends, overwhelming chosen the latter." And still do, in the Southern Baptist and Roman Catholic Churches, though no longer in most mainline Protestant polities.

The immanent stance must be worldwide, of course. What of faith traditions beyond Christianity in America? The Church of England has admitted female priests for two decades, and approved the first female Bishop in December 2014, despite determined opposition and the likelihood of schism from affiliated branches within England and, particularly, in Africa. Indeed, the worldwide Anglican Communion overseen by the Bishop of Canterbury is currently in the process of transitioning to a loose association bound together by prior history, rather than doctrinal commonalities.

Islam, like most widespread faith traditions, contains a diversity of polities and opinion within itself. While we in the West seem to think mainly of the more established schools, and terrorists appropriating the vocabulary of the tradition, there are sectors of Islam showing evidence of traits associated with the immanent worldview. For example, in March of 2014, the highest Islamic clerical body in Indonesia issued a religious fatwa against the illegal hunting and trade in endangered animals in the country. The Ulema Council declared such activities "unethical, immoral and sinful."

"All activities resulting in wildlife extinction without justifiable religious grounds or legal provisions are *haram* (forbidden). These include illegal hunting and trading of endangered animals. Whoever takes away a life, kills a generation. This is not restricted to humans, but also includes God's other living creatures, especially if they die in vain."

At the other geographic end of Muslim-majority countries, Islamic scholar Hama Jaiteh told a Gambia youth conference on female genital mutilation (FGM) that the practice, widespread in northern Africa, was not justified by either the Qur'an or the traditional sayings of the prophet in the *sunnah* or *hadith* traditions.

Directing himself to the opinions of "venerable so-called Islamic scholars," Jaiteh declared "There is no valid *hadith* they can bring to support their claims (for FGM)...He who created a woman knows the benefit of that thing there, leave it. Let everybody go back and read, conduct research. Islam is Islam, it is here to preserve the interests and rights of the woman. This FGM is completely against Islam."

Islamic imams and scholars will be the best judge, of course, on how the faith tradition might embrace a more immanent tone through the various aspects of its living practice

The oldest of the Abrahamic religions, Judaism, contains many members with an open readiness to contemporary revelation complementing that of traditional sources, particularly in the Reform school, where female rabbis are common and highly respected. This school will, I think, be a model of a faith tradition moving wisely in an immanent direction as the urgency of the modern situation is better understood. The 2016 months-long topping of nonfiction book lists in Israel of astrophysicist Elia Leibowitz's *New Readings in the Old Testament* is pertinent, since the God he describes is primarily the source of creation, neither vengeful nor beneficent—a positively Muir-like emphasis.

The Hindu faith tradition of India exhibits little tendency to anthropomorphize the deity; indeed, in its embrace of a variety of embodiments of the sacred in the animal world, it seems friendly to the immanent worldview. The harsh misogyny of the society in which Hinduism is imbedded, however, along with its persistent caste outlook, would seem to challenge its ability to move in an immanent direction. Again: Hindu pandits, pujaris, and scholars will be the best judge of what can be accomplished.

Buddhism's original stance on the illusory nature of the world of *samsara*, and its stated goal for humans to escape the rack of existence into another realm, *nirvana*, would seem rocky ground for the cultivation of the immanent. Yet within the many schools of the Buddhist faith tradition there is an enormous variety of views, and a profound receptivity to different ways of thinking. Stephen Batchelor's 2015 *After Buddhism: Rethinking the Dharma for a Secular Age* is an example. My Buddhist friends are very open to the world and how best to live; it seems likely their religion might welcome movement toward an immanent stance.

Scholars, theologians, and practitioners of all these religions must consider how to bring their respective concepts of God or divinity more in line with the immanent stance. Cannot modern theological development consider a God less like an old human male, whether loving or jealous of his laws and strict obedience to them? Surely the creator of the universe would be larger than this Abrahamic conception, more of an awesome, dynamic, creative Presence, concerned equally with all creation, rather than any one creature among the teeming millions of the earth—and elsewhere in the universe.

The folk Taoism of China and folk Shintoism of Japan (as distinct from the official state-sponsored versions) are of course very much attuned to the immanent worldview, uniquely so among the world's faith traditions. These Eastern religions and their practitioners are already "there" in terms of immanence (though not infrequently accompanied by an extensive overlay of what we Westerners would term superstition—which bothers me not at all).

The bottom line: all must lead, environmentalists, scientists, foundations, and religions, if humanity is to come into a new, respectful relationship to the earth, and forestall the worst of the climate-change calamity bearing down upon it. Widespread adoption of the immanent worldview is necessary, and with due haste, whether it be embodied in Earth Wisdom, Taoism, Darwinism, Indigenous cosmologies, or immanentized existing religions.

Only as the world's peoples make known their conviction that the earth is our true home, that we are kin to all other creatures, and that yin feminine traits are as important as yang masculine ones—only then will the groundswell push leaders to the economic, social, and political restructuring that alone can save humanity's future on this lovely planet.

Epilogue. Two Paths, and a Choice

"These are the falling years,
They will go deep,
Never weep, never weep.
With clear eyes explore the pit.
Watch the great fall
With religious awe."

—ROBINSON JEFFERS

"This star, our own good earth, made many a successful journey around the heavens ere man was made, and whole kingdoms of creatures enjoyed existence and returned to dust ere man appeared to claim them. After human beings have also played their part in Creation's plan, they too may disappear without any general burning or extraordinary commotion whatever."

—JOHN MUIR

A terrible arc is looming over the history of humans on this planet. The decisions we make in the next two decades will determine how far down this impending path we travel. There are six stages we can envision in the story of humanity's relation with the climate change it has brought about. In the first, **Challenge**, the necessary measures to reduce carbon emissions upon James Hansen's alarm in 1988 could have been relatively easily accomplished, and a sustainable human future ensured. We failed to do so in the three ensuing decades.

We are currently in the early years of the second stage, **Crisis**. In the several years ahead, steadily expanding occurrences of drought, early famines, increases in severe weather episodes, and migrations of climate refugees will further dislocate the current world order. These factors will continue their rise until they constitute a constellation of problems bringing about substantial damage to the world's economy and social fabric, problems that will intensify by the year.

Although world leaders have promised to respond, as in the Paris UN conference at the end of 2015, the existing economic elite, particularly fossil fuel and mining corporations, have successfully brought pressure to bear on politicians long accustomed to funds channeled to them to sustain the existing order. This resistance to serious efforts to combat climate change has led to the faltering of 2015's blossoming of hope, and locked in continued rises in carbon emissions which ensure our passage to the early developments of the third stage: **Desperate Struggle**, which we will enter within two decades.

In this stage, ever-increasing heat and drought will render many countries uninhabitable, particularly in a wide equatorial band through Africa and South Asia. Production of grains will plummet worldwide as the floods and droughts intensify, especially in the now-salty river deltas of Asia, and amid the searing heat of tropical regions. Famine will hit the increasing human population very hard, first in Africa and South Asia, then in South America. Hundreds of millions will die in the famines, followed by further hundreds of millions in the ensuing epidemics as fragile third-world health systems are quickly overwhelmed.

Great waves of humanity will surge north from the unbearable heat, famine, and disease of the tropics to the temperate countries. America, China, Russia, and Europe will be besieged by hundreds of millions of clamoring climate refugees. These northern countries, already dealing with their own climate problems, and unable to support huge additions to their populations, will resort to constructing fences with armed towers along their entire borders, through every hill and valley. Still the desperate migrants will come, rioting and forcing their way across the barriers.

Quickly the border towers will be manned by military personnel, machine guns placed every several hundred yards, in the same crossfire pattern deployed so devastatingly in June 1944 on Omaha Beach. Desperate and fleeing for their lives from impossible conditions, the southern refugees will persist in attempts to surmount the barriers. Soon the borders will be marked by piles of corpses, mounds of death that grow daily. Within months, grotesque heaps of dead bodies will stretch continuously along the entire extent of the borders, thousands of miles of killing fields on three continents.

Rats, crows, and vultures feeding on the corpses will soon spread formerly tropical diseases into the now-hotter northern countries. Epidemics of a range of diseases will quickly rack the northern countries, spread widely also by mosquitos, viruses, and bacteria. High human populations and hence densities fuel the epidemics, to either side of the contested borders.

These northern countries will in addition be dealing with their own droughts, food shortages, and widespread flooding of coastal regions due to ocean rise of one to two meters. Internal climate refugees will overtax their social fabric. Democracy disappears across the world mid-century as partisan-fueled paralysis utterly fails to address the burgeoning constellation of emergencies. Martial law will be declared by every country, and authoritarian regimes assume power to cope with the dire conditions. The world order begins to unravel as countries arbitrarily employ force to win access to dwindling water and food sources.

The early developments of this third stage are already locked in with near certainty, thanks to the victories of the climate deniers in the past four decades, the lack of compulsory reductions in emissions at the December 2015 UN climate meeting, and the intransigence of fossil fuel and mining corporations and their political servants frustrating meaningful responses to the climate change upon us.

How deeply into this stage human society plunges, and whether the fourth stage follows, depends entirely upon what we do in the next decade. If the current anthropocentric worldview persists, with its smug assumption of human superiority and exemption from the travails of the planet, then the will of the plutocrats controlling the world's economy will persist unchanged and the full extent of stage three will occur, followed inexorably by successive stages. If, on the other hand, a worldwide popular movement insisting on the Gaiacentric stance emerges in the next decade, to transform the world's political and economic order, then perhaps only the early components of the third stage occur. The next decade will tell.

The fourth stage of **Catastrophe** is only likely, not yet certain. Without prompt and urgent changes in our current worldview and economic order, though, humanity will surely slide into this fourth stage, with chaos and disorder reigning throughout the world in human affairs, as climate change and its results intensify. Decades of drought withering forests and scrublands lead to raging fires across entire continents, enveloping the planet in smoke for months on end, affecting even oceanic systems. Creatures and ecosystems which had flourished for a hundred million years—sequoias and redwoods in California and China, coral reefs worldwide—disappear from the planet forever. Temperatures continue to rise due to the vastly increased densities of carbon dioxide in the atmosphere.

The conflagrations swell the ranks of internal and external refugees and wipe out the last vestiges of social order. Nations disintegrate into separate regions ruled by brutal warlords. Warfare is the common state worldwide. The bloodletting is particularly extreme in the former United States, where the millions of assault rifles and automatic handguns fuel widespread slaughter. Here the distinction between good and bad blurs, morality disappears, and survival is the only concern. Roving bands of heavily armed men scavenging food and supplies are the norm throughout the continent.

As the old "countries" disappear worldwide, border controls fail and climate refugees swarm freely into the habitable northern areas in the hundreds of millions. In the resulting universal social disorder, human society loses the last vestiges of sanitation systems, water supplies, and electricity generation. Populations plummet as fires, warfare, epidemics, famine, and extreme weather reduce humanity to a state of barbarism. Even now, climate change intensifies, as unrestricted burning of easily-obtained coal soars, the only available source now of fuel for cooking, and for winter heating in the north.

The occurrence of any of several ecologic tipping points in either stage three or stage four will make recovery—that is, stopping the slide into succeeding stages—impossible. We do not know enough about the planetary systems of climate and cycling to have any confidence that all tipping points have been identified, but among those we can foresee is the melting of the arctic permafrost, which will release massive amounts of the potent greenhouse gas methane, an amount calculated to be equivalent to 205 gigatons of further carbon dioxide in the atmosphere. Temperature would increase at least another 0.5°C at this point. Another tipping point would be the melting of the Greenland and polar ice sheets, leading to precipitous increases in ocean level and the complete reconfiguration of the old continents as vast inland seas open up.

"Game over," in the chilling words of early climate scientist James Hansen.

In the early years of stage five, **End of Human Civilization**, the continuing savagery among warlords, along with the continuing droughts, floods, famines, and epidemics of the unrelenting global warming, bring about further decreases in human populations. Humans exist now only in isolated bands in the remaining habitats that can support human life: favored valleys and canyons, the few plains that have reliable water and are defensible from other bands.

The great time of killing in stage four, and the unraveling of civilization, have depleted the ability to produce further metal-based weapons or ammunition. At midpoint of this fifth stage, warfare wanes. The widely scattered human groups remaining are led not by warlords, but by handy, practical men and women skilled in the creation and maintenance of mechanical water pumps, simple irrigation systems, wheeled vehicles such as carts and bicycles, and cultivation of soil and crops in large-scale gardens. Literature and music have long since disappeared from human society. Mere survival is uppermost, now.

As human populations plummeted to low levels in stage four, the spread of disease abated, due to the isolation of the remaining stage five bands, and the natural immunity of the survivors. But the pathogens are still present, and mutating, themselves. For each surviving group, it becomes statistically likely that, given enough time, a combination of the ever-continuing drought, famine, and random introduction of a pathogen into the band by some vector will kill its last remaining members. The number of bands in the habitable locations worldwide dwindles from thousands to hundreds. To dozens.

To a dozen.

One by one, the surviving human bands flicker out. The last human disappears from the planet in the waning years of the 21st century. Perhaps her name is Eve.

The earth is quiet, now. Never again will human laughter, or singing, or murders occur. Stage six, **Human Extinction**, has arrived.

This is the arc of history upon which humanity is currently traveling. *There is another path, if humans can muster the will to take it.* This second path is the unlikely path, the difficult path. Although we have passed stage one (Challenge), are currently in the first years of stage two (Crisis), and have locked in our passage to an early stage three (Desperate Struggle) by our continuing carbon emissions, we may avoid the succeeding stages if this other path is chosen within the next decade or so.

Here is what could happen. Somehow, due to the persistent efforts of scientists, environmentalists, educators, and a few religions in the late second and early third decade of the 21st century, more and more people throughout the world—mainly youths—begin to question the old anthropocentric worldview and practices, and embrace the Gaiacentric Earth Wisdom, Darwinism, Taoism, and the immanent philosophy. Females have leading roles as these movements swell in the early 2020s.

Investors made nervous by the early signs of climate change shift their capital into renewable energy, and products independent of the metals of extractive mining operations. As humanity enters into the early travails of the third stage, Desperate Struggle, the immanent, Gaiacentric movements swiftly gain strength, form alliances, and demand changes in the economy through massive civil disobedience throughout the world.

In some countries, governments respond to popular will and transition to policies fully addressing the climate crisis. In other countries, where governments are dominated by climate-denying plutocrats of fossil fuel and mining corporations, the response is brutal force against the popular will. Blood is shed and martyrs made. Yet still the massive demonstrations surge forward, implacably demanding the rule of life rather than the rule of death. Within a decade—*in the mid-2020s*—world governments have no choice but to accede, even in authoritarian regimes, and take previously unimaginable actions.

Coal plants are closed, and planned ones canceled; coal, oil, and gas reserves remain in the ground. Large scale mining of metals and ores ceases. Renewable production of electricity soars, even as demand for metals plummets with reuse and recycling now the norm. Production of food and goods becomes thoroughly localised; long-range shipping of food and freight plummets. By the end of the first full decade along this path—*in the mid-2030s*—carbon emissions are reduced to the level of a 1.75°C world. Surprisingly, humanity tiptoes past the major "tipping points" by virtue of prompt, firm action.

Sea levels rise by two meters, but no more. Though thousands of miles of coastline are abandoned due to their reconfiguration, and storm- and tidal-surges in a dozen great cities worldwide render large areas uninhabitable, the economic repercussions are merely daunting, not catastrophic. Locked-in results of carbon emissions up to 2030 render many areas of Africa and South Asia uninhabitable due to intense heat and lack of water, but the dramatic drop in emissions in the century's fourth decade limits the temperature increase, and thus its effects in the equatorial countries.

Migrants number only 30 to 50 million spread worldwide, and the horrific killing fields at the northern countries' borders disappear within a decade. More migrants are absorbed by neighboring countries adjacent to the equatorial zones, assisted by now-generous aid from northern countries shaken by moral repugnance at the killing fields.

As a series of pathogens travel from the tropics into the temperate regions to the north, vastly improved (and funded) health systems crank out vaccines and treatments quickly, reducing mortality to levels judged tragic, but not devastating. Even formerly prosperous northern nations struggle with decreased food supplies due to the heat, drought, and storms. But they avoid massive death tolls, in large part because their populations have already declined steadily due to population control measures in the third and fourth decades of the century.

The authoritarian regimes which got humanity through the early years of Desperate Struggle relax their controls as conditions slowly improve. Soon a semblance of democracy returns in places, particularly in the West, one markedly less partisan due to the shock of the third stage's travails.

As the new century approaches, human civilization is fragile, but survives. Human populations are stable, though distributed mainly in the northern and southern temperate zones now. Renewable sources of energy and raw materials are well established and economically viable, thanks to research and development fueled by the early shifts of capital by canny investors.

Tensions remain, of course, centering on equitable distribution of fresh water and the continuing integration of migrants into temperate zone countries. Demands for more democracy are a constant from the populace in the West and in China, particularly. But human civilization, chastened by the challenges midcentury, remains determined to follow the lessons of Earth Wisdom, Taoism, Darwinism, and the immanent worldview.

Humanity abides on a slowly recovering earth, half of whose land and ocean is now set aside as natural preserves. Babies are born, and grow strong in societies marked by love and respect for the earth, acknowledged now as our true home. The countryside is rich with a new abundance of trees, mammals, birds, and insects, fully accepted as kin and fellow benefactors of the earth's abundance. Females and males alike have important roles in the surviving societies, often though not always the same, but equally respected and valued. The yin qualities of cooperation, acceptance, nurturing, and the feminine are fully integrated into human society.

Humans understand that no species has escaped extinction in the four billion years of life on earth. But they accept the time they have, with gratitude. For as long as it may last.

Acknowledgments

My wife and four children have kindly showered me with their love and their company on many adventures (and a few misadventures) in the natural world. For this, and more, I thank them. My colleagues in the Chico Cohousing community of Valley Oaks Village introduced me to many of the joys of the immanent life, particularly in our father-kid backpacking trips into the High Sierras, in the congenial and skilled company of Richard Perelli, Bill Travers, Cal McCarthy, Michael Cross and a passel of delightful (mostly) kids.

Various journeys to China, Taiwan, and Japan as "independent travelers" were enlivened by my travel buddies AJ Dickinson and Kyle Brown. Liu Ming was an early and appreciated guide to Taoism. Yale college roommate George Scarlett inspired me to a serious study of John Muir only a decade ago, to provide a chapter for a book on spiritual exemplars which he was editing. The essay bloomed (or metastasized, some might say) into the current volume, and George was patient and encouraging during the whole process (though he does not concur with the entirety of my conclusions). My heartfelt appreciation to him.

Gary Anderson has been a perceptive editor of the manuscript through several versions; his ideas contributed significantly to whatever coherence and fluidity the story contains. His assistance in the design of the cover is also much appreciated. Baine Kerr and Cindy Carlisle rescued me from an early impasse by kindly opening their studio on the Big Island to me for a month.

Counsel on Muir's travels in the Sierra was provided over topo maps by mountaineers Richard Perelli and Jerry Snodgrass, lubricated by Scotch, the memory of piney smells, and tall tales of their own mountain adventures, some of which may be true. Ongoing immersion into the immanent glories of America's West has been kindly provided by kayaking and camping buddy Al Vogel. Early musings on Muir and Earth Wisdom were welcomed into Chico State University honors classes of Donald Miller and Kristen Mahlis.

Constructive criticism of early drafts was freely given by George Scarlett, Cindy Carlisle, my wife, and youngest daughter. My former agent Michael Larson, founder of the San Francisco Writer's Conference, shared his thoughts on the shaping of a later draft. Karma Ganzler provided invaluable help with graphics, photos, and cover design. Chico State colleague Aiping Zhang assisted with romanisation and translation of Chinese material.

Thanks to all.

Appendix One. Moving Society and Religion Toward the Immanent Stance

First: More Earth, living here and now;
     Less Heaven, living in the future and elsewhere.
Second: More Kinship with all earth's creatures;
     Less Human superiority and focus.
Third: More Yin traits expressed; Less Yang dominance.
   (More cooperation, acceptance, nurturing, and feminine;
  Less competition, dominance, destruction, and masculine)

Existing examples of the immanent worldview:

Earth Wisdom of John Muir	Darwinism of Science
Taoism of China	Cosmologies of Indigenous Peoples
Elements of current religions	

Throughout Part One, and often in succeeding chapters, I make use of material in several of the biographies of Muir. I rely heavily on two sources in particular, the first and the last (as of this writing) of the formal biographies: Linnie Marsh Wolfe's *Son of the Wilderness: The Life of John Muir*, and Donald Worster's *A Passion for Nature: The Life of John Muir*.

Muir's daughters Wanda and Helen had asked their California friend Wolfe to edit Muir's unpublished journals decades after his death, which led to *John of the Mountains* in 1938. (Some journal material had already been published as separate books: *My First Summer in the Sierra* in 1911, *Travels in Alaska* in 1915, and *A Thousand Mile Walk to the Gulf* in 1916). So pleased were Muir's daughters with *John of the Mountains* that within a year they commissioned Wolfe to write a biography of their father as well, giving her complete access to his letters, and assistance in securing interviews with his surviving friends and colleagues. Though Wolfe had never met Muir, she interviewed a large number of Muir's contemporaries, and *Son of the Wilderness* was published in 1945, promptly winning the Pulitzer Prize. Her biography is a jewel: clear, succinct, and accurate, alive with not just the stuff of Muir's life but his spirit as well.

Worster's 2008 biography is different in several ways. Unlike Wolfe, Worster is an academic historian, with many well-received articles and books to his credit, particularly relating to environmental topics. Worster came to his task nearly a century after Muir's death, and benefited from the considerable corpus of scholarly study on Muir and the environmental movement during that interval. Though *A Passion for Nature* is longer than Wolfe's biography, and crammed with more references and a much longer bibliography, it reads easily and, like Wolfe's volume, captures the spirit of Muir well.

Other useful biographies consulted include the accomplished mountaineer Michael Cohen's 1984 *The Pathless Way: John Muir and American Wilderness*, and Thurman Wilkins' 1995 *John Muir: Apostle of Nature*. I have also used material on Muir's life found in the annotated material of four edited volumes of his writings: Wolfe's 1938 *John of the Mountains*; Robert Engberg and Donald Wesling's 1980 *John Muir: To Yosemite and Beyond*; Jean Hanna Clark and Shirley Sargent's 1985 *Dear Papa: Letters Between John Muir and His Daughter Wanda* (Clark being Wanda Muir's daughter); and Bonnie Johanna Gisel's 2001 *Kindred and Related Spirits: The Letters of John Muir and Jeanne C. Carr*.

Befitting a volume that focuses primarily on the "hidden Muir" revealed in his journals and correspondence, the vast majority of the quotations I cite are drawn from Wolfe's *John of the Mountains*, Muir's own *A Thousand Mile Walk to the Gulf*, *My First Summer in the Sierra*, and *Travels in Alaska*, and Gisel's *Kindred and Related Spirits*. Sources are attributed below by chapter.

Opening Quotations

Muir quote is from *John of the Mountains*, dated "late 1872" by editor Wolfe. The quote of 7th century BCE reformer Guan Zhong (Kuan Chung) is found in the second volume of Joseph Needham's *Science and Civilization in China*, Chapter 10, section (d) (1), the translation being Needham's. Another possible translation would treat "wan wu" as a metaphor: "Reaching the highest state of spirituality, you understand everything." Pope Francis' quotes are from part II of Chapter 3 and part II of Chapter 6 in his encyclical on the environment. Yeager quote is from "'Suspended in Wonderment': Beauty, Religious Affections, and Ecological Ethics" *in J. of Christian Ethics* 35 (2015). The quote of the 8th century BCE Jewish prophet Isaiah is from the Old Testament's *Isaiah*, chapters 40 and 60.

Chapter 1. The Wanderer: a thousand mile walk (1867)

The quotations in this chapter are all from the 1916 *A Thousand Mile Walk to the Gulf*, taken from Muir's early journals as edited by his Sierra Club friend William Frederic Bade. As a first-hand description of postbellum Southern society, the book is fascinating, and always colorful. One is struck by Muir's even-handed treatment of whites and Negroes, as well as his assiduous avoidance of derogatory terms.

Chapter 2. Sierra Nevada Geologist, Botanist (1869)

The "floweriest piece of world I ever walked" quotation is from Muir's July 26, 1868 letter to Jeanne Carr. The "might have stood as a portrait of the angel Raphael" quotation is from Therese Yelverton's novel *Zanita, A Tale of the Yosemite*, published in 1872.

Chapter 3. Discovery of a Living Glacier (1871)

Wolfe has the best general account of Muir's 1871 discovery of the first Sierra glacier. Muir describes his finding the Black Mountain glacier in an October 8, 1872 letter to Jeanne Carr, which was the basis of a short *Overland Monthly* article that December. His actual descent into the icy *Shrund* womb of the glacier was described in his later article "Living Glaciers of California" for *Harper's*, quoted in Cohen's *The Pathless Way* (where it's located at adjoining Red Mountain).

Chapter 4. Tracing the Sierras to Mt. Whitney (1873)

The material on Galen Clark, including Muir's assessment of him as "the best mountaineer I ever met", is taken primarily from Shirley Sargent's 1981 *Galen Clark: Yosemite Guardian*. Quotations describing the journey from Clark's Wawona inn to Mt. Whitney are taken from Muir's journals in Wolfe's *John of the Mountains*. The riveting account of Muir's adventure on Mt. Whitney is taken from Wolfe's biography *Son of the Wilderness*.

Several months after my reconstruction of Muir's route from his terse journal entries of his successful scaling of Whitney October 19-21, I encountered the 1965 *History of the Sierra Nevada*, by two-time Sierra Club president Francis Farquhar.

To my relief, his judgment on the details of Muir's route to the summit from the north is the same as mine.

Chapter 5. A Jubilee of Mountains and Rivers (1877)

The "No one of the rocks seems to call me now" quotation is from a long, extraordinary September 1874 letter to Jeanne Carr. The account of the trip to Mr. Shasta with Gray and Hooker, including the memorable "Look at the Glory!" fireside episode, is recounted in Wolfe's biography. Muir's Thanksgiving stuffing by the Strentzels is described in Worster's biography.

Chapter 6. Alaska, Land of Glaciers (1879-1890)

The quotations recounting his adventure on the Brady Glacier with the dog Stickeen are from chapter 15 of *Travels in Alaska*. The tale became famous, and Muir often retold it at dinner parties and gatherings. A charming children's version with breathtaking illustrations is Donnell Rubay's 1998 *Stickeen: John Muir and the Brave Little Dog*.

Louie Strentzel Muir's letter to Muir is quoted in Wolfe's biography. Muir's extraordinary reflections while sledding on the Muir Glacier are from his 1890 journal entries in Wolfe's *John of the Mountains*. Quotations of Muir's canoe adventures in Hugh Miller Fiord are from chapter nineteen of his *Travels in Alaska*.

Chapter 7. Singing the World's Heart

The "could only have been executed by genuine genius" and "I could have been a millionaire" quotations are from Wolfe's biography. The other quotations are taken from Wolfe's *John of the Mountains* and Muir's *My First Summer in the Sierra*.

Chapter 8. Nature as Healer of Broken Humans

The quotations here are mainly from Wolfe's *John of the Mountains*. Muir's surprise visit to the professor and the general in Yosemite Valley, and his later reflections on it, are from *My First Summer in the Sierra*. The "Plain, sky, and mountains" quotation is from *A Thousand Mile Walk to the Gulf*.

Chapter 9. Gaiacentrism: "Lord Man" overthrown

Quotations here are from *A Thousand Mile Walk to the Gulf* and Wolfe's *John of the Mountains*.

Chapter 10. Death: no longer the great enemy

Quotations in this chapter range from *A Thousand Mile Walk to the Gulf* to *My First Summer in the Sierra* to Wolfe's *John of the Mountains*. The "This death, disease, and pain business" quotation is from Wolfe's biography.

Chapter 11. How Nature Works: Muir the scientist

Quotations here are from Wolfe's *John of the Mountains* and *My First Summer in the Sierras*. The "Glaciers do not so much mold and shape" quotation is from Wilkins' biography.

PART II. THE TAO OF MUIR: EARTH WISDOM, EAST

In general, I employ the modern pinyin romanisation system for Chinese terms, often giving the more familiar, older Wade-Giles romanisation in parentheses. The only exception: the terms *Tao* and *Taoism*, where the original Wade-Giles version is so thoroughly entrenched in Western popular culture that it would be confusing to employ the newer versions (*Dao* and *Daoism*, respectively). In quotations, I retain whatever version is used in the original quote.

Chapter 12. Echoes

The Li Bo and Wang Wei poems are from Witter Bynner's *The Jade Mountain*, a 1964 edition of the famous three hundred leading poems of the T'ang dynasty. Note that I have retranslated the Li Bo poem. The Lin Bu poem containing "Its spare shadows are horizontal and slanted" is quoted in Maggie Bickford's charming *Bones of Jade, Soul of Ice*, charting the intersection of the Flowering Plum cult and Chinese art.

The best scholarly introductions to the complex set of phenomena we in the West label "Taoism" are Kristofer Schipper's *The Taoist Body* and Isabelle Robinet's

Taoism: Growth of a Religion. The best popular introduction is my *Relax, You're Already Home: everyday Taoist habits for a richer life*. For those wishing to dive deeper into a bracing intellectual adventure, the long chapter on Taoism in Joseph Needham's second volume of *Science and Civilisation in China* is incredible, packed with insights and quotations (mostly translated) from Greek, Latin, Chinese, Persian, and Sanskrit. A much-abridged version is Colin A. Ronan's *The Shorter Science and Civilisation in China: 1.*

Unless otherwise noted, my quotations from the two primary sources of philosophical Taoism, the *Daodejing* (*Tao Te Ching*) and the *Zhuangzi* (*Chuang Tse*), are from the translations by Gia-fu Feng and Jane English.

Chapter 13. Mountains: the Two Perfected Lords

Chinese cultural views of mountains are explored in Kiyohiko Munakata's *Sacred Mountains in Chinese Art*. The striking description of Hsi Wang Mu is given there, where its original translation in Suzanne Cahill's 1982 UC Berkeley Ph.D. thesis on the goddess is acknowledged. The activities and quotations regarding The Two Perfected Lords of Mt. Hua-kai are based on Robert Hymes' 2002 *Way and Byway: Taoism, local religion, and models of divinity in Sung and modern China.*

The Muir quotations here are from *My First Summer in the Sierra*; *Travels in Alaska*; and *John of the Mountains*.

Chapter 14. Water: the Black Dragon King

Adam Yuet Chau's *Miraculous Response: Doing Popular Religion in Contemporary China* is the source for the material on the Black Dragon King and his festival in Shaanxi province. The estimate of over a million visitors over the festival's week comes from an email to me from Dr. Chau of May 14, 2014.

Muir quotations are from Wolfe's *John of the Mountains* and *My First Summer in the Sierra*.

Chapter 15. Cycles, Flow, Transformation

The Muir quotation is from Wolfe's *John of the Mountains*.

Chapter 16. Humans: one part of the spectacle

The Muir quotation is from *A Thousand Mile Walk to the Gulf.* I first heard the Taoist view of humans as "nothing extraordinary" in a talk by Liu Ming, the founder of the San Francisco Bay-area Da Yuan Circle. His views are amplified in a *Yoga Journal* article in June, 1995 (vol. 122).

Chapter 17. Death: "A natural transformation"

Muir quotations are from *My First Summer in the Sierras.* The Taoist view of *hun* and *p'o* souls is from Schipper's *The Taoist Body.*

Chapter 18. The Yin and Yang of Muir

The "I sat down beside them and wept for joy" quotation is from the *Kindred and Related Spirits* volume of correspondence between Muir and Jeanne Carr, and is contained in a letter from Muir that Wisconsin University professor J. D. Butler forwarded to the *Boston Recorder.*

Muir's antics with his daughters are recorded in Wolfe's biography and that of Wilkins. His daughter Wanda's succinct "Father was the biggest, jolliest child of us all" is from *Dear Papa*, as is Muir's account of his New York City "night on the town" with Robert Underwood Johnson and the inventor Nikola Tesla, the prototype "mad scientist." (Tesla, interestingly enough, commented often upon the deleterious consequences of women being denied full rank in society, and stated his belief that women would become the dominant sex in the future, thus conforming with the third pillar of Muir's Earth Wisdom.)

Wolfe's biography contains some examples of the doggerel that flowed between Muir and John Burroughs. Wilkins' biography recounts the exchange between Muir and Sarah Hodgson, as well as Therese Yelverton's description of the character Kenmuir from her novel.

The Muir quotations in this chapter are from Wolfe's *John of the Mountains.*

Chapter 19. Muir's God and China's Tao

The Muir quotations here are from *A Thousand Mile Walk to the Gulf; My First Summer in the Sierras*, and many from Wolfe's *John of the Mountains.*

The various translations I cite here include James Legge's *Tao Teh Ching*; Gia-fu Feng and Jane English's *Tao Te Ching*; Burton Watson's *Complete Works of Chuang Tzu*; and Tsai Chih Chung's *Zhuangzi Speaks*.

Chapter 20. Open Eyes, Open Mind, the Immanent

Needham, in volume two of his *Science and Civilization in China*, remarks upon the implications of the term *guan* to designate Taoist temples.

PART III. A BLUEPRINT FOR HUMAN SURVIVAL

Chapter 21. The Hetch Hetchy Battle (1909-1913)

My review of early Sierra Club history, including the active role of women in its founding and outings, is based on the "History: Origins and Early Outings" section of the Sierra Club website (www.sierraclub.org), which is itself based on Michael Cohen's *The History of the Sierra Club: 1892-1970*.

Worster's biography has an excellent account of the entire battle against the Hetch Hetchy dam, including the important role of women in the campaign, the "short-haired women and long-haired men" slur on the opponents of Hetch Hetchy, and the cartoon of Muir with a broom. Muir's letter to Colby, recounting his "long, hearty, telling talk with the President" is from Wolfe's biography, as is his poignant question in a letter to his daughter Helen: "I wonder if leaves feel lonely when they see their neighbors falling."

Chapter 22. Environmentalism's Flawed Model

Robert Underwood Johnson's eulogy to Muir is given in the *Sierra Club Bulletin* of January 1916. "The battle we have fought" is from a speech to the Sierra Club by Muir Nov. 23, 1895, published in the *Sierra Club Bulletin* the following year. "The conscience of the whole country..." from Jan. 1, 1914 letter to Robert Underwood Johnson quoted in Worster, *Epilogue*. "I have precious little sympathy..." is from *A Thousand Mile Walk to the Gulf*.

David Brower material is culled in part from John McPhee's 1971 *Encounters with the Archdruid* (referring to Brower) and *Wikipedia* biography. Material on Greenpeace, Sea Shepherd Conservation Society, and Earth

First! is drawn from their respective websites and *Wikipedia* entry on "Radical Environmentalism."

The rise of the pro-business wing of the environmental movement is described in Ch. 6 of Klein's *This Changes Everything*, including the quotation of the EDF's Fred Krupp. Environmental groups worldwide are catalogued in Doyle and MacGregor's 2013 2-volume *Environmental Movements Around the World*.

Chapter 23. Ignoring Climate Change (1988-2012)

Sherlock Holmes stating he "follows docilely wherever fact may lead" is from *The Reigate Squires* in *The Memoirs of Sherlock Holmes*. The Nov. 1992 Union of Concerned Scientists' *World Scientists' Warning to Humanity* can be uploaded on their website (www.ucsusa.org). Evidence of Exxon's knowledge of global warming and its effects in 1980s detailed in *Los Angeles Times* articles Oct. 9 and 15, 2015.

Activities of the Heartland Institute are detailed in Klein's Ch. 1 and its footnotes, including funding from fossil fuel sources to various individuals. The Institute's leaked internal documents detailing further funding to individuals were published by the global warming blog *DeSmogBlog* on Feb. 14, 2012; vetted by the *NY Times, The Guardian, UPI*, and *AP*; and covered in articles in *The Guardian* (Goldenberg) on Feb. 15 and 16, *The Christian Science Monitor* (Pappas) on Feb. 15, the NY Times (Gillis and Kaufman) on Feb. 16, and *UPI* on Feb. 18, 2012.

"The Death of Environmentalism" can be uploaded on The Breakthrough Institute website (www.thebreakthrough.org) in its archives.

Thompson quote from Introduction to Klein's *This Changes Everything*.

Tipping point from melting permafrost releasing up to 205 gigatons equivalent of carbon dioxide: announced in Woods Hole Research Center policy briefing October 2015, covered in *The Guardian* (Abraham) Oct. 13, 2015. The briefing was based on two studies: Schuur et al, "Climate change and the permafrost carbon feedback," *Nature* 520: 171-179 (April 9, 2015); and Schaefer et al, "The impact of the permafrost carbon feedback on global climate," *Environ. Res. Lett.* 9 (2014) (IOP Publishing Aug. 15, 2014).

The 2009 U.N. climate change conference in Copenhagen, the wave of studies on global warming from 2010 to 2012, the predicted consequences of climate change, and Brad Werner's fall 2012 presentation are treated in the Introduction and Conclusion, particularly, of Klein's *This Changes Everything*, and fully referenced in her footnotes.

Chapter 24. (2012-2015) Hope Dawns, Blossoms...

The Sierra Club's increasingly active stance under Michael Brune is detailed in ch. 10 of Klein. The early history and activities of 350.org are colorfully described in founder Bill McKibben's 2013 *Oil and Honey*. The Blockadia movement is described by Klein in ch. 9 and the Conclusion, from which I draw the quotations of indigenous peoples.

Negative reaction in America to Pope Francis' environmental stance is covered in a Sept. 18, 2015 article in *The Guardian* (Gajanan). Pope Francis' encyclical, *Laudato Si'*, can be uploaded at https://laudatosi.com/watch or ordered as a paperback publication.

The 2015 U.N. Conference on the Environment in Paris was extensively covered by all newspapers and magazines. Summaries and reactions to its accomplishments—or lack thereof—were reported in numerous articles in *The Guardian* (Harvey; Vaughan; Jacobs; Goldenberg; Taylor; McKibben; and editorial) on Dec. 12, 2015 and the following week, as well as *The Economist* Dec. 19 edition.

Chapter 25. ...and Falters (2016)

Shell Petroleum looks to solar 35 years in the future, and meanwhile adds offshore leases in Brazil and Gulf Mexico: *The Guardian* (Neslen) Sept. 28, 2015. Ten oil companies pledge to "play their part" in limiting emissions, and Greenpeace comment: *The Guardian* (Willsher) Oct. 16, 2015. ExxonMobile decades-long deception over effects of global warming: *LA Times* articles Oct. 9 and 15, 2015. Full text and signatories of 350.org petition to DOJ to investigate ExxonMobile deception: https://350.org/the-department-of-justice-must-investigate-exxonmobil/. New York state Attorney General investigating ExxonMobile: *NY Times* article Nov. 6, 2015.

ExxonMobile counterattack of spring and summer 2016: House Committee on Science, Space, and Technology press release May 18, 2016; *InsideClimate News* March 2 and 30, 2016, and June 2, 2016; *U.S. News & World Report* March 29,

2016; *NY Times* May 23, 2016. Fossil Fuel donations to 13 Republican members of Science, Space, and Technology: *Media Masters* June 21, 2016. TransCanada NAFTA suit against U.S.: *NY Times* (Austen) Jan. 6, 2016.

Coal corporation bankruptcies: *SNL Financial News* (Kuykendall) June 4, 2015. World Bank President warning on Asia coal-fired power plants: *The Guardian* (Goldenberg) May 5 and (Elliot) Oct. 9, 2016. Chevron CEO rejects C tax, asserts need to help world's poor escape poverty (!): *SF Chronicle* (Baker) May 26, 2016. Clean Energy Ministerial conference May 31 to June 3, 2016 in San Francisco: *SF Chronicle* (Baker) May 31, 2016. Bill McKibben and zombie-killing: *LA Times* (McKibben) op-ed, Jan. 19, 2016; McKibben on the crisis as World War III: *The New Republic*, Aug. 15, 2016; on the dying oceans: *The Guardian* (McKibben) Sept. 7, 2016. Megadroughts in the American Southwest: *The Guardian* (Milman) Oct. 5, 2016. Lord Stern on infrastructure overhaul: *The Guardian* (Milman) Oct. 6, 2016.

Chapter 26. The Immanent: how to kill a zombie

"By looking" from *Daodejing* stanza 54. Darwin quote from *Origin of Species*, Recapitulation and Conclusion.

Tool use in animals: the definitive work is Shumaker et al's 2009 *Animal Tool Behavior: the Use and Manufacture of Tools by Animals*. See also Pierce's 1986 "A review of tool use in insects" in *The Florida Entomologist* 69: 95-104. The interesting example of the coconut octopus is described in Finn et al's 2009 "Defensive tool use in a coconut-carrying octopus" in *Curr. Biol.* 19 (23): 1069-1070. Use of mirrors to gauge consciousness in animals: *The Economist* Sept. 12, 2015, "What is Consciousness: The Hard Problem." The subject of animal emotions is treated in 2015's *Beyond Words: What Animals Think and Feel* by Carl Safina.

The best treatment of the dualism of yin and yang—ever—remains that of Joseph Needham in vol. 2 of his magisterial *Science and Civilization in China*, especially the section on "The water symbol and the feminine symbol" within "The Approach to Nature."

Chapter 27. A Rough Map to the Immanent Society

"Awe in the fact of mystery" and "To perceive something as beautiful" quotes of D.M. Yeager from *'Suspended in Wonderment': Beauty, Religious Affections, and*

Ecological Ethics, in *J. Soc. Christian Ethics* 35, 1 (2015). "Throw some tea and bread" quote recounted in Introduction to Teale's 1954 *The Wilderness World of John Muir.* Pope Francis quotes from *Laudato Si'*.

The pernicious effects of addiction to smartphones and social media are well-documented, for both kids and adults; see, for example: MIT sociologist Sherry Turkle, "The Networked Primate," *Scientific American* Sept. 2014; Schumpeter column in *The Economist* Jan. 3, 2015 "Getting Hooked: how digital firms create products that get inside people's heads;" and Silicon Valley entrepreneur Nir Eyal's *Hooked: How to Build Habit-forming Products* (2014).

"Overpopulation, environmental degradations and drought, followed by famine and disease" quote regarding collapse of Maya civilization from William Carlsen's 2016 *Jungle of Stone.*

Resistance to Pope Francis' attempts to lead (nudge? drag?) the Roman Catholic Church in an immanent direction is explored in "Hearts, Minds and Souls," *The Economist* July 30, 2016.

Circulatory urbanism in India: *The Guardian* (Echanove and Srivastava) Sept. 16, 2015. *Neoruraux* in France: "Village croissant," *The Economist* Oct. 24, 2015.

Chapter 28. It's the Economy, Stupid: general traits

Chrystia Freeland quote: E.J. Dionne Jr. column Oct. 26, 2015. The text of FDR's "economic bill of rights" in his 1944 State of the Union speech can be accessed at http://www.fdrlibrary.marist.edu/archives/stateoftheunion.html. Automation concerns and Denmark's "flexicurity" system: *The Economist* leader, June 25, 2016, "March of the Machines."

Robert Reich, in a *SF Chronicle* column March 20, 2016, suggested "a much larger Earned Income Tax Credit (effectively, a wage subsidy for lower-income workers)" to offset spotty employment. Resurrecting charters for corporations: *How Good We Can Be: Ending the Mercenary Society and Building a Great Country* by Will Hutton (2015), and Oxford management professor Colin Mayer in 2015 lecture to the British Academy.

Carbon tax as tool to decrease carbon dioxide, British Columbia experience: *The Economist* Dec. 5, 2015, "Free Exchange: the best is the enemy of the green." True cost of coal in Chinese economy: summarized and report accessible at http://www.greenpeace.org/international/en/campaigns/climate-change/coal/the-true-cost-of-coal/.

America's abandoned mines, the Gold King Mine spill into Animas River, and EPA and BLM statistics: "Toxic Heritage" (Bridget Huber of Fairwarning.org) *SF Chronicle* Dec. 28, 2015. Collapse of "holding" dams in Minas Gerais mines: *The Guardian* (Douglas) Nov. 13 and 23, 2015.

Substitutes for hydrocarbon products: Brazil forest industry looking into eucalyptus timber use in plastics-like product being developed in Canada, *The Economist* March 26, 2016.

Chapter 29. The Immanent Economy: getting there

Heinberg and Fridley studies on achieving the transition to sustainable economy in U.S.: "Life After Oil," Spring 2016 *YES! Magazine* (Heinberg). Transport ships adopting new wind-powered technology: "Ship propulsion: We are sailing," *The Economist* April 9, 2016.

Dissatisfaction with modern capitalism: see Adair Turner's 2015 *Between Debt and the Devil: Money, Credit, and Fixing Global Finance* ("Free financial markets left to themselves are bound to create credit in excessive quantities and allocate it inefficiently, generating unstable booms and busts"); Akerlofff and Schiller's 2016 *Phishing for Phools: the Economics of Manipulation and Deception* (the pernicious iron grip of profits); "The slumps that shaped modern finance," essay in Financial Crises series in *The Economist*, April 12, 2015 (several-centuries history of financial busts); "Capitalism and its discontents," Schumpeter column *The Economist* Oct. 3, 2015 (general overview).

New elements in American capitalism: "Reinventing the Company," *The Economist* leader Oct. 24, 2015; "Reinventing the Deal," *The Economist* Oct. 24, 2015; "The business of business: An old debate about what companies are for has been revived," Schumpeter column, *The Economist* March 21, 2015; "Corporate governance: Change, or else," *The Economist* July 30, 2016.

Chapter 30. Who Will Lead?

Thompson quote from Introduction to Klein's *This Changes Everything*. Pope Francis' attempts to lead the Roman Catholic Church in an immanent direction (not always successfully) are explored in "Hearts, Minds and Souls," *The Economist* July 30, 2016. U.S. Episcopal changes, and presiding bishop Katharine Jefferts Schori's comments, covered in *The Guardian* (Goldenberg) March 24, 2015. Various versions of the Common Doxology (including that of the United Church of Christ and Disciples of Christ) are given in the *Wikipedia* article on "Doxology." Jimmy Carter's classic and oft-quoted essay, "Losing my religion for equality," was originally published in 2009 in *Observer*, and can be accessed at http://www.theage.com.au/federal-politics/losing-my-religion-for-equality-20090714-dk0v.html.

The Church of England's general synod decision to admit women bishops is described in *BBC News (UK)* July 14, 2014. Archbishop of Canterbury Justin Welby's proposal to replace the worldwide Anglican communion with a "much looser grouping" is covered in *The Guardian* (Brown) Sept. 16, 2015.

The fatwa against illegal hunting and trade in Indonesia's endangered animals is treated in *The Guardian* (France-Presse) March 5, 2014. The denunciation of female genital mutilation by a Muslim scholar in Gambia is described in *The Guardian* (Topping) Oct. 8, 2014.

Epilogue: Two Paths, and a Choice

The Robinson Jeffers quote is from *For Una*, published in 1941, referring originally to the early turmoil of World War Two in Europe, but presciently evocative of today's crisis. The Muir quote is from his *Thousand Mile Walk to the Gulf*.

I postulate six stages of humanity's relation to the crisis of climate change, based on my own readings, scientific judgment, and extrapolations. The stages emerge from an inextricable welter of science and imagination, and are meant as general predictions, whose timing and features are impossible to specify with precise accuracy. Notwithstanding these *caveats*, I believe the scenario has a high degree of probability as a whole.

Among recent studies since 2015 corroborating the many earlier ones indicating climate change does, indeed, threaten human civilization and the survival of the species: Bill McKibben's "A World at War" in *New Republic* Aug. 15, 2016; NASA's 2015 "State of the Climate" report, *AP* Aug. 3, 2015; "Climate Urgency: we've locked in more global warming than people realize," *The Guardian* (Nuccitelli) Aug. 15, 2016.

Climate change stressing Giant Sequoia groves: Sept. 5, 2015 *The Guardian* (Carswell); coral reefs: see http://earthjustice.org/irreplaceable/coral-reef? for overview regarding effects of increasing ocean temperature and acidification. James Hansen's "game over" quote is from his "Game Over for the Climate" op-ed piece in the *NY Times*, May 9, 2012, referring originally to the Keystone XL pipeline. Higher temperatures even now rendering Gulf climate uninhabitable by humans: *The Guardian* (Carrington) Oct. 26, 2015; *The Economist* Aug. 6, 2016.

Eminent entomologist and sociobiologist E. O. Wilson proposed that approximately half the earth be set aside as natural areas in his spring 2016 book *Half Earth: Our Planet's Fight for Life*. See *NY Times* (Dreifus) Feb. 29, 2016 and *Smithsonian Magazine* (Hiss) Sept. 2014.

Raymond Barnett grew up in Tulsa, Oklahoma. At Yale University he studied the Chinese language and graduated *magna cum laude* in Chinese history. After studying theology for a year at New York City's Union Theological Seminary, Barnett served with the U.S. Army in the Republic (*sic*) of Vietnam at Long Binh, working in the Surgeon General's Office at Headquarters, U.S. Army Vietnam.

Upon earning his Ph.D. in evolutionary ecology from Duke University, Barnett spent the next three decades on the Biological Sciences faculty at California State University, Chico. During this time he worked with community leaders to found Chico's Gateway Science Museum. When he retired, the museum Board proclaimed Barnett "Father of the Museum." Barnett and his wife were among seven founding families of Valley Oaks Village, a cohousing community in Chico, California.

Barnett's interests include snorkeling and tide pooling in Hawaii and California, kayaking California's coast and rivers, backpacking in the High Sierra, mystery stories (particularly Sherlock Holmes, Lord Peter Wimsey, and Judge Dee), the culture of traditional China (particularly the tea cult and porcelain), and music of the Baroque in Europe (particularly Antonio Vivaldi and J. S. Bach). Descriptions of his fiction and nonfiction writings can be found at www.raymondbarnett.com.

CPSIA information can be obtained
at www.ICGtesting.com
Printed in the USA
LVOW08s2256070517

533653LV00006B/96/P